HEGEL FOR SOCIAL MOVEMENTS

Studies in Critical Social Sciences Book Series

Haymarket Books is proud to be working with Brill Academic Publishers (www.brill.nl) to republish the *Studies in Critical Social Sciences* book series in paperback editions. This peer-reviewed book series offers insights into our current reality by exploring the content and consequences of power relationships under capitalism, and by considering the spaces of opposition and resistance to these changes that have been defining our new age. Our full catalog of *SCSS* volumes can be viewed at https://www.haymarketbooks.org/series_collections/4-studies-in-critical-social-sciences.

HEGEL FOR SOCIAL MOVEMENTS

ANDY BLUNDEN

Haymarket Books
Chicago, IL

First published in 2019 by Brill Academic Publishers, The Netherlands.
© 2019 Koninklijke Brill NV, Leiden, The Netherlands

Published in paperback in 2020 by
Haymarket Books
P.O. Box 180165
Chicago, IL 60618
773-583-7884
www.haymarketbooks.org

ISBN: 978-1-64259-192-7

Distributed to the trade in the US through Consortium Book Sales and
Distribution (www.cbsd.com) and internationally through Ingram Publisher
Services International (www.ingramcontent.com).

This book was published with the generous support of Lannan Foundation and
Wallace Action Fund.

Special discounts are available for bulk purchases by organizations and
institutions. Please call 773-583-7884 or email info@haymarketbooks.org for
more information.

Cover design by Jamie Kerry and Ragina Johnson.

Printed in United States.

10 9 8 7 6 5 4 3 2 1

Library of Congress Cataloging-in-Publication Data is available.

Contents

PART 2
The Logic

PART 3
The Philosophy of Right

Acknowledgements

I owe a debt to countless friends and comrades, both activists like myself and Hegel scholars, thanks to whom I have developed my understanding and interpretation of Hegel over the past 30 years. In particular, I want to thank the participants in my annual Hegel Summer Schools 1998–2011 and in my Hegel Reading group 2014–2018, and three people in particular: Darren Roso, Daniel Lopez and Brecht de Smet, who encouraged me to write this book.

Figures

PART 1

Introduction

∵

CHAPTER 1

Why Hegel

§1   For Hegel, Ideas were Forms of Activity

Anyone who is interested in social movements should study Hegel. And that includes someone who is committed to fighting for (or against) a particular social movement, as well as anyone with a wide-ranging interest in social movements and social change in general. If you are looking to plant an idea in the world, Hegel is your guide.

As a philosopher, Hegel's subject matter is ideas, concepts. But for Hegel an idea is not something which exists inside your head (though he did have a Psychology as well, and even 200 years later it stands up to criticism very well). Hegel sees concepts as forms of human social activity – ideas exist and live in the practical activity of human communities, as *forms* of that activity. The consciousness with which people act is an irreducible part of their action: so a behaviour which is unconnected with a person's consciousness, like a hiccup or goose bumps, is not action in this sense. And so-called thoughts which have *absolutely* no manifestation in action, but are mere chimeras, mirages – they do not exist. Hegel does not deal with ideas empirically, as psychological objects; he deals with ideas *logically*. But his Logic is something very different from what usually goes by the name of logic. When Hegel is talking about thoughts he is talking about forms of practice, of social life and his logic is the logic of social action. But at the same time, these concepts are entities you can *reason* with, make logical arguments, explain things and draw conclusions with.

It is not that you first observe social life, abstract patterns from what you observe and then apply them to describing and predicting social life. That is the model scientists typically have of the processes and concepts they study – you could read Hegel's *Logic* and never notice that the subject matter is human activity because Hegel makes only occasional reference to thought as activity. Forms of thinking originate in our practical activity and as we grow up we learn to apprehend these forms as things in themselves abstracted from the practical activity in which they are realised. And we learn through experience what follows from what, how far an idea can be stretched, how to distinguish a concept which is stable and reliable from a bad concept which will collapse under the least criticism. We think in the concepts which we have acquired through participation in the various projects which have made up our life, so the logic of social life manifests itself for us in the logic of concepts.

For example, you may hear that "All immigrants are the same," but if we are a reflective type of person we will know that such an idea is rooted in contact with immigrants which is only superficial, and the same person might soon be heard to say something like: "There are good and bad in every community," and so on ... Hegel calls this "how identity comes to difference" and it is one of hundreds of conceptual transitions found his Logic. And Hegel shows that this is not an oddity of social psychology, but a movement which is inherent in the concepts of identity and difference themselves. But *formal* logic will tell you that either they are all the same or there are differences, one or the other – there's no *becoming* there.

Formal schooling however inculcates *formal logic*, teaching us to categorise things according to their various features, and then carry out simple syllogistic logical operations using these categories. "Fish are like that, birds are like this." The ubiquity of multiple choice tests is evidence that this mode of thinking remains as pervasive as ever. The slightest life experience, however, is usually sufficient to convince us that life does not work like those classroom exercises. The kind of formal thinking which is instilled, mainly through maths and science classes, is of precious little use in handling the kind of problems which we come across in social life. The more complex the situation the less room there is for formal logic. By contrast, Hegel's dialectical logic comes into its own in concrete, realistic and complex situations, the kind we live in all the time, a world where there are always unintended consequences and porous boundaries, where one and the same action often evokes a different response, and so on.

This is the kind of world in which activists live. Governments and bureaucracies, on the other hand, get by with formal logic because they are set up to work that way and using mass production techniques they can impose their way of thinking on to everyone who has to deal with them: every interaction requires a form to be filled out, boxes to be ticked and responses are routinely fixed according to legislation and rules with an appropriate quantitative allocation of resources. So the formal thinking which the school system instils trains the next generation of bureaucrats and teaches people how to interact with the bureaucracy. But this kind of formal thinking is useless for what we have to do as social change activists. When the time comes to build new institutions though, there is always a place for procedures and formal ways of thinking.

Hegel's Logic is a wonderful achievement which has never since been modified or updated. If you have worked in social movements or in other activities which oblige you to deal concretely with a changing reality, you will already be familiar with much of what Hegel teaches us, but it helps a great deal to make this knowledge explicit and develop a systematic understanding of it. On the other hand, without such life experience, it will be difficult to understand Hegel's philosophy.

§2   'Thought' Means Norms of Human Activity

Now, an important corrective to what I have said above is necessary. When I say that concepts are forms of human activity and that Hegel's logic is a logic of action, it is not actual actions which are meant here. People sometimes do things which are quite 'illogical' and idiosyncratic, and Hegel does not provide us a 'logic' which can predict such behaviour. It is the *norms of human activity* which are the subject matter of Hegel's logic.

Natural science works like this, too. For example, when Galileo discovered that a sphere rolling down an inclined slope had (up to a point) a uniform acceleration, he well knew that every time he repeated the experiment, the measured acceleration would be slightly different – air resistance, surface friction, misshapen spheres, delays in starting the clock, etc., etc., all led to differences in each individual measurement. But what he discovered was the *essential principle* of uniform acceleration. Behind all the individual measurements there was a uniform law and it was this law which he sought to reveal. Stretching the meaning of the term somewhat, we could say that this uniform acceleration according to the angle of the slope was the *norm* for rolling down inclined slopes.

So a scientific understanding of human activity requires us to understand the norms of human activity, how they come to be contested and how they change. The subject matter of the Logic is indeed an ideal object – norms – rather than the actual material movements; for empirical data, physics, biology and psychology are also required. Hegel refers to these changing norms of human activity as 'thought', something which has led to no end of confusion among his modern-day interpreters. But it makes sense doesn't it? Understanding human activity (and deciding what to do in a given situation) is not a matter of being able to give a physical description of movements through space and time, but of perceiving the norms which people are instantiating in the activity – the norm is an ideal quality implicit in the activity. Our ideal representation of that action, our thought, therefore, is an 'in-growing' of the relevant norms; thought is also an essential part of carrying out that action. And not only that, norms may take the form of material objects, artefacts. As Hegel put it: "the tool is the norm of labour." So when Hegel is talking about 'thought' he is not talking about some kind of ethereal or spiritual substance but simply the norms manifested in human activity and embodied in artefacts.

Norms mean not only *practical* norms (what people ought to do in a given situation – laws, customs, etc.), but also *theoretical* norms, or norms of belief (all kinds of metaphysical, scientific and common sense beliefs about how the world works), and *semantic norms* (the meaning attached to words, signs and gestures). These three kinds of norm characterise human activity in any given culture and the social change which we are interested in is constituted by changes in these norms. This is not to suggest that norms are homogeneous in any community; on the contrary, Hegel is very much concerned with how norms are contested and undergo change.

I hope this makes clear why I say that Hegel is the philosopher for social change activists.

Norms are grasped as *concepts* and Hegel's approach is to subject these concepts to logical criticism. By this means he demonstrates how every concept at some point falls into contradiction with itself and gives way to a new concept which arises from the ruins of that contradiction. Thus the scientific study of social change takes the form of a logic. Of course, our task is more than logical criticism of the status quo, we have to make a 'practical critique', but as it happens, practical critique also involves a lot of arguing.

Whether your aim is to realise feminist norms of the concept of woman, or maybe to obliterate abstract "essentialist" concepts of gender altogether, or to shift the norms economic life to socialist norms and to recover the concept of the proletariat or recover a valid concept of the relation of humanity to Nature ... then you need to study Hegel.

The way Hegel sees social life has nothing in common with 'crowd psychology'. The 'thought' which is manifest in social life is the practical, theoretical and semantic norms which are not the product of subjective thought as such, but the rational and necessary unfolding of cultural and social activity, appropriated by individuals, and entering into the consciousness of individuals in the course of their participation in social practice.

This is not to say that history unfolds along an invariant and predictable line, however. Nothing changes unless people actually challenge existing norms, and the outcome is predictable only to the extent that it is already visible in embryo. Dialectical logic is 'open ended' in that sense.

I should mention at this point that my reading of Hegel in terms of Spirit being human activity is not entirely unique. Others like Walter Kaufman, Charles Taylor and Robert Pippin also read Hegel in more or less this way.

My approach differs from that of others in that I use a specific concept of 'activity' appropriated from the Soviet Cultural Psychologists and Activity Theorists, for whom 'activity' is essentially synonymous with 'social practice'. But I make no claim to able to tell the reader what Hegel really meant. What I offer is an interpretation of Hegel's writings which is appropriate to the needs of the social change activists of our own times.

§3   Hegel's Influence on Modern Philosophy is Immense

Hegel was one of a series of philosophers in Germany in the late 18th and early 19th century who developed their philosophy in reaction to Immanuel Kant. Kant was himself a giant of philosophy and to this day his system provides the philosophical underpinning of mainstream analytical science and secular ethics. Kant invented the modern philosophical language, and called his philosophy "critical philosophy," in contrast to the sceptical and dogmatic philosophies which had previously fought for dominance in philosophy. It turned out, however, that Kant's philosophy contained a number of troublesome dichotomies and dualisms. Nevertheless, Kant's philosophy *encouraged* criticism rather than simply creating 'followers' who would extend and apply his ideas. The German Idealists criticised Kant's system itself and built new systems in an attempt to overcome the contradictions in Kant's philosophy. The most well-known figures in this tradition are Johann Gottlob Fichte, Friedrich Schelling and Georg Wilhelm Friedrich Hegel himself, who could be regarded as having completed the project of critique of Kantian philosophy by 'negating' it.

Hegel's influence on modern philosophy has been vast. He was very popular in Germany during own life time, or at least during the last 15 years of his life, and for a decade after his death, thanks to the radical "Young Hegelians." In 1841, the Prussian government launched a campaign for the "expurgation of Hegelianism," and Hegel's defence was taken up by Marx and Engels, and, mediated through Marx's appropriation and more recently through modern French philosophy, Hegelianism has become possibly the most influential social philosophy in the world.

Hegel's direct influence in the English-speaking countries was marginal until quite recent times, but during recent decades, many writers coming from a variety of different directions have returned to a study of Hegel's philosophy in the original, rather than being content with the Hegelianism implicit in Marxism. Some of these more recent readings of Hegel are tinged with Marxism to different degrees, with writers reassessing the relation between Marx and

Hegel; others have been influenced by French philosophy, where interest in Hegel blossomed as a result of Alexander Kojève's lectures on Hegel's *Phenomenology* in the late 1930s, published after the War.

All the well-known names of radical philosophy are Hegelians of one type of another – Simone de Beauvoir, Jean-Paul Sartre, Herbert Marcuse, Jürgen Habermas, Jacques Derrida, Jacques Lacan, Michel Foucault, Slavoj Žižek and Judith Butler, as well as all the Marxists, along with the anarchists, whose founders – Pierre-Joseph Proudhon and Mikhail Bakunin were also Hegelians. Now, it is obvious that these philosophers are an extremely diverse bunch who would find very few points of agreement amongst each other and their reading of Hegel reflects that diversity. A commitment to Hegelianism does not commit you to any particular line of social or political criticism. Indeed, Hegel himself was politically fairly conservative by our standards – he favoured a constitutional monarchy and the patriarchal family – though in the context of his time he was a committed progressive. Even Pope Benedict XVI and right-wingers like Francis Fukuyama count themselves as Hegelians. Hegel's social and political views reflect Hegel's social position and the times in which he lived. However, it is not his social and political views which we wish to appropriate, but his Logic. The conceptual apparatus which Hegel developed transcend his times. You don't have to be an advocate of constitutional monarchy and the patriarchal family to use Hegel's Logic, any more than you need to be an advocate of world government to use Einstein's Theory of Relativity or be an anti-Semite to use Frege's analytical logic.

Like all the German philosophers of his time, Hegel was an Idealist, ranking ideas as more important in social life than material conditions as such. Marx, it is said, was a materialist, emphasising the historical importance of developments in technology rather than thinking, and this difference is real enough. But for all Marx's denunciations of Hegel's idealism and the endlessly repeated aphorisms about Marx standing Hegel on his head, etc., the difference between Marx and Hegel is by no means a simple one, and political and social views aside, Marx's methodological and philosophical views are far closer to Hegel than is generally recognised.

It is unsurprising that no-one since Hegel has tried to construct an *Encyclopædia of the Philosophical Sciences*, wrapping up all of human knowledge in a single, logical system without any appeal to empirical evidence. Hegel marked the end of an era when a philosopher could aspire to that kind of systematic, encyclopædic knowledge. Whether you agree with Marx or not, some kind of reorientation of Hegel's philosophy was going to be necessary if it was to retain its usefulness. The relation between Marx and Hegel will be treated in some depth later on and I will not attempt to sum it up in a few words. There has been enough confusion generated by such simplifications already.

§4   Hegel is Very Difficult to Read

Hegel's life spanned from 1770 to 1831. That's a long time ago, and although Hegel was witnessing the emergence of modern capitalist conditions, it was a very different world he lived in. Even in his own day, Hegel's philosophy was notoriously difficult to understand, and it is even more obtuse for the present-day reader. Partly this difficulty arises from Hegel's idealism, his propensity go on and on about abstraction upon abstraction with precious little reference to anything factual. More significantly this obtuseness arises from the nature of his subject matter. In elaborating a Logic whose domain is to be real and concrete social processes, rather than the simplified scenarios that mathematicians prefer, and in expressing himself in such a way that his Logic will stand up across the widest imaginable range of contexts, such abstractness is unavoidable. The concrete examples I will use to illustrate Hegel's Logic, taken from natural science, everyday life or history, are easy to understand; but each example has only a limited truth. None of those examples can substitute for the general rule; the more concrete the claim the more restricted its scope. So conversely, a rule which is to have universal validity, good in any context, must be maximally abstract.

My aim here is to make Hegel's philosophy accessible and relevant for today's social change activist, without shying away from challenging the reader to wrestle with unfamiliar ideas. We are told that in his lectures, Hegel richly illustrated his points with examples and I will also endeavour to put flesh and bones on to Hegel's abstract, idealistic prose by means of contemporary examples.

But I *do* recommend that the reader also tackle reading Hegel in the original, in English translation if you are not fluent in German. Hegel is such a dense writer. Almost every line is a quotable quote. I hope that you will learn enough from this book to make Hegel's own writing comprehensible, but it is always going to be hard work.

It is fashionable nowadays, following the French philosophers, to begin reading Hegel with the *Phenomenology of Spirit*. The *Phenomenology*, published in 1807, was the book with which Hegel first made his name as a philosopher and it remains an essential component of his works, but it is also the most difficult of all Hegel's books to read. Partly this is because Hegel's systematic thought was only just in the process of crystallisation at the time he wrote it. As a result, the structure of the *Phenomenology* is complex and arcane, which is in sharp contrast to Hegel's later works in which the Table of Contents is itself a good read. A further difficulty is the polemical character of the *Phenomenology*, drawing the reader into arguments and historical analyses with which the reader may not be familiar. I recommend that you do not tackle the *Phenomenology* until after you have mastered the works covered here.

Hegel's second book, completed in 1816, was the *Science of Logic* – 840 pages of dense logical argument completely lacking in illustration or more accessible explanation. It would be madness for a novice to attempt to read the *Science of Logic* from the beginning to the end. However, as its subject matter is logic, it has stood the test of time very well. Although formal logic has much improved since Hegel's day, the concepts in the Logic are much the same today as they were 200 years ago. It is also astoundingly systematic in its structure which makes the individual paragraphs easier to understand because you find them in their logical context, and every transition is fully spelt out and explained.

In 1817, Hegel published the *Encyclopædia of the Philosophical Sciences*, after a short introduction criticising the main currents in the history of philosophy, we have the *Logic* (known hereafter as the *Shorter Logic* or *Enc. Logic*), the *Philosophy of Nature* and the Philosophy of Spirit, composed of the *Subjective Spirit* (his psychology), the *Objective Spirit* (his social theory) and Absolute Spirit, covering Art and Religion and finally a brief reflection on Philosophy.

Whereas the *Phenomenology* was never revised, and the *Science of Logic*, was revised only once, a year before Hegel's death, the *Encyclopædia* was continuously updated throughout his life, because he used it as the basis for his lectures. Further, Hegel's editors have included useful notes in the *Encyclopædia* provided by his students based on Hegel's lectures which he illustrated with examples.

In 1821, Hegel published *The Philosophy of Right*, an expansion of the *Objective Spirit* from the *Encyclopædia*, which has sufficient detail to make Hegel's argument comprehensible, as well as the useful notes and some additions Hegel added later, also arising from his lectures. But unlike the *Science of Logic*, the subject matter – modern social life – is by its nature more accessible than the *Logic*. The *Philosophy of Right* is still argued *logically*, but the content of the logical categories is explicitly social, whereas the connection of the *Logic* with human life is mystified by Hegel – it's just one abstraction upon another upon another.

Thanks to its length and its density, the *Science of Logic* rigorously explains every single step in Hegel's argument, whereas in the more accessible *Shorter*

Logic some of the steps are skipped over and some of the arguments are so truncated that they are not entirely convincing and sometimes unclear.

So here is my plan for an outline of what the social change activist needs to know of Hegel's writing which will be covered in Parts II and III to follow.

§5   Plan of this Book

To complete this introduction (Part 1) I will give a brief sketch of the times in which Hegel lived, the social problems which occupied his attention, and the motivations which underlay his philosophical work. There are many biographies of Hegel available and the interested reader may consult any one of these for details of Hegel's life.

Hegel wrote the *Phenomenology of Spirit* as the introduction to his then yet to be elaborated philosophical system. It is an introduction in more than one way: it tells the story of how Hegel's philosophy came about in three different intertwining ways: (1) how the subjectivity of an individual develops from naive common sense to philosophical reflection, (2) how philosophy itself has developed from the ancient Greeks to modern times, and (3) how 'objective thought' in the form of institutions and the constitution of states has risen from antiquity to modernity, including critical analysis of the French Revolution. I will use a synopsis of the Preface to the *Phenomenology* to give an overview of Hegel's idea of science and philosophy and then try to explain the principal ideas of the *Phenomenology of Spirit* and the sense in which the *Phenomenology* provides the starting point for a philosophical system which is to begin with the *Logic*. I will then flesh out my claim that Hegel is the philosopher of social movements.

Part 2 is devoted to the *Logic*. I will begin with some generalities about the Logic, then explain the content of its various sections and move on to take the reader point by point through the whole of the logic. Like Lenin, I will be reading the *Science of Logic* and the *Shorter Logic* side-by-side, using material from one or the other work to illustrate a point according to the suitability of each text to my purpose. The reader should end up with a fairly detailed knowledge of the Logic by the close of this section and be in a position to read either version for themselves and make good sense of it.

At the conclusion of Part 2, I will provide a very brief summary of the *Philosophy of Nature*, which follows the *Logic*, and I will begin Part 3 with a fairly brief account of the *Subjective Spirit*, which is the connecting link between the *Philosophy of Nature* and *The Philosophy of Right*. This should help the reader to gain an appreciation of the structure of the *Encyclopædia*.

Part 3 will focus on *The Philosophy of Right*, and following the same approach as I use in Part 2, I will begin with an overview of the subject matter of *The Philosophy of Right*, and then summarise each of its divisions before moving to a detailed treatment of the whole work chapter-by-chapter.

Part 4 will begin with a critical overview of Hegel's philosophy, but now in the light of a shared understanding of Hegel's philosophy in some detail. I will point to the weaknesses of Hegel's philosophy as a philosophy for our times but at the same time defend aspects of Hegel's philosophy which are, in my opinion, frequently subjected to unfounded criticisms or misunderstood.

Part 4 will conclude with essays on three special topics of interest to social change activists – an overview of Marx's criticism of Hegel and the relation between Marx's *Capital* and Hegel's *Logic*; the appropriation of Hegel's philosophy by the Soviet Cultural Psychologist, Lev Vygotsky (1896–1934) and the Soviet Activity Theorists; a proposal for emancipatory politics derived from my study of Hegel and Marx.

By the time you have read this book, you will know quite a lot about Hegel. In what follows I will quote liberally from English translations of Hegel, so you will also be accustomed to tackling Hegel's difficult prose. But it is my hope that readers will continue on to read at least the *Shorter Logic* and *The Philosophy of Right* for themselves. You cannot have a firm grasp of Hegel until you have read him for yourself, first hand. Only by reading him for yourself will you be able to claim your knowledge of Hegel as your own and be able to defend it and deepen it. But if you complete this book, you will have already begun to read Hegel.

The main thing is to get the hang of Hegel's logic and to be able to see how this logic is manifested in social and cultural development.

CHAPTER 2

The Young Hegel and What Drove Him

§1   Germany was Fragmented, and Socially and Economically
      Backward

In order to understand what Hegel was doing with his philosophy, we should first look at the circumstances of his life and the situation in Germany at the time.

Hegel was born in Stuttgart in 1770, just 620 km from Paris. So he was 18 at the time of the storming of the Bastille and his earliest writing, an essay on the prospects for advancing the Enlightenment by launching a "folk religion," were penned while a seminary student in Tübingen 1793. Shortly afterwards, Robespierre launched his own manufactured religion of the "Supreme Being." This project fell flat and Robespierre was himself sent to the guillotine soon after. Mainly under the influence of his friend, the poet Hölderin, Hegel abandoned his youthful disdain for the Christian religion and came to the conviction that, for all its faults, it was Christianity which had ultimately opened the way for the Enlightenment and modernity.

He completed his first published book, the *Phenomenology of Spirit*, in Jena, just as the town was occupied by his hero, Napoleon Bonaparte – "The World Spirit astride a horse" (Hegel 1806/1984). Napoleon was born the same year as Hegel, but, defeated at Waterloo in 1815, died in 1821 shortly after the publication of Hegel's *Philosophy of Right*, which culminates in the section on World History where Hegel describes such world-historic heroes as "living instruments of the world mind." Napoleon introduced the modern *code civile* into Germany and smashed up its ancient feudal structures. The reform movement Hegel hoped would complete what Napoleon had begun, capitulated to reaction. As Hegel wrote: "the world spirit has given the age its marching orders. These orders are being obeyed. The world spirit ... proceeds irresistibly like a closely drawn armoured phalanx ..." (1816/1984).

The French Revolution had a profound impact on Hegel's life; he supported the Revolution but had profound misgivings about both process and outcome. The movement to ban the slave trade swept across Europe during the 1790s and culminated in the British Abolition Act in 1807. Wealthy Germans continued to invest in slavery and this outrage contributed to shaping Hegel's views, and Hegel became a participant in the Reform movement.

However, the first uprisings of the French proletariat against the misery of early capitalist development in France began only in the 1830s, after Hegel's death, and although the industrial revolution in Britain roughly coincides with Hegel's lifetime, 1770–1830, the Chartist Movement began the fight back only in the late 1830s.

Hegel saw the revolutionary impact of capitalism and the misery it brought with it. He followed the revolution of slaves in Haiti, but he never saw a modern labour movement. Also, some of the most brilliant of the classical feminists of his time were amongst his circle of friends, including his mother and sister, but Hegel never saw a mass women's movement and never accepted the claims of feminism. In fact, he had dreadfully patriarchal views.

Germany did not have a state. Until 1815, Germany was part of what was still called the Holy Roman Empire, which stretched from Nice up the French border to Calais, across to Gdansk, bordering the Russian Empire down through Prague to Rome. Court life rested on the exaction of agricultural surplus by feudal blood-and-soil relations. Life in the towns, however, was self-regulated by corporations and guilds, which bound the people into a myriad of complex networks of mutual though unequal obligation. Ruling all this was a fragmented nobility.

The Holy Roman Empire was made up of a patchwork of over 300 small principalities, some Catholic some Protestant, each with their own class structure and traditions and with no solidarity between each other or from their own subjects. England to the North, Revolutionary France to the West, Imperial Russia to the East and Austria-Hungary to the South. The armies of these great powers marched back and forth across Germany, pushing the German princes around like pawns in a power game in which the Germans had no say whatsoever. None of the princes of these little statelets could count on their citizens to take up arms in their defence. Germany was helpless, mere spectators of history, and wallowed in social and economic backwardness while Revolutionary France made history with its armies and its politicians, and the English built an empire with their money and their inventions. But this was the Germany of Goethe and Schiller and Beethoven.

Hegel was forced to the conclusion that if Germany was going to modernise it would have to be done with philosophy rather than with guns and mobs. And it was only relatively late in life (aged 28) that Hegel resolved to become a philosopher, began to build his own system and was appointed to a professorship at the age of 46, in 1816. It was the fate of his own country, the problems of modernisation and freedom for his native Germany, which was his central concern.

The Holy Roman Empire was brought to a close by Napoleon in 1806 just as Hegel completed the *Phenomenology*. As the last volume of the *Science of Logic* went to press, the Congress of Vienna convened in the aftermath of Napoleon's military defeat, and the German Federation was created with just 38 components, each with an average population of about 600,000 – less than the population of Paris at the time. This situation suited Hegel (although he had earlier advocated for a united Germany under an Emperor), and generally speaking, the most creative period of Hegel's life was the period of the Napoleonic Wars, 1804–1815.

We should also recall that Hegel never knew Darwin. *The Origin of Species* was published almost thirty years after he died, and microscopes were not yet powerful enough to reveal the microstructure of organisms. Although he was familiar with the theory of Lamarck, he positively rejected the idea that human beings had evolved out of animals – indeed Darwin was the first person to *witness* natural change in a species, let alone one species changing into another. He knew of Lyell's theory of geological formation and accepted that the continents were products of a process of formation, but he insisted that there was change but no development in Nature. He knew nothing of the pre-history of humanity and as surprising as it may seem for the historical thinker *par excellence*, he claimed that:

> even if the earth was once in a state where it had no living things but only the chemical process, and so on, yet the moment the lightning of life strikes into matter, at once there is present a determinate, complete creature, as Minerva fully armed springs forth from the head of Jupiter.... Man has not developed himself out of the animal, nor the animal out of the plant; each is at a single stroke what it is. The account of the creation given in Genesis is still the best ... Man has not formed himself out of the animal, nor the animal out of the plant, for each is instantly the whole of what it is. (*Philosophy of Nature*, §339)

At the time, natural science offered no rational explanation for the appearance of organic life out of inorganic life or of the origins of the human form with our linguistic and tool-making abilities. It is to Hegel's credit that he did not try to resolve a problem for which he had no viable alternative to the Biblical story. He relied almost entirely on the *intelligibility of human activity* as he saw it to reveal what was *necessary* in the existing forms of Nature, but lacked any scientific theory for the transformation of one natural form into another – something which in any case had never been observed.

In Nature, Spirit is merely *in itself*; in human life, Spirit is *for itself* and here there is evolution and development, as Hegel saw it.

His misogyny and racial prejudice, which led him to exclude women and the peoples of less developed nations from being creators of culture, derived from his blindness to the fact of the cultural origins of the human form itself. Although this is a limitation in his natural philosophy, it is one which is very easy to correct for given all that we know today, 200 years later, and has little impact on his Logic, which rests on the domain of Spirit, where development and evolution are the norm.

§2   Hegel was a Modernist Opponent of Liberalism

Hegel presents a contradictory figure. He was an enthusiastic proponent of the Enlightenment, and before his career as a professor of philosophy took off, he was briefly a newspaper editor and then for seven years, headmaster of a secondary school in Nuremberg. He was dedicated to the ideal of *Bildung* – a German word usually translated as 'education' but carrying a much stronger connotation of personal development and participation in the cultural life of a community. He saw himself somewhat as a foot soldier for the Enlightenment. But it was the combination of witnessing what Kant in particular, but also Fichte and Schelling, achieved as proponents of philosophical systems and as university professors, and the increasing awareness of the unsatisfactory nature of the systems of these, his predecessors in German philosophy, which impelled him to construct a philosophical system of his own.

The Enlightenment entailed the promotion of Reason over superstition and tradition and the expansion of individual freedom, but unlike other proponents of the Enlightenment Hegel was *not* a liberal (i.e., libertarian). That is, he did not identify freedom with the absence of constraint on individual action, and he did not see the individual subject as the arbiter of Reason. Hegel fully embraced the Enlightenment values of rationality and freedom, but he was critical of the liberal-individualistic conception in which these ideals were framed. Liberalism was only the first phase in the development of Freedom which could only be realised through the moral development of a whole people which in turn would depend on the development of rational systems of social regulation and collaboration.

At best, an individual only has the power of the whole community of which they are a part. The citizen of a nation like Germany, which had no state, has no freedom. Individuality can be only realised at that historical moment when the contradiction between right and welfare is overcome, that is, when a state has developed to a point where what every person strives for is only the welfare of all.

In order to understand Hegel, we have to suspend our conception of the state as an instrument of class oppression, other than in the case of the domination of a people by a foreign power. And we have to reject the notion of the state as a limitation on individual freedom and grasp the sense in which the state is also an instrument of its citizens and an expression of their freedom. Hegel did not know of the idea of the state as an instrument of *class rule*, and he conducted a life-long struggle against all those theories which promoted a libertarian, or 'negative' idea of freedom. For him, the state occupied the space that it would occupy for the people of Vietnam and other nations which emerged from the national liberation struggles of the post-World War Two period: that of a *social movement* expressing the aspirations of an entire people. What he describes in his *Philosophy of Right*, for example, is not of course a social movement in the usual sense of that expression, but a state, complete with hereditary monarchy and a public service. However, at the deepest level, the level which we find in the Logic, his philosophy is the philosophy of a social movement, people organized around a common cause or 'project'. Ideas exist as permanent processes of development, inclusive of the formation of states instantiating a certain way of life.

But Hegel wasn't simply a communitarian, who, like Durkheim saw social solidarity arising from homogeneity or from mutual dependence among citizens. He was deeply concerned for the full development of individuality and how the self-determination of an individual person could be realized in and through the acquisition of the culture of a whole community. Such an achievement entails the moral development of the whole population as well as elaborate structures of mediation and collaboration.

The real limitation on Hegel's conception of a social movement is that, as remarked above, he never saw nor ever conceived of a social movement of the *oppressed* which aimed to *transcend* the existing state, rather than *escape* from it or succeed in being *included* in it. He fully understood the need for an oppressed people to emancipate themselves from foreign domination, but he saw no reason to believe that 'the mob' (*Pöbel*) could or should liberate themselves from the elite. Hegel believed that participation of the educated elite was essential to the development of a social movement. However, all modern theories of self-emancipation presaged on the formation of collective self-consciousness rather than individual 'self-help' originate from Hegel's theory. The state is the expression of collective self-consciousness *par excellence* and in working out the relation between individual action, collective activity and the state, Hegel laid the basis for understanding social movements and the institutions which arise from those movements. One could go further than that. Hegel was deeply concerned with the role of individuals in bringing about social change, but the conception of the individual which he developed was a radical break from those which had gone before and in sharp contradiction to present day conceptions of individuality. Even 'world-historical figures' like Napoleon, as living instruments of the World Spirit, played an important role in Hegel's conception of historical change.

§3   The Main Difference between Hegel and Marx is the Times They Lived In

The philosophical difference between Hegel and Marx is a topic which has been hotly disputed for over a century. The differences between the philosophical approaches of Hegel and Marx will be dealt with in detail later on, but the essential difference between Marx and Hegel is the times they lived in.

Given the economic, social and cultural peculiarities of Germany in Hegel's day there was some basis for Hegel to believe that it would be through philosophy that Germany could modernise itself. Today, this stands clearly exposed as an 'idealist' position - to believe that an economic, social and cultural transformation could be led by a philosophical revolution, rather than the other way around. But this does not invalidate the choice Hegel made in his day. After Hegel's death in 1831, his students drew the revolutionary conclusions that were implicit in their teacher's philosophy. Hegelianism spilt over the walls of the academy as his students popularised his teachings and translated them into the language of politics – or more correctly, translated politics into the language of Hegelianism. In 1841, the Prussian government moved to "expunge the dragon's seed of Hegelian pantheism" from the minds of Prussian youth. A newly-appointed Minister for Culture mobilized Friedrich Schelling (the last surviving representative of German Idealism, and now a conservative) to come to Berlin and do the job. His lecture in December 1841 was attended by Engels, Bakunin, Kierkegaard and notables from all over Europe but manifestly failed to quell the spread of radical ideas and revolutionary agitation.

It is a remarkable fact that almost all the revolutionaries of the 19th and 20th century were either students of Hegel, Hegelians of the second or third philosophical generation or influenced by other figures of German Philosophy of the time – Kant, Fichte and Schelling, but above all Hegel – whether in the form of Marxism or other critical philosophical currents. So Hegel was not entirely mistaken.

By the time that Marx resigned the editorship of the *Rheinische Zeitung* in 1843, France had been rocked by a series of working class revolts and Paris was seething with revolutionary ferment, the English working class had constructed the first working class political party in history (the National Charter Association) and were challenging bourgeois rule in Britain, and an advanced industrial working class was emerging in Germany. It was obvious that change would come in Europe through political struggle springing from the industrial working class. Capitalist development was disrupting all the old relations and it was going to be the industrial working class who would lead the transformation. Furthermore, the leaders of the labour movement were not just demanding inclusion in or reform of the state, or aiming to replace it with one of their own, but aimed to *smash* the state. This was something unimaginable in Hegel's day.

On reflection, it will be seen that all the political and philosophical differences between Marx and Hegel arise from the changes that took place in Europe in the interval between Hegel's last years and Marx's entry into radical political activity.

§4   The "Spirit of a People" was Rooted in an Historical Form of Life

It was this concern to find a route to modernity for Germany which led Hegel to an investigation of the source of the differing spirit of peoples and the fate of each nation. Hegel did not invent this study. Before him Kant and in particular Johann Gottfried Herder, who had coined the terms *Volksgeist* and *Zeitgeist*, had made investigations into the problem. By studying the history of a people, the young Hegel hoped to discover why one people would make a revolution, another build an empire, while another would wallow in disunity and backwardness.

Herder's ideas became important in the development of cultural anthropology in the 19th century and helped shape ideas of people like Franz Boas, but modern multicultural nations are not cultural entities in the same sense as the peoples of early modern times. Hegel, whose interest was in the fostering of both social solidarity and individuality, realized this. At best the concept of *Volksgeist* – based on the historical experiences of a people and the principal forms of labour – could be useful in characterisation of an ancient city state or of an isolated community perhaps, or to explain particular *aspects* of the character of different nations. In today's context such a project would be seen as reactionary, firstly because it tends to erase differences of class, gender and so on within a people, and secondly because it reeks of "cultural racism."

But remember firstly that the question of the sovereignty and Spirit of a people was posed from the point of view of the *excluded*, in this case, the German people, who were being ridden roughshod over by the European powers and denied a say over their own affairs, and this makes a difference. It is not a justification for empire.

But further, it asks a legitimate question, and *Volksgeist* was a *first step* towards understanding the specific nature of a modern community and its relation to the psychology of the individuals who make it up. And it was a radical break from trying to understand the problem of freedom through the study of eternal categories of Reason as Kant had done.

Hegel's early work, particularly the 1802–03 work, *System of Ethical Life*, is especially important because in it we see Hegel working out his conception of spirit in terms of the experiences of practical daily life. Taking the lead of his predecessors Kant and Fichte, and Descartes for that matter, he aimed to make no presuppositions other than experience. However, instead of turning inwards to the contemplation of 'clear ideas', or making appeals to mathematical-type axioms, he took as his given datum ordinary, living people creating and reproducing themselves and their communities.

Now it is true that this kind of consideration is less obvious in his later works, certainly the Logic, which moves almost entirely in the domain of abstract thought forms, but there is no reason to suppose that he abandoned his view of the construction of Reason through labour and strong evidence that he remained of this view, albeit with a very broad conception of 'labour' which included speech and the raising of children as well as production. Philosophy in general and logic in particular has to stand on its own ground and cannot appeal to other domains for its proof. But Hegel's early investigations did not lead him to a kind of social psychology, to do with how people *acquire* an idea, but a radically new conception of what an idea *is*.

Somewhere between the writing of *System of Ethical Life* and the next version of his system, which is sometimes called the *Philosophy of Spirit* (1805–06), an important change took place in his idea of Spirit. Whereas up till this time he had been interested in the spirit of a times or the spirit of this or that people, and looked for its origins in the day-to-day activity and experiences of people. In line with the pressure which comes to bear on every builder of a philosophical system, he began to talk about "Spirit" as such. So instead of having the spirit of this or that people arising from an historical form of life, forged through the experience of victory or defeat at war, through the raising of crops or the hunting of animals, we had *Spirit*. Spirit *manifested* itself in the activity of a people, developed as that people fulfilled their destiny, but then, if that nation faced a crisis and proved incapable of making the transition to a new principle, the further progress of Spirit would be the task of another people. So without any change in the conception of spirit itself, spirit became something that pre-existed the form of life in which it was instantiated. Spirit was one and the same process which found a different form at a different time in a different people.

This move greatly facilitated the construction of a systematic philosophy. All German professors of philosophy have to have a system. It's part of the job description, and by this time, Hegel had his sights on becoming a professor of philosophy. But it moved his philosophy into a more theistic direction. At the same time, it is a move which, for our secular times, is rather easily reversible. You don't need to have a conception of Spirit as pre-existing human life, and *manifesting* itself in human activity, to use the concept of spirit – the character of human activity in this or that epoch, in this or that nation, this or that social movement.

The other implication of this conception of Spirit was that it really emphasized the unitary character of spirit: everyone, however marginalised, shares in the culture of a people, its language, its forms of production and distribution, its institutions and its religion. It is this shared character of spirit as Hegel conceived it, which comes to the fore, rather than a concern with analysis of differences. But the point is: should we proceed like Hobbes and Fichte and present-day analytical philosophers, beginning from the *individual*, and from the nature of the individuals deduce the nature of the state, the society? Or should we on the contrary, begin with a conception of the *whole* community, its institutions and its various activities and sections, and from there deduce the nature of the individual persons. Surely Hegel was correct in beginning with that shared form of life. We all share, even if unequally, in the language, the science, the art, technology and production, the political and social institutions of our society; we constitute and modify them in our own activity together with others. We all have our own particular take on that culture, but it remains a cultural life which is shared at the global level through the nation whose laws we all share, etc., down to more restricted contexts, brought to light if we bring a magnifying glass to bear on the consciousness of different classes, subcultures or natural groupings within society. But at whatever level, we have to be able to deal with individuals constituting a shared form of life and themselves as a part of that.

§5   *Zeitgeist* Remains a Widely Accepted, if Problematic, Concept of Spirit

There is some basis for associating Hegel with notions of progress and 'cultural evolution' in which all the people of the world are subsumed into a single narrative. But to criticise Hegel for this would require a blindness to the obvious *relative* truth in the idea. The kind of ideas and activities which flourished in the 1930s sink like a lead balloon in the 2000s, and conversely, the fashions, values, prejudices and beliefs which are widespread today were either taboo or unknown in earlier decades and will be again in future decades. And these obvious changes in the *Zeitgeist* severely limit was is politically possible and not possible in our times. A political actor who ignores the spirit of their times is doomed to irrelevance. And we need to be sensitive to changes in the *Zeitgeist* as they develop. And the *Zeitgeist* also varies from place to place, within limits. Wouldn't it be good to understand the 'mechanics' of how the *Zeitgeist* changes?

Hegel worked out an approach which can illuminate the individual psyche and its structure by beginning from studying the dynamics of national institutions, politics, movements in art and philosophy and so on. The current fad among social psychologists for talking about the psychology of entire generations is a very lame attempt to do this. Lumping together an entire cohort of people born in a certain decade as if they shared common goals and experiences is questionable to say the least. And the same goes for any grouping of people according to one shared attribute like 'white collar employees' or 'suburbia' – abstract categories which have no collective self-consciousness at all, mere similarity. Hegel's approach is much more powerful.

This brings us to the issue of individuality and individualism. Nowadays we commonly hear people talking about 'two levels', the level of the individual and their immediate associates, versus the level of institutions and social forces. On one hand, we have individuals with ideas, motivations, consciousness and personalities of their own, able to decide what they do from one moment to the next. On the other hand, we have impersonal social forces, such as the economy governed by the invisible hand of the market, politics governed by public opinion, large impersonal institutions, and economic, social and historical forces and laws. Psychology is in one department of the university, whilst Sociology is in another – the conceptual apparatus we need to understand human beings is split between at least two incommensurable sets of concepts.

What Hegel's concept of spirit gives us is a set of concepts, all interconnected with one another in his Logic, which deal throughout with the character of human beings en masse. "Spirit is the nature of human beings en masse," and the study of spirit is nothing other than the study of the activity of human beings en masse. Individuals do not build civil societies and states, only human beings en masse do that. But in dealing with human beings en masse Hegel does not obliterate the individual or reduce the individual to a member of a group or a bundle of personal attributes.

'Spirit' is a word people don't like to hear too much these days. It summons up notions of extramundane substances. But it is undeniably real, and to present Hegel's Logic simply as a philosophy "without presuppositions," deleting any reference to "spirit" would be to deny Hegel's philosophy its very subject matter.

§6   In What Sense was Hegel an Idealist?

(a)   *Hegel Described Himself as an Idealist*
Hegel was the final product of the philosophical movement known as "German Idealism," which arose in Germany in response to Immanuel Kant's Critical Philosophy. Kant had aimed to resolve the impasse between largely British Empiricism and largely French Rationalism. These philosophical currents were driven by problems which had arisen from the rapid development of natural science since Galileo, chiefly the nature of reality, and the sources and limits of human knowledge of Nature. Kant had proposed that a thing existed "in itself" but human beings could have knowledge only of phenomena, i.e., appearances, while the nature of the thing-in-itself remained beyond experience and unknowable. Kant's approach generated many troubling dualisms and contradictions, and the German Idealists attempted to resolve these contradictions by focusing on *forms of knowledge*, rather than by speculating on the nature of a reality outside of human practice, which was the preserve of the Materialists.

Hegel put it this way:

> The proposition that the finite is ideal constitutes Idealism. The idealism of philosophy consists in nothing else than in recognising that the finite has no veritable being. Every philosophy is essentially an idealism or at least has idealism for its principle, and the question then is only how far this principle is actually carried out. ... A philosophy which ascribed veritable, ultimate, absolute being to finite existence as such, would not deserve the name of philosophy; the principles of ancient or modern philosophies, water, or matter, or atoms are *thoughts,* universals, ideal entities, not things as they immediately present themselves to us, ... in fact what is, is only *the one concrete whole* from which the moments are inseparable.
>
> Science of Logic, §316, HEGEL, 1812

So the archetypal materialists were the ancient Greek Atomists – everything, including human life, was the result of interactions between atoms. Modern materialism, which arose *after* Hegel, has a broader concept of material reality which is inclusive of social relations, but earlier materialists tended to be blind to the social formation of knowledge and consciousness.

It was the Idealists, Hegel in particular, who discovered the *social character* of consciousness and knowledge, not the materialists. However, the idealists did not make forms of practice explicitly the subject matter of their systems; rather they took logical categories, concepts, ideas, etc., as their subject matter, thus justifying their description as "Idealists." A critical reading of Hegel will show however that *content* of these ideal forms is *forms of activity*.

Not all forms of idealism are the same. In particular, Hegel distinguished between *subjective* idealists like Bishop Berkeley, and objective idealists, such as himself and Schelling. That is, for Hegel, thought forms were not chimera existing only inside your head, but existed *objectively*, in activity and material culture, independently of any single individual, and which individuals acquired in the course of their activity.

(b)   *Hegel Emphasised the Active Side rather than Passive Contemplation*
The very first expression of Marxism – Thesis 1 of Marx's *Theses on Feuerbach* – is referring to Hegel in particular when it speaks of "idealism":

> The main defect of all hitherto-existing materialism – that of Feuerbach included – is that the Object, actuality, sensuousness, are conceived only in the form of the object, or of contemplation, but not as human sensuous activity, practice, not subjectively. Hence it happened that the active side, in opposition to materialism, was developed by idealism – but only abstractly, since, of course, idealism does not know real, sensuous activity as such. Feuerbach wants sensuous objects, differentiated from thought-objects, but he does not conceive human activity itself as objective activity. ...
>
> *Theses on Feuerbach*, MARX, 1845

Not only did the Idealists see perception as an *active* process, they also saw the interpretation of one's experience, how you conceived of and reacted to a situation, as an active process. The contrast with the materialist attitude to the social formation of human beings is set out in "Thesis 5":

> The materialist doctrine that men are products of circumstances and upbringing, and that, therefore, changed men are products of changed circumstances and changed upbringing, forgets that it is men who change

circumstances and that the educator must himself be educated. Hence this doctrine is bound to divide society into two parts, one of which is superior to society. ... (*op. cit.*)

On the other hand, we see that Marx lambasted the philosophers for merely *interpreting* the world rather than seeking to change it, partly because "idealism does not know real, sensuous activity as such," being concerned with concepts rather than activity – the shadows rather than the real activity itself. So Marx presents us with the contradiction that it is the idealists who based themselves on the struggle to change reality as the source of knowledge of reality, rather than passive contemplation of reality like the materialists. But like all professional philosophers, they merely "interpreted" the world, rather than acting to change it.

Overall, Marx's *Theses on Feuerbach* is a *defence* of Hegel's idealism.

(c)   *Hegel Took the Social Elite to be the Agents of Change*
Having witnessed social change in Britain thanks to industrialisation, and in France thanks to the guillotine, Hegel looked forward to a less traumatic and chaotic revolution in Germany which would be led by the social elite – philosophy professors, enlightened monarchs and a meritocratic civil service, rather than the blind destruction wrought by mobs and factories. Although he supported the right of slaves and oppressed nations to throw off their oppressors, he wanted his native Germany to achieve modernity through the perfection of a state which would guarantee the freedoms of its citizens. He saw states as guarantors of freedom, not instruments of oppression and was resolutely opposed to destructive, revolutionary methods of achieving social progress. He regarded the poor and working class as incapable of being agents of social progress – their misery was a *social problem* which could be solved only by the intervention of the enlightened elite.

When a work process is improved is it thanks to the supervisor who devises the improved method, or is the improvement implicit in the work process itself? Should we credit the workers or the supervisor for the improvement? When a social problem is solved by the passing of a new law, do we credit the parliamentarians who passed the new law, or the demand for change by the suffering? Do we get to a better world by (at least some) people forming an image of that better world and then going out and fighting for it, or does the better world arise out of contradictions inherent in the present state of affairs which drive people into actions irrespective of whether or not they can foresee the outcome? We call those people "idealists" who think that the social class whose business is plans and ideas are the agents of change, rather than the masses who act out those ideas. We call those people "materialists" who see social change arising directly out of the conditions of life with ordinary people as its unconscious agents.

But recall *Thesis 5* quoted above: if, as materialists, we see people as products of their social conditions we reduce them to passive objects of change, leaving consciousness of change to the intelligentsia or the Party. Hegel and the Idealists erred on the side of change-from-above, but exclusive focus on change-from-below is equally mistaken because it makes the people passive objects of structural forces beyond their control.

(d)   *Hegel Believed that Institutions Tend to be True to their Concept*
Anyone will recognise that over the years automobiles have come to better accord with their concept than they used to, conveying passengers to their desired destination in comfort without breaking down; likewise, washing machines have become more and more likely to wash your clothes and not wreck them since they were first invented in 1908. Hegel believed that this idea, which has been called "normative essentialism," applies to social institutions as well as useful artefacts, and is crucial to his social philosophy.

Although states originate in violence, according to Hegel, the concept of the state is Freedom – freedom from crime, famine and outside attack, freedom for personal development and the enjoyment of culture. That is to say, a worthwhile concept, once it comes into being, will tend to realise itself in increasingly perfect forms and only falls into crisis when its concept no longer makes sense. In this sense, Hegel sees the logic of ideas and concepts as the driving force in history. Marx responded:

> *History* does *nothing*, it "possesses *no* immense wealth," it "wages *no* battles." It is *man*, real, living man who does all that, who possesses and fights; "history" is not, as it were, a person apart, using man as a means to achieve *its own* aims; history is *nothing but* the activity of man pursuing his aims.
>
> *Holy Family*, 1845

Marx here is expressing a materialist position, in which people are not to be seen as captive of ideas but real actors. But if Marx is not to be accused of voluntarism, we must take account of his aphorism:

> Men make their own history, but they do not make it as they please; they do not make it under self-selected circumstances, but under circumstances

existing already, given and transmitted from the past. The tradition of all dead generations weighs like a nightmare on the brains of the living.

The Eighteenth Brumaire, 1852

That which is "transmitted from the past" – the institutions, symbols and beliefs, the norms built up by a people over centuries – unfold in a way ably described by Hegel with his dialectical idealist philosophy. But how people *make use of* those conditions is not always logical; people do not always do what they have to do, so to speak, so Marx's insistence that the realisation of an idea is a matter of *struggle* is an important corrective to the Idealist vision of history unfolding according to rational principles. The fact remains however that Hegel's Idealism is a powerful principle of historical development and historically, it has always been the idealists who have emphasised human agency in social change.

(e)   *Hegel Minimised the Effect of Mundane Relations on Institutions*

In his *Philosophy of Right*, Hegel is sometimes unbelievably naïve: he thinks that the civil service is a meritocracy which serves the public good, and doesn't even consider that civil servants look out for themselves like everyone else; it doesn't seem to matter to him how judges are appointed or from what social class they are drawn, because it is their concept to apply the law to individual cases, not further their own class interest or political agenda; that the constitutional monarch, as the traditional owner of the land, is an extremely wealthy person does not cause Hegel to suspect that their judgment might be prejudiced by their wealth.

Marx ridicules this idealism, commenting wryly: "The man within the civil servant is supposed to secure the civil servant against himself" (*Critique of Hegel's Philosophy of Right*, 1843), noting that a 'civil society' necessarily operates *within* the civil service. Hegel seems to think that officials will act according to their job description; Marx does not believe this. Everyone knows that the remuneration structure determines an employee's actions far more effectively than the organisation's mission statement.

In the USA everyone seems to accept that Supreme Court judges act according to their own political agenda, and that lower courts can be relied upon to discriminate against African Americans. However, in most developed countries, despite the fact that judges are always drawn from the most privileged section of society, the law is generally developing and applied in a rational fashion worthy of writing up in the law books, rather than being naked expressions of class prejudice. What is more, when decisions are made which *are* expressions of naked class prejudice, there is public outrage, appeals and political pressure, and even if it takes centuries, there is some merit in the aphorism: "The truth will out." In the long run, Hegel's idealism in this sense often turns out to have more merit than a cynical materialism would suggest.

(f)   *Hegel Overestimated Speculative Reason Relative to the Social Process Itself*

Hegel first published his *Encyclopædia of the Philosophical Sciences* in 1817. In this monumental work he aimed to prefigure (among other things) the entire development of natural science. But natural science did not progress by the writing of ever more perfect encyclopaedias; rather individuals and groups beavered away on narrowly defined problems, all the while lacking any sophisticated view of the whole (c.f. the definitions of idealism and materialism mentioned above in §1), and gradually, over the decades, the separate strands more and more came into contact with one another, and over time viable overall scientific visions began to emerge.

Each strand of research has been influenced by the discoveries and theories and techniques and tools produced by the others; the scope and complexity and interconnectedness of human activity developed further and further, throwing up new insights, new techniques, new theories, new forms of experiment, new possibilities endlessly, way beyond the capacity of a single mind to plan or predict. Every insight, every discovery is the product of a human mind, but the process as a whole is a gigantic worldwide social process.

At each moment, the latest discovery to come out of the endless unfolding of human practice is intelligible in the light of what has gone before, what has already been discovered. And who can tell what the next discovery will be?

When Marx wrote the *Communist Manifesto* he left many questions unresolved. One of these was the question of whether the workers' movement could could seize power and how they would use that power. Marx did not attempt to work this out in advance. He had to wait until the Paris Commune demonstrated what the workers movement would do. He then amended the Manifesto accordingly – adding to the 1872 Preface to the *Manifesto* the words: "One thing especially was proved by the Commune, viz., that "the working class cannot simply lay hold of the ready-made state machinery and wield it for its own purposes."

Likewise, in the writing of *Capital*, Marx took as his starting point not the concept of value as such, but the simplest social form in which value was manifested, the exchange of commodities. Living in England, at that time the most advanced capitalist country, it was possible to *observe* the unfolding of the value relation from practice of exchanging commodities. A "concept of value" was observable in the writings of the political economists, but *exchange of commodities* is a real act which can be witnessed and grasped viscerally by anyone. He could make the development of capital intelligible by means of his analysis of exchange, but he made only the most general and qualified predictions of where it was headed based on his clear view of where it was at the moment. But he could not predict the successive transformations of capital which would flow through the economy after his death, and Marx knew this.

But compare Marx's analysis with Hegel's naïve analysis of value (See §16.1 below).

As an Idealist, Hegel falsely believed that Logic would allow him to foresee what was as yet outside social experience. Given that he was writing in 1817, before the Michelson-Morley experiment, the microscope and Darwinism, and the burgeoning of natural scientific investigation during the 19th century, it is obvious to us that the project of the *Encyclopaedia* was untenable. Only the social process itself as a whole can work out and reveal the real content of a concept; this insight is available to the theorist to the extent that they can observe and make intelligible what exists or is already at least in the process of development.

This is the difference between Idealism and Materialism in terms of method.

§7   Spirit and Material Culture

In the Knox translation of §264 of *The Philosophy of Right*, we have the very succinct definition: "Spirit is the nature of human beings en masse." But when we go to the original German which Knox was translating, it has to be said that this is a very liberal translation. A more correct translation would have: "The nature of human beings en masse is spiritual (*geistig*)," and Hegel goes on to point to the "doubled aspect" (*gedoppelte Moment*) of *Geist*: the for-itself knowing and willing of individuals at one extreme and public knowing and willing (*Substantielle wissenden und wollenden Allgemeinheit*) in the form of rights and institutions at the other extreme. The implication of this is that neither individuals, in that hypothetical 'state of nature' (in which humans or their forebears are supposed to have lived in small bands with no language, civil society, institutions or culture of any kind), nor institutions which are 'defunct' (in the sense that they play no part in general social life) are 'spiritual'. *Geist* implies both knowing, willing individuals, and active public institutions or culture. Only human beings en masse manifest Spirit in this sense.

It is easy to miss some of what this entails. It is well known that a person left to grow up on their own, isolated from contact with other human beings, will not grow up to be a human being in any real sense. But this is only the half of it. If you dropped a few hundred people into the jungle *together*, but without the benefit of the *material culture* built up by preceding generations (including a common language), the result would be just as bad. When we are talking about human beings en masse, then we are talking not only about so many human beings, and the forms of organisation and cooperation that they are involved in, but also the material culture that they have inherited, created, modified and use together. This includes language, both spoken and written, means of production from factories and mines through to crops and tools, and domesticated animals and soils which are as much a product of human culture as are our own bodies and our basic needs. Language is not only necessary for communication between individuals, but individuals use language to coordinate their own activity. But it is something we inherit, culturally, from previous generations.

For Hegel, all the objects of material culture are 'thought-forms' (*Denkbestimmung*, or thought determinations), as are the semantic, practical and theoretical norms the material culture underpins. It is true that the material culture entails 'externality': even words require a medium, whether air or paper or optic fibre. (Hegel's aphorism: "The tool is the norm of labour, the word is the norm of reason" sums this up nicely.) But the psyche is only able to interact with other psyches to the extent that it can act through such artefacts. So the material substratum of culture is as much a part of Spirit as the actions utilising it. And a word is what it is only in connection with other words and its use by human beings and the same is true of a chair or a key or a rosary. That is, Spirit is an organic whole.

One of the difficulties that Hegel had to overcome was the problem of *dualism*. Descartes operated with a mind/matter dualism, and Kant's philosophy got around mind-matter dualism at the cost of introducing a host of other dichotomies and the need to overcome these dichotomies in Kant's philosophy was one of the main drivers for Kant's critics, such as Fichte and Schelling and Hegel. For Hegel, it was all 'thought'. We will presently come to how Hegel arrived at difference from this abstract beginning, but the idea of thought, of Spirit, shaping the world, served as a foundation upon which to build a philosophical system.

Hegel was an idealist, but he was an *objective idealist*. That is, 'thought' was not for him something subjective or inward, something opposite to and distinct from 'matter'. Thinking is the activity of the human mind, but the content of that thinking is objective, it is given from outside the individual, the individual's 'second nature'. The objects around us which are the content of our perception and thoughts are the objectifications of the thought of other people and ourselves. We live in a world not natural material objects, but of 'materialised thoughts' – artefacts. But what makes a key a key is not its shape or its substance, but the fact that there's a lock somewhere that it opens. What makes a chair is not its shape or the material of which it is made, but its use in the practice of sitting and the comfort and social status acquired by sitting in a chair rather than on the floor. Artefacts are objectified norms.

One of the most popular approaches to modernizing Hegel today is what is known as 'intersubjectivity'. 'Intersubjectivity' begins from the same observation that "spirit is human beings en masse," but reduces human activity to momentary, unmediated communicative actions between individuals. The human body is taken for granted and subsumed as part of the acting 'subject', language is comprehended as the performance of individuals without regard for the objective prior existence of a common language. The entirety of material culture – technology, land, domestic animals and all the material relations involved in the reproduction of the species – is pushed into the background. An interpretation of human life which marginalises the material reproduction of society and of the species itself, and the entirety of material culture self-evidently fails to capture the notion of human beings en masse, of Spirit. Hegel was not an intersubjectivist in this sense. In his effort to understand spirit, these artefacts (the material culture present to everyone) are very much included in the picture.

In Hegel's words:

> If thought is the constitutive substance of external things, it is also the universal substance of Spirit. [*Das Denken, wie es die Substanz der äusserlichen Dinge ausmacht, ist auch die allgemeine Substanz des Geistigen*] (1830/2009, §24 note)

CHAPTER 3

Hegel's Idea of Science and Philosophy

Hegel completed the *Phenomenology of Spirit* in 1807, and wrote the Preface after completing the work itself, before rushing the manuscript off to the printer. It seems to me that it was only after writing the *Phenomenology* that Hegel achieved clarity about his system, and then summed it up succinctly and brilliantly in the Preface. The Preface is, accordingly, both a summary and an introduction to the whole of his philosophy which was only fully elaborated with the publication of the *Encyclopædia of the Philosophical Sciences* in 1817, and refined over the following decade. The Preface is not an easy read, but it is well worth the effort of a Hegel novice to read it for themself. Below is a summary of the main ideas.

§1   The Subject Matter of Philosophy

Previous European philosophers had posed the problems of philosophy – the limits and validity of knowledge, the meaning of existence, etc. – in terms of an individual philosopher confronting a natural object. These issues were dealt with in distinct disciplines, the classical disciplines of epistemology and ontology, alongside ethics, logic, the history of philosophy, and theology. Hegel's approach was quite different.

Rather than posing the problems of philosophy in terms of an individual subject confronting a natural object, Hegel posed science in terms of what we could call a 'subject-object', a subject whose object is constituted by the subject's own activity.

If an individual, abstracted from their being part of some definite community in some definite historical period, is confronted by an object, of which they are supposed to have no previous knowledge – what can he or she make of it? Such an approach would be a totally abstract and unrealistic posing of the problems of epistemology and ontology. Every community has some form of life and as an integral part of that form of life they recognize this and that type of thing; the meaning of these things is given in the same forms of activity in which the individuals themselves have been shaped. To a member of a hunter-gatherer community a mark in the soil is as meaningful as the words on the pages of the Bible are for a member of a Church congregation, while a public health system makes a lot of sense for a British worker, but makes little sense for a stock broker living in a leafy suburb in the USA. Generally speaking, everything that is found in a given form of life makes sense within that form of life. By taking the entire form of life as his starting point, Hegel made the sciences of epistemology and ontology obsolete as distinct sciences.

What this means is this: instead of having a subject on one side (typically an individual person) and an object (typically a natural object) on the other, we have a subject-object – a system of life with its various aims and means of achieving those aims. Taken separately, the objects and the activities make no sense at all, but taken together they make a form of life, valid and transparent within its own terms. Insofar as this form of life is a stable, self-sufficient, self-reproducing whole, it can be said to be an *identical* subject-object. That is, the conceptions and motivations of the various individual actors are the mirror image, so to speak, of the social processes and artefacts they produce and reproduce. It is "equal to itself."

However, it is generally *not* the case that a community lives like this in perfect harmony with their natural and cultural environment. At some point, someone does something obviously wrong without breaking a law (or vice versa) or observes an inexplicable phenomenon, a crop fails or some other event brings to light some contradiction or gap inherent in their life-world. Suddenly, problems of epistemology and ontology are posed. People have to answer questions like 'Why can't I do this?', 'What kind of object is this?', 'How do I know this?' The problems of philosophy therefore arise out of the gaps, limitations and contradictions within a whole form of activity, exposing contradictions implicit in the nature of the subject-object itself. Robert Brandom rightly defined the subject matter of philosophy as *norms*. What is ultimately called into question then is not some finite fact or the validity of some proposition, but the validity of the entire form of life or the activity as a whole.

Philosophy is a particular kind of activity, giving a certain kind of voice to the community of which it is a part, and not a way of life in itself. Centuries of historical development are required for philosophy as a special form of activity to develop to the point where Hegel can have a readership for a book like the *Phenomenology of Spirit*. Nonetheless, "every one is a son of his time; so philosophy also is its time apprehended in thoughts" (1807/1910 Preface). Philosophies unfold historically in a coherent and intelligible manner, building on what has been achieved by past generations, but need to be understood within their own terms. Questions of epistemology and ontology taken out of this context are meaningless.

§2   The Diversity of Philosophical Views are Parts of a Single Whole

The above would seem to lead us to some kind of relativism.

Ideas and practices can only be understood or criticised within the terms of the form of life of which they are a part, *insofar* as the relevant form of life is an isolated, self-standing system of concepts and practices. These are very important provisos, however.

The basic idea of relativism is both true and false. In the first place, there is nowhere in the world, no form of life, which is isolated from the rest of the world – all peoples actively participate in a world system of social interaction (whether they want to or not). On the other hand, all cultures are diverse within themselves and always in a process of change. And these two qualifications are connected with each other.

So for example, the claim that it is OK that women in Saudi Arabia can't go outside without a male relative as chaperone because that is 'part of their culture' is wrong because there are Saudi women who strongly object and appeal to well-known international norms to validate their claim. Saudi Arabia could not exist as it is other than through its connections with the rest of the world, so the appeal to international norms is valid, and these women deserve our solidarity. And in any case, Saudi Arabia is developing towards modernity and has an economy thoroughly penetrated by trade, and is consequently riven with contradictions, reflecting the conflict between its traditional and bourgeois norms.

On the other hand, some Saudi women who wish to claim their rights appeal to the Quran to show that this repression is not in fact mandated by Islam, but is rather a remnant of traditional non-Islamic norms. All the great religions of the world have reconciled with traditional practices in the various countries where they have taken root, and traditional and theistic ideas have merged in a single, national way of life in each country. People are generally unaware of these contradictions inherent in their own system of beliefs. But inevitably, internal critics will discover these contradictions and open them up to bring about change, whether for better or worse. This criticism from *within* a culture, in its own terms, either *by* someone who is part of that culture, or in solidarity with internal critics, is what is called "immanent critique" and we owe this idea to Hegel, though it was Georg Lukács who coined the term in 1923.

The Absolute and the Relative

So (absolute) relativism is based on the untenable idea of ways of life (systems of concepts) absolutely isolated from all other cultures and absolutely lacking in internal contradictions, and therefore static and eternally unchanging. Hegel's is not this kind of relativism.

Hegel takes up the problem by reflecting on the diversity of philosophical systems. People expect that a philosopher should either agree with a proposition or disagree with it. People want to know whether a given claim is true or false. But according to Hegel this demand is misplaced. A claim by a philosopher *and* its negation are both necessary moments[1] of an organic whole. An example is what I just said above about relativism. Relativism's claim, that any practice which is valid within a given culture cannot be criticised from outside, turned out to be both wrong (every culture is also part of a world system of interaction) and correct (internal critics must appeal to internal norms in order to win their claim). No matter how valid some claim might be, even within its own community, there is always some truth in the very opposite claim.

The point is to understand the *limits* of any truth beyond which it becomes a falsehood. For example, I have said that a practice cannot be criticised from outside a culture unless there is a party within the culture which is challenging it. But it would be going too far to condone slavery on that basis; slavery is an absolute crime, a crime under international law, and even if no slave objects to their enslavement it is wrong, absolutely. There is an absolute within the relative. But to condemn slavery in antiquity on that basis would be ahistorical and wrong. There is always a relative within the absolute.

Opposing moments do not necessarily sit side by side as if calmly understanding their own limitations. Necessary as the opposition between two principles may be, their opposition becomes a contradiction which must be resolved. What contradictions reflect is that all philosophical systems (and this goes for political opinions as well) are part of an organic unity which needs to be understood as the progressive evolution of the truth. By 'truth' Hegel just means what comes out or prevails at the end, when the ground of the conflict between two opposing principles is revealed. Once the 'truth' of a conflict is revealed, it is somehow overcome with a principle for which the opposing sides are seen as partial, one-sided views. The earlier positions are therefore not to be disparaged, as having been refuted and disposed of, but on the contrary appreciated as necessary steps towards achieving a sounder system, and are actually implicit within that more developed system. It may be inconvenient from the point of view of polemic to grant that one's protagonist has some truth in their claim, and you may never be reconciled to your opponents'

---

1   More on this later, but a 'moment' is an essential aspect of a whole or essential phase of a process. Unlike a part, a moment cannot exist separately from the whole, nor the whole without its moments.

claim, but sooner or later the dispute will most likely fade into the background, overtaken by a deeper difference.

Consider for example, the tendency of thinkers of our times to disparage the idea of 'progress' so treasured in past times, a scepticism which is often associated with the label 'postmodernism'. If, after all this time, philosophy has arrived at an understanding of the limits of the concept of 'progress', then it is surely thanks to these progressive thinkers and their critics that we have achieved this understanding. And does this not prove that, after all, progress *has* been achieved? 'Progress' is a valid ideal insofar as it looks to the improvement of *specific aspects* of life, but invalid insofar as it neglects that such progress always has a downside.

Now it needs to be said that there is a danger inherent in Hegel's view that philosophies, and the ways of life which they express, are bound together in "the progressive evolution of truth." There is an undoubted truth within this claim – every change within a system of life (unless the system simply collapses) and every development in a philosophical dispute happens because it successfully resolves some contradiction. But it must not be overlooked that this progress almost invariably happens at a cost. So for example, the introduction of a new method of production may solve some problem in the given branch of production, but may at the same time degrade the quality of the product or undermine the quality of life of the producers. There is a general rule: you *cannot compare totalities*. I may decide to emigrate from Australia to the US in order the benefit from the better pay for writers, but that doesn't mean I think the US is a "better country"; I may, for example, return to Australia when it's time to raise my kids. Comparison presupposes the abstraction from a totality of some quantity, because only quantities can be compared. Whole ways of life, entire cultures, cannot be compared because they are qualities. Nonetheless, Hegelianism may be in danger of slipping into dogmatism by means of the historical comparison of ways of life: was feudal Britain necessarily superior to ancient Britain because it historically overtook it? This would be a category error. Hegel himself could be accused of this error in that he recognises the right of the more modern civilisation to overthrow a more primitive form of life – it was on this basis that he supported Napoleon's army in Germany and the slave revolution in Haiti. The same claim could be made with respect to a protagonist's argument, saying that it is an 'old' argument which has been overtaken by history. This is a form of dogmatism which is prevalent today (and indeed is expressed in the objective working out of history itself), but one which the readers of this book will recognise for the dogmatism that it is. Hegel himself was subject to this kind of dogmatism in the place he gave to historical necessity in his system, but this does not oblige us either to follow him in this nor throw out the entirety of his philosophy as a result. Hegel himself gives us the means to rid ourselves of this kind of dogmatism.

§3   From Where to Begin?

An ongoing problem in the history of philosophy is "From where to begin?"

The scholastics looked to revealed religion or the writings of the ancients for an authoritative starting point.

Modern philosophy began with Descartes' claim that, like the mathematics of his day, philosophy must begin from some certainty which could provide a foundation on which to build reliable knowledge. Descartes observed that despite the work of philosophers over centuries, there was nothing which was not still in dispute. Therefore, he resolved "never to accept anything for true which I did not clearly know to be such ... commencing with objects the simplest and easiest to know." As a result, he determined that "I think therefore I am" (1637/1911, Pt. II) (i.e., that because he was thinking, he could be sure that he existed, even if his thinking was delusional) was the only claim that he found to be beyond dispute, and made this the starting point of his philosophy.

On the other hand, the Empiricists held that the only reliable knowledge was that given by the senses. Kant however observed that "though all our knowledge begins with experience, it does not follow that it all arises out of experience," (1787/2007) and agreed with the Rationalists that the data of the senses is unreliable, and sought a secure foundation in what could be warranted by Reason alone, a priori.

Hegel Took a Completely Different Approach

Rather than seeking the elusive axioms from which an edifice of certain knowledge could be deduced, Hegel recognised that *science always begins from a falsity*. A philosopher begins their work by criticising the philosophical wisdom of his or her own times, pointing out defects in it, and working out concepts which overcome those defects. In doing so, the philosopher needs to recognise that the target of his or her criticism has itself arisen as a solution to philosophical problems of the past.

Before Philosophy (or any branch of science) is born there will be a period of gestation during which the problem cannot yet be explicitly formulated. The philosophy is born with the first formulation of the problem. Then there is a process of 'maturation' (rather than the correction of errors) in which what was implicit in one system is made explicit in the next, subjected to criticism and resolved in various ways. The history of philosophy is therefore more like a process of successive approximation than a mathematical theorem beginning from axiomatic truisms. Truth always issues from falsity.

In the course of this development, different *particular* points of view are expressed. These particular positions are not 'wrong', but rather *incomplete*, and await subsumption into a more complete system of ideas. In this way, what begins as very abstract ideas – i.e., simple concepts, lacking depth and content – are overtaken by more and more *concrete* ideas, systems of concepts which are rich in nuances and interconnections. For example, Darwin's original idea of evolution was: natural selection under conditions where offspring resemble their parents. That's all. Nowadays, ideas like genes, random mutation, ecosystem, co-evolution, the 'selfish gene', punctuated evolution and so on are all built into the concept of evolution of species. Each of these innovations was made in response to problems which arose with the concept of evolution as it stood.

So the history of philosophy is not at all a sorry tale of mistaken ideas from the past which have been refuted, but rather a series of efforts to overcome problems which have in turn brought to the surface deeper contradictions. It is this history which gives meaning and depth to the philosophy of one's own time. Making sense of the history of philosophy is therefore the most important task of the philosopher who wants to understand the philosophy of her own times and solve the problems of her own times.

The question which lies at the beginning of a philosophical endeavour is a *given*, it comes from outside that endeavour itself, providing it with its starting point. So philosophies (sciences, systems of ideas) are not closed circles, but on the contrary are linked together as parts of an organic whole.

Therefore no philosophical proposition stands on its own; its real meaning is contained in the whole process which led up to its formulation as a more or less satisfactory resolution of a series of problems. Feminism is not therefore a state of the world in which women have an equal place with men (or any such formulation), but the whole process, the long drawn out struggle of women to throw off their oppression and reshape the world and their place in it. Likewise, socialism is not a state of the world in which the exploitation of labour by capital has been abolished, and nor is it just a set of principles, but rather the centuries-long struggle by labour to free itself from capital. In short, Hegel "does away with the contrast between result and the process of arriving at it."

Philosophical propositions are not therefore to be taken as static assertions of the relation between a subject and a predicate, but rather expressions or concepts which can be shown to contain within them contradictions. As a result propositions must be seen as inherently self-moving. Logic has a dimension of time.

This is how Hegel viewed the history of philosophy, and political or social movement activists should adopt the same attitude towards the movements of the past and their protagonists of the present, even if on many occasions they have manifested perverse expressions of a social problem rather than satisfactory solutions.

Hegel's real innovation, though, was that he adopted the same approach to the structure of *his own* philosophy – he took the dynamic he observed in the history of philosophy and made it the moving force of *his own* philosophical system, rather than attempting, like Descartes or Spinoza, to construct his philosophical system like a geometric theorem.

Hegel begins each of the topics he addresses with an abstract concept which has arisen from the real history of philosophy and subjects it to immanent critique. By this means, Hegel does not 'refute' the principle, but on the contrary transforms it into a concrete concept which embraces an entire science (just as Darwin's original idea of natural selection did). The science is therefore an integral whole, with every part bound together with every other through the action of critique.

"Knowledge," according to Hegel, "is only real and can only be set forth fully in the form of science, in the form of system." Consider for example any law taken from Physics or Chemistry such as 'bodies fall at a uniform rate of acceleration under the influence of gravity'. On its own this is a relative truth – friction for example is not taken account of – and it seems to belie the fact that a satellite may circle the Earth in a circle with uniform speed. The principle of uniform acceleration under gravity stands up only as part of a whole system of science, not as a stand alone principle.

Likewise, the claim of women for equal pay is only valid in the context of recognition of the equal worth of women's work and the overcoming of the gender division of labour. On its own, it is just a very abstract principle.

§4   The *Phenomenology* and the *Logic*

The *Phenomenology of Spirit* was Hegel's first book and the book which made his name in Germany, and was intended to be an introduction to his philosophical system. The printed title of the book was "System of Science. First part. The Phenomenology of Spirit," with the second part containing the Science of Logic, Philosophy of Nature and the Philosophy of Spirit (i.e., the *Encyclopædia*). At the time he wrote the *Science of Logic* in 1812 he saw it as a "sequel" to the *Phenomenology*.

But the *Phenomenology* is not an Introduction in any normal sense – giving an outline of the text to come and how it relates to other treatises on the same subject, written by his predecessors or his contemporaries. In any case, the philosophical system which it introduces had not yet been written. Rather, in accordance with the spirit of his philosophy it traces how Mind[2] (i.e., *Geist*) comes to philosophy, and invites the reader to follow. The *Phenomenology* deals with material which is given empirically. A "phenomenon" is the *appearance* of something, so he claimed to be writing a book about the appearance of Spirit. But because Spirit is appearing *to itself*, he describes it as "Science of the *experience* of consciousness" – the book's working title before it went to the printer. The appearance of spirit is demonstrated via a number of themes in turn: the development of individual consciousness making its way from naive realism to philosophical consciousness; the history of philosophy from antiquity to modern philosophy; the historical development of state-forms; the evolution of religion, art and philosophy – each of which are manifestations of the appearance of unfolding consciousness. Taking 'consciousness' as something manifested in these diverse domains of reality, each of them empirically verifiable, was a revolutionary step. The *Phenomenology* culminates in a section called "Absolute Knowledge," in which knowledge understands itself as the resolution of the successive problems manifested and overcome in coming to this point in the development of human consciousness – capable of formulating and understanding Hegel's philosophy.

But philosophy as such (as Hegel sees it) begins with the *Logic*. Hegel's philosophy is systematic like no other philosophy before or since. It begins with the first category of the Logic, Being, and proceeds by means of immanent critique, concluding with a passage cited, in the original Greek, from Aristotle's *Metaphysics*:

> thought thinks itself because it shares the nature of the object of thought; for it becomes an object of thought in coming into contact with and thinking its objects, so that thought and object of thought are the same;

thus completing the circle, from bare, abstract concept of Being back to Being, but Being now turns out to contain all of human experience implicitly within it.

---

2 In using a capital-M for "Mind" I am following the common practice among Hegelians. In German, all nouns begin with capitals, but the conventions for using capitals in English are rather odd. Apart from proper nouns, we use capitals for Nature, God, South, New Year, Socialism, etc. But it may look strange when we write Being or Appearance. The convention I use is that I retain the capital for categories in the context of writing about Hegel's philosophy, and in addition, when referring to a concept such as "Science" in a context where it is acting as an *agent*, just as we would for the proper names of organisations. For example, "The Liberal Party is the enemy of Science."

There is no place *within* this system for the *Phenomenology*, it is not a part of the system. What the *Phenomenology* gives us is the "objective, demonstrated science" from which the need and possibility for philosophy arises along with the material from which it is nourished. As Hegel explains in the first preface to the *Science of Logic*:

> It is in this way that I have tried to expound consciousness in the *Phenomenology of Spirit*. Consciousness is spirit as a concrete knowing, a knowing too, in which externality is involved; but the development of this object, like the development of all natural and spiritual life, rests solely on the nature of the pure essentialities which constitute the content of Logic.

Note well: "the pure essentialities which constitute the content of Logic." I take "pure essentialities" to mean something akin to "laws of motion," as if an astronomer had presented all his observations of the positions of all the heavenly bodies and then demonstrated Kepler's laws of planetary motion. We will return to this question in Part 2, on the Logic.

Nevertheless, the *Phenomenology* is an essential part of Hegel's work, but somewhat in the same way that Engels' observations on the practice of capitalist businesses could be said to be part of Marx's *Capital*. Over and above this, however, it does do the job Hegel intended for it, of introducing the reader to Hegel's approach. But the structure of the *Phenomenology* is arcane and, at the time of writing it, Hegel was not yet clear about some of the categories and their relations to one another.

Ideas and Forms of Life

One of the ideas which are introduced by the *Phenomenology* which is crucial to Hegel's contribution to how we understand thought, is expressed, in his own words:

> The mind's immediate existence, conscious life, has two aspects – cognition and objectivity.

That is, Mind (i.e. *Geist*) as Hegel understands it is both *subjective* (i.e., the mental activity of individual human beings) and *objective*. By objective Mind Hegel means the 'constellations' of artefacts – land, tools, buildings, machines, books, art work, spoken words and so on, and the *actions*, manifesting the subjective mental activity and using these artefacts – the economic, social, political and military activities of the community and their artistic, religious and philosophical practices. Not only is Spirit (or Mind, they are just two translations of the German word, *Geist*) both objective and subjective, but there is an important triad here: the way of thinking, the forms of activity, and constellation of material culture of a community. The third moment, material culture, is explicitly referred to only rarely by Hegel. I say 'constellation' because the meaning of the relevant objects is not intrinsic in the objects themselves, they are "thought determinations," constituted as part of a whole by their use in human activities.

This idea raises the question of how Hegel sees the relation between how an individual acquires the knowledge of their times and how that knowledge is acquired originally as a cultural and historical conquest by the person's forebears. Hegel put it like this:

> The particular individual, so far as content is concerned, has also to go through the stages through which the general mind has passed, but as shapes once assumed by mind and now laid aside, as stages of a road which has been worked over and levelled out.
>
> 1807/1910, Preface

My friend, Lynn Beaton, once described the Women's Liberation Movement in similar terms:

> The project of women's emancipation is a road which began long ago as a narrow and perilous track. Each development has improved the road but the second wave feminists built the highway we now travel.
>
> BEATON, 2013

Hegel expressed the significance the *Phenomenology* this way:

> All the various moments appear as modes or forms (*Gestalten*) of consciousness. The scientific statement of the course of this development is a science of the experience through which consciousness passes.

That is, all the concepts which the philosopher must analyse are given empirically in social formations; the philosopher's job is to understand why and how the given formation changes and passes away, knowledge provided by the study of the manifestation of these concepts (i.e., phenomena) in the various domains of thought as outlined in the *Phenomenology*. The purest form of each moment is given by the philosophers of the time, as expressed in Hegel's aphorism:

> Each philosopher expresses the thought of their times.

CHAPTER 4

The *Phenomenology* and 'Formations of Consciousness'

The key concept of the *Phenomenology* is the 'formation of consciousness' (*Gestalt des Bewußtseins*), which we referred to earlier as a 'subject-object'. I shall critically examine how a 'formation of consciousness' can be conceptualised and the various entities which can be subsumed under the idea of a 'formation of consciousness'. Finally, I shall give an outline of the master-servant narrative.

§1   How can We Conceptualise a 'Formation of Consciousness'?

Terry Pinkard, a highly regarded contemporary translator and interpreter of the *Phenomenology*, sees a 'formation of consciousness' this way:

> A 'formation of consciousness' in Hegel's sense is composed both of the ways in which a form of life takes certain types of reasons (or, to put it more generally, norms) as authoritative for itself and the ways in which it articulates to itself why it is legitimate for those reasons to count for it as authoritative, non-optional reasons.
>
> PINKARD, in HEGEL 1807/1996

Pinkard's point is that a formation of consciousness cannot be characterised in a behaviourist manner simply in terms of what people *do*. The reasons people give for what they do is just as important and is what makes the actions intelligible to themselves and others.

Pinkard agrees with the Pragmatist Robert Brandom that a formation of consciousness is characterised by the norms, whether implicitly or explicitly recognised by the actors, including norms of inference and judgment, as well as semantic norms and theoretical norms reflecting metaphysical beliefs.

When I refer to 'practices', I take it that 'practice' includes the thinking that goes along with the behaviour and makes behaviour intelligible, but the emphasis given by these authors give to the reasoning is warranted. We cannot understand a system of practices without listening to why people are doing this or that, what is meant by this word or that, and building up an understanding of the whole system of concepts and metaphysical beliefs which make the practices intelligible to the actors themselves.

So if we wished to conceptualise patriarchy as a formation of consciousness, then it would not be sufficient to enumerate the behaviours which demean, stigmatise and discriminate against women; we want to get at the concepts whereby those who are part of the patriarchy justify these behaviours to themselves and others.

I don't think Hegel's idea of using 'formation of consciousness' as a key concept for understanding the world is anything like as idealistic as it sounds at first hearing. A shared system of actions, i.e., a *practice*, is made intelligible by means of the concepts organising the activity. Nevertheless. I will often refer to *social formation* synonymously with *formation of consciousness*.

However, there is more to it than that. *Every act is a judgment.* Every time I do something (and by 'do' I mean 'act purposively') I am making judgment on the entirety of my purposes and everything bearing on my situation. The various concepts and perceptions which contribute to this judgment are, in general, implicit, so if asked to rationalise my action, my explanation may not withstand criticism very well. "I didn't ask for Peter's opinion while ignoring Mary waving her hand because I valued Peter more than Mary, it just happened that he caught my eye first."

So there is a tension here; the "subject-object" is not an "identical subject-object." I am saying that it is necessary to utilise the "inferentialist" interpretation of formations of consciousness, which conceives of a formation of consciousness entirely in ideal terms, because we reason with words and our actions are governed by norms. Insofar as our actions are rational we endeavour to think things through and then act accordingly. I can't write a book here which is filled with actions not words. We communicate with words, both with ourselves and others. This does not take away from the fact, however, that when people act in the world they do so with a *practical intelligence* that may surpass what even the most sophisticated theory, including their own self-understanding, could make explicit.

I propose that a 'formation of consciousness' can be conceived of as a formation (or system) of actions, but that each of these actions can be understood as a judgment, so as a result, a formation of consciousness can be grasped in its own theoretical terms, as well as being subject to objective observation and analysis. And we recognise that there is a tension between the two – self-consciousness and objective analysis.

§2   How do We Conceive of a Formation of Consciousness as a *Whole*?

In the expression 'formation of consciousness', 'formation' is a translation of the German word *Gestalt*, which carries the connotation of being an integral *whole*. The question is: how do we conceive of a formation of consciousness as a *whole*? The first part of the answer to this question is that we must identify the *units* of which the *Gestalt* is composed, and we have said that the units are actions, which can be conceived of as judgments. The second part is to answer this question: what binds all the units of the *Gestalt* into a single whole?

Inferences by their very nature are linked together in logical chains and networks: 'this is so because this and this are so, but because this is so, and so on'. Such chains of justification will come back to some settled norms which are 'beyond question'. Hegel showed with his Logic that such networks of inference unfold out of a single concept, I will call it the *Urbegriff*, or Urconcept, of the *Gestalt*. The Urconcept can be conceived of as an identity which 'seeks to realise itself' or as a grounding principle. For example, all scientific activity, if called into question, has to justify itself as being Science – i.e., the fundamental concept of what constitutes scientific activity – evidence, logic, peer review, verifiability, etc., connecting it to other scientific activity.

Actions are also, by their very nature, linked together in aggregates called activities or projects, and what unifies an aggregate of actions is the purpose (*Zweck*); each action has its own goal which differs from the purpose of the activity as a whole, but which together with all the other actions serves the common purpose which is definitive of the *Gestalt*. We can use the same example: Science. Every action which counts as part of science contributes to the accumulation of scientific knowledge and is subject to the norms of Science.

I will discuss what Hegel tells us about the dynamics of formations of consciousness in §4, but there is one other issue about the conceptualisation of a formation of consciousness which needs to be dealt with first. This is the question of the artefacts which mediate the actions making up the *Gestalt*. Hegel makes this issue almost (but not quite) invisible in all but his earliest writings and it is an aspect of Hegel's philosophy which is ignored in all other interpretations of Hegel. However, it is the necessity of using material objects which means that human action is always subject to Nature and the changes which have been made in Nature by our forebears. Otherwise, our actions appear to be utterly subjective, unrestrained and without consequence. (See Part 1 of Hegel's Theory of Action, below).

I refer to the artefacts mediating the activity of a formation of consciousness as a 'constellation of artefacts' because, like astrological constellations, the relations between the objects and their meanings is not inherent in the material existence of the artefacts themselves: the meaning is *imputed* to the objects by human activity; nonetheless, no human action is possible without the mediating role of this constellation of artefacts.

For example, a nation almost invariably uses a tract of land as a central mediating artefact binding it together. There is nothing inherently 'Australian' about the land mass to the south-east of the Indonesian archipelago, but by millions of actions over centuries this land mass has been 'marked' as 'Australia' and plays a pivotal role in all activities constituting the nation of Australia. Likewise, there is a mass of written and spoken words which define everything from the laws of Australia to all the concepts of which the English language is a carrier, etc.

By noting that the formation of consciousness requires the coincidence of not two, but three elements – briefly, the actions, the objects and the means – we open our eyes to further dimensions of the potential for contradictoriness in a formation of consciousness.

For example, a man might denigrate a woman by his actions without being aware of having violated a norm; or alternatively, he might inadvertently use a word which was inappropriate in the given situation, even when his meaning was valid.

On its own, a constellation of artefacts, such as exemplified by the material culture uncovered by an archaeologist or the literature of a past epoch cannot be considered as a 'formation of consciousness'. Following Hegel we could refer to this as a 'system of unconscious thought' or using Schelling's term, 'petrified intelligence'. The activity of living human beings is essential to what is meant by a 'formation of consciousness'.

§3   What can be Called a 'Formation of Consciousness'?

Archetypically, a 'formation of consciousness' is taken to be a nation or a people. Sometimes the term 'community' is used. But 'nation' or 'people' or 'community' *cannot* be conceived as it is normally conceived, as a collection of *people* – it is an aggregate of *actions* or *judgments* united by common norms and rules of inference. Consequently, it can only approximately correspond to a nation or any group of people. A bureaucrat might be satisfied with an alphabetical list of all citizens as an adequate definition of a nation, but we would not. Nations outlive all of their citizens, and include dual citizens and citizens who have no real connection with the country. The nation is defined by the *principle* which determines citizenship, not who are actually citizens at a given moment.

A 'formation of consciousness' can also be a way of conceiving of a single person. A person's actions are all unified as the person's identity, by means of their own body (an artefact) and the series of their actions.

But it is at the 'meso-level' that the concept of 'formation of consciousness' is most useful. Here a 'formation of consciousness' corresponds to a collaborative project such as a capitalist firm, or a social movement, or at the broadest level, institutions like Science or the Catholicism.

In each case, there is an aggregate of actions, generally carried out by different individuals, all subject to the shared norms characteristic of the project and directed towards the realisation of a shared ideal.

§4   The Dynamics of 'Formations of Consciousness' is in the *Logic*

The dynamics of 'formations of consciousness' is understood as a rational, i.e., intelligible process, and the logic which applies to these dynamics is what is elaborated in Hegel's Logic, the subject matter of Part 2 below. But there is one idea which should be mentioned from the outset.

Every 'formation of consciousness' has at its centre a concept, what I have called the Urconcept, which is the most fundamental principle and the principle definitive of the 'formation of consciousness' and which constitutes its identity.

Like any concept, the Urconcept undergoes a process of concretisation as it interacts with the broader reality and faces challenges of various kinds, both internal and external. The Urconcept acts as a kind of 'court of last appeal' against which any dispute must be decided.

Through experience, what begins as an abstract concept becomes more and more concrete, what was a 'general idea' becomes rich in corollaries, qualifications and nuances. For example, second wave feminism began with a rejection of sexism. Any proposal or claim which was deemed 'sexist' would be rejected by feminists. But this came under internal criticism from, among others, women of colour who declared that not all women had the same experiences of sexism and nor did they share the same interests. As a result of a series of such challenges, the idea of feminism became much more nuanced and qualified.

At a certain point in its realisation, *every* concept falls into contradiction with itself. In adapting to each challenge the concept becomes more concrete, but at some point it either collapses or is taken over by a new concept, and the entire formation is restructured.

Those familiar with Thomas Kuhn's "The Structure of Scientific Revolutions" (1962) will recognise this process. According to Kuhn, in the development of a branch of science there is an accumulation of observations which cannot be satisfactorily explained in the existing 'paradigm'; someone formulates a new paradigm which provides a satisfactory description of the relevant observations; the old paradigm fights back fiercely insisting on the absurdity of the new paradigm; eventually, the new paradigm wins the day and supplants the old; but then the science is left with a plethora of unanswered questions; then follows a period of 'puzzle solving' guided by the new paradigm; gradually new anomalies build up until a new crisis is reached, requiring a new scientific revolution. And so on. Kuhn was a sociologist of natural science, but what he describes essentially corresponds to Hegel's idea about a formation of consciousness.

All social movements go through crises like these. The result may be a transformation of the movement, which can surmount the crisis and further develop, or the movement may collapse, split or wither away. Hegel's Logic is the science which gives us insights into this process.

§5   The Importance of the Master-Servant Narrative is Exaggerated

I don't wish to go any further in the interpretation of the *Phenomenology*, but there is one issue which must be dealt with before moving on.

Some interpretations of Hegel take as their point of departure the master-servant relation, §§178–196 of the *Phenomenology*. Leaving aside academic Hegel specialists who are familiar with the whole of Hegel's work, there are those who take master-servant relation (and possibly the *Phenomenology* altogether) as their essential Hegel and those who take the *Logic* (and possibly also *The Philosophy of Right*) as their essential Hegel. Very broadly speaking these are two almost mutually exclusive schools of thought. What is special about the master-servant relation is that it is an apparently *unmediated* confrontation between two parties lacking any third party to mediate between them. By contrast, the *Logic* is all about mediation, beginning from the observation that "There is nothing, nothing in heaven, or in nature or in mind or anywhere else which does not equally contain both immediacy and mediation." There is hardly a passage of the *Logic* in which the problem of mediation does not figure.

In fact, this is also true of those 19 paragraphs of the *Phenomenology*.

The master-servant dialectic makes its first appearance in Hegel's first sketch of his system in 1802/3, *The System of Ethical Life*, in which it features *twice* (both in the case of the formation of a state, and in the case of employer-employee relations). It reaches its most extended exposition in the *Phenomenology* in 1807, where it takes the form of a foundation myth, apparently as a parody of state-of-nature narratives like those of Rousseau and Hobbes. Subsequently, a much attenuated version is relegated to Hegel's Psychology, within the *Subjective Spirit* section of the *Encyclopædia*, where it is embedded within the intricate structure representing the the transition from Nature to self-consciousness, while other aspects are dealt with in the *Objective Spirit*.

The passages which follow master-servant narrative ('Lordship and Bondage') in the *Phenomenology* – Stoicism, Scepticism, Unhappy Consciousness – describe a series of transformations of the slave's consciousness in becoming reconciled to their social position. It is a very interested narrative which has proved a rich mine for academic and political interpretation over the past 80 years or so. But for me, as a student of Hegel's mature work, I don't look to Hegel for 'models' and scenarios like this.

In the *Subjective Spirit*, the subsequent episodes of the master-servant narrative in the *Phenomenology* are absent. Instead, we have a finely graded structure representing the formation of self-consciousness: Consciousness proper, Self-consciousness (Appetite, Self-consciousness recognitive, universal self-consciousness), Reason. Hegel remarks here:

> To prevent any possible misunderstandings with regard to the standpoint just outlined, we must here remark that the fight for recognition pushed to the extreme here indicated can only occur in the natural state, where men exist only as single, separate individuals; but it is absent in civil society and the State because here the recognition for which the combatants fought already exists. For although the State may originate in violence, it does not rest on it; violence, in producing the State, has brought into existence only what is justified in and of itself, namely laws and a constitution. What dominates in the State is the spirit of the people, custom and law. (*Philosophy of Right*, §432)

The *Phenomenology* was Hegel's first published book, composed at a time when his ideas were still in gestation, and written in a rush to meet the publisher's deadlines. Only 250 copies were printed during Hegel's lifetime, and he used to give copies as presents to friends. At the time of his death, 25 years later, Hegel abandoned work on a second edition of the *Phenomenology*, and wrote on the manuscript: "Characteristic early work not to be revised – relevant to the period at which it was written ..." The *Phenomenology* and Hegel's earlier work are important for understanding how to read Hegel's later works, especially his *Logic*, but in this writer's view, they are immature representatives of Hegel's thought, which have been largely superseded by his mature works.

The master-servant relation is about how two subjects, lacking any third party, common language or system of law to mediate between them, still somehow manage to mediate their relation. The mediating element in this extreme case is the Servant's labour, which meets the desires of the Master. This can be expressed in terms of two subject-objects confronting one another, each *duplicated* by the separation of subjectivity and objectivity; the subjectivity (desires) of one subject (the master) mediates between the objectivity and subjectivity of the other ('delayed gratification' for the servant) while the objectivity of the servant (the servant's labour) mediates between the master's needs and their satisfaction (its objectivity). The servant's needs are modified and met within the activity of the master subject-object. They mediate each other.

Thus by the separation of the once-immediate relation between needs and their satisfaction by a division of labour in which the labour of one subject is directed by another subject, who appropriates a surplus, relations of material interdependence are created. But these relations of mutual dependence are formed on the basis of the forceful subordination of one subject by another.

In the absence of a shared system of norms, unless a subject has some surplus product which another subject needs, then there is no basis for any relationship between them at all. In the event that two such subjects were to come across one another (as if you came across a wild animal), either one would kill the other, or they would recoil from one another and peacefully go their own way.

But if, contrariwise, one subject is capable of producing a surplus product, and is therefore ripe for exploitation, but is unwilling to fight to the death to defend their freedom, then it is a matter of historical record that the one will be enslaved by the other. Hegel puts a lot of store by the willingness of either party to fight to the death, and he may be right in this. While Hegel was writing the *Phenomenology,* Toussaint L'Ouverture's and Jean-Jacques Dessalines' army were fighting in Haiti under a banner realistically inscribed "Liberty or Death."

Once the slave and the master are incorporated into a single system of social reproduction, Right (property relations and a customary or formal system of law) replaces relations of force on the foundation of this mutual interdependence of subjects – even if slavery only "occurs in a world where a wrong is still right." (1821/1952, §57ad.).

Whereas Rousseau asked "How is that man is born free but is everywhere in chains?" Hegel showed that, on the contrary, that although human beings are inherently free, the state begins with slavery and human beings *become free* only through the perfection of states, states which mediate the relations of person to person and foster the development of socially conscious individuals.

§6   How the *Phenomenology* was 'Rediscovered'

Until Alexander Kojève gave his lectures on Hegel at the École des hautes études in Paris, 1931–1939, no-one had made any interpretation of the master-servant relation at all. Marx mentions it in three words in a table of contents of the *Phenomenology* in his 1844 Manuscripts, and that is as far as anyone went in interpreting these 18 paragraphs. Outside a select group of Hegel scholars it was quite unknown until Kojève's lectures were published in 1947. Up till then, French speakers had known Hegel only via a very poor translation of the *Encyclopædia* by the Italian, Augusto Vera, which resulted in a distinct lack of interest in Hegel among French speakers. Internationally, all the attention of Hegel scholars had been directed at the *Logic* and the *Encyclopædia*, and among specialist readers, his Lectures on Philosophy of History, History of Philosophy, Religion and the Aesthetics. In the English-speaking world, Hegel was known almost exclusively through the *Logic*. Almost no-one read the *Phenomenology*.

In 1947, France was facing national liberation movements as it struggled to recover its colonies in North Africa and Asia, so with Kojève's lectures and the publication of Hyppolite's excellent French translation and his book on the *Phenomenology* also published in 1947, we can see how Hegel caught the imagination of French intellectuals. Simone de Beauvoir's *The Second Sex*, was published in 1949 and utilised themes from the master-slave narrative. Thanks to Kojève, suddenly everyone wanted to read the master-servant narrative.

Since 1947, this highly eccentric passage, which is very uncharacteristic of Hegel, became the touchstone of French philosophy, and then spread to the world, to such an extent that today, even many educated people still think that Hegel was someone who had a theory about the master-slave relationship, and even that he saw it as the archetypal interpersonal relationship. Hegel scholars know this is a myth, but the strength of the myth is such that it is difficult to dispel. Familiarity with the master-servant narrative is a *sine qua non* for admission to polite philosophical society. And the mythology does not stop at Hegel. Thanks to Marcuse and others, the idea established itself that Karl Marx had built his theory on the master-servant dialectic. This is utterly untrue. Marx hardly knew the passage existed. Likewise, Alex Kozulin is responsible for the myth that Lev Vygotsky (1896–1934) modelled his Psychology on the master-servant dialectic, though it is certain that Vygotsky knew nothing of this work.

Nonetheless, there is good reason for the master-servant dialect having become popular among the Left in post-War France and for the growth of interest in it in following decades. The relation between a colonial power (such as France) and an emergent post-colonial consciousness among the colonised people is exactly represented in the master-servant dialect, insofar as international law and institutions were absent or ineffective in those conflicts. When the colonialist arrives on the shores of a foreign land, the local beliefs and languages (their subjectivity) are invisible to him and simply destroyed; it is, just as if the indigenous people were wild animals,. The land and labour of the colonised (their objectivity), however, is subordinated by the coloniser and transformed into an objectification of their own needs. This results in a kind of dual personality for those who are colonised, and the struggle to overcome this can be seen in terms of the master-servant narrative.

The master-slave dialectic may reflect the experience of subordinated groups in a state when they put forward a claim for recognition, such as in the case of the ethnic minorities, feminists and other identity claims. However, the effectiveness of the master-servant relation in shedding light on the trajectory of a social movement (such as the workers' movement, the Women's Movement, the Civil Rights Movement, the Peace Movement, etc.) is more than questionable. These movements work within a system of law in which the individuals concerned have rights and such movements have invariably sought to use the courts in prosecuting their aims, not to mention making every effort to capture the institutions of governance and sought to transform the system of law by embedding a new concept within the dominant culture. This is not what happens in the master-servant narrative. It is in the *Logic* and *The Philosophy of Right* that we find a conceptual foundation for understanding how a state can be transformed by a radical subject which challenges its norms.

CHAPTER 5

Hegel as Philosopher of Social Movements

§1   It is Hegel's Logic which Makes Him the Philosopher of Social Movements

My claim that Hegel is the philosopher for social movements is not based on Hegel's political ideas or his social theory. It is based on his *Logic*. This is not to say that Hegel's social and political ideas are not of interest. Part 3 of this book is devoted to a reading of *The Philosophy of Right*, which is Hegel's book about politics and social theory and there is much of interest there, over and above seeing how Hegel himself puts his Logic to work in analysing social questions.

There are two aspects to the value of Hegel's Logic for the social movement activist. The first is that the Logic is the logic of social change. The Logic provides a very detailed and fine grained 'physiology' of the transformations through which concepts and the corresponding forms of social action pass as an idea is realised in the world. There are 214 different categories in the *Science of Logic* and we have not yet touched upon these at all; they are the subject matter of Part 2, and so far we have only dealt with generalities. The second aspect is that Hegel's Logic is itself a logic relevant to the scientific consideration of concrete, realistic problems, in contrast to syllogistic or mathematical logic which have only a very restricted domain of applicability. As such it is useful for our own critical thinking and problem solving in the course of fighting for ideas.

The concepts of the Logic are very abstract and their relevance to social movement activity is not obvious. Few of the categories of the Logic have any obvious connection to social categories until you get to the later sections of the book. It is my intention to use frequent illustrations so that the connection between the abstract logical concepts and social categories will become familiar to the reader. But it is not immediately apparent.

On the plus side, Hegel's Logic is, broadly speaking, as valid today as it was in Hegel's lifetime. There are aspects of the Logic which are dated, and these issues will be dealt with in Part 4, but on the whole the problems with the Logic do not undermine the validity of the concepts elaborated in the Logic nor the transitions between them. But there are limits to their validity which were not visible to Hegel. On the other hand, all the other parts of Hegel's writing, which were of literally encyclopaedic extent, have suffered with the passage of time and appear dated in the context of the progress of natural scientific and other branches of knowledge over the past 200 years.

That said, we should look at what Hegel knew of social movements in his own lifetime.

§2   Hegel Knew Emancipatory Social Movements, but No Labour Movement

The Slavery Abolition Movement

Hegel's life spanned from 1770 to 1831. This period roughly corresponds to the Industrial Revolution in Britain, and the most significant social movement of this period was the Slavery Abolition movement.

From the mid-17th century, the use of slave labour in the Americas made the trade in slaves and their exploitation in plantations, especially sugar, the major source of the growing wealth and power of the European bourgeoisie. Although the maritime powers – Britain, Holland, France, Spain, Portugal, Belgium and Denmark – were the main players in this trade, the German bourgeoisie were deeply involved through their business connections with slave-trading nations, and slavery was a major social issue in Germany. While denouncing their own 'enslavement' by their own nobility or foreign powers, Enlightenment thinkers had been mostly blind to the involvement of their own bourgeoisie in *real* slavery. Slavery financed the pinnacle of mercantile capital, and would only be finally eradicated with the triumph of industrial capital in the mid-19th century.

Although slavery had been outlawed in Vermont and other Northern states in the 1770s, and was briefly abolished by France in 1794, but reinstated in French colonies by Napoleon in 1802, it continued in America until 1861. The turning point in the Abolition movement was the successful slave rebellion in Haiti led by Toussaint L'Ouverture and Jean-Jacques Dessalines which defeated French troops and established an independent, constitutional republic in 1805. There had been slave rebellions since antiquity, but this was the first time that the slaves had succeeded in establishing their own state, and what is more, they modelled their state on the ideals of the French Revolution. This not only struck fear into the slave-owners and inspired emulation by slaves everywhere, but put paid to the racist mythology used to exclude Africans from the universal, humanist categories of the Enlightenment. The Haitians fought under the banner of "Liberty or Death" and there is every reason to believe that they took this quite literally. Toussaint's victory tipped the balance in the struggle for the abolition of slavery. The British Slave Trade Act of 1807 reflected the change in the balance of bourgeois opinion, though slavery was not banned in the colonies until 1833, after a protracted struggle by the Abolitionist movement.

Hegel was throughout his life an avid reader of the press, especially the more progressive journals and was an active commentator on political affairs. He subscribed to the German-language journal *Minerva* which was a consistent advocate for the Abolitionist cause and provided blow-by-blow reporting of the revolution in Haiti. So there is no doubt that Hegel was well informed about the realities of Germany's involvement in slavery in general and the Haitian revolution in particular. Further, the Haitian Revolution roughly corresponds to the period of writing the *Phenomenology* and the famous master-slave narrative.

Several aspects of what Hegel wrote about slavery are worth noting here. Firstly, unlike some others of his time, he did not qualify concepts of universality to accommodate slavery, even though his attitudes to non-European cultures was tainted by racial prejudice. Secondly, he insisted that slaves could only be emancipated by *their own struggle*, and further, that self-emancipation entailed "Liberty or Death." Thirdly, however, he favoured a *gradualist* approach which would make it realistically possible for a republic of emancipated slaves to appropriate the cultural and social gains of their former oppressors, rather than the total eradication of the former state and its culture. Hegel further believed that slaves did no wrong in breaking laws which enslaved them and that a state which rested on slavery forfeited any rights as against a foreign power seeking to overthrow it and abolish slavery.

While the Haitians set a new benchmark in ridding their constitution of racism, their history since has been somewhat of a sorry tale, and Haiti has never enjoyed the benefits of democracy and modernity. So even if we do not go along with Hegel's gradualism, it has to be recognised that the opposite policy did not work out too well.

The majority of what Hegel has to say about slavery is not in the *Phenomenology*, however, but in *The Philosophy of Right*. It will often be the case that the reader will not be able to abide Hegel's conservative approach on matters which seem to demand revolutionary solutions, but any reader who fancies themself a revolutionary would do well to heed Hegel's warnings.

The French Revolution

Undoubtedly the most significant social event of Hegel's lifetime was the French Revolution, the entire course of which Hegel observed, as we noted above, from just 620 km away, while he was a seminary student, along with his friends Hölderin and Schelling. The French Revolution was to them what May '68 was to my generation and the Russian Revolution was for my grandparents – hopes sky high, but followed by disappointment. The Great Terror shattered their dreams.

But the Revolution produced Napoleon and the young Hegel hoped that Napoleon's armies would unite Germany and modernise its social system – in other words, do for Germany what Germany could not do for itself, dragging them by force into modernity. But Napoleon was defeated. After the Congress of Vienna in 1815, the reforming Prussian Kaiser promised to introduce a constitutional monarchy, much along the lines of what Hegel sketched in his 1817–18 lectures which later became *The Philosophy of Right*. The *Zeitgeist* shifted however, and the promise was revoked and censorship was imposed. Hegel was forced again to re-evaluate the prospects for modernising Germany.

Hegel's analysis of the French Revolution is found in typically obscure form in the sections of the *Phenomenology* on Individuality and particularly in the section entitled "Absolute Freedom and Terror."

According to Hegel, the Revolution destroyed the state in order to implement Rousseau's philosophy forthwith from above, replacing the state with an immediate identity between individual consciousness and the universal consciousness. In its urge to realise absolute freedom and equality, society was atomised into individuals each of them taking themselves as an incarnation of the Revolution. All distinctions of rank and class were eradicated, all familial, communal and vocational ties were dissolved. In this situation the government was merely the momentarily victorious faction, which, since it had failed to implement absolute freedom would have to be overthrown. The value of individual human lives was set at zero alongside the requirements of the Revolution. The result was the Great Terror in which the Revolution went from eradicating all the pillars of the old society to devouring itself at the guillotine. The essential reason for this tragedy was the determination to impose an abstract philosophical conception from the top down.

By 1819, Hegel's life had been characterised by a series of disappointments. Hegel's early hopes for a modern, united Germany to be created by revolutionary means or from above were abandoned and he thereafter favoured smaller states and *organic* development. Hegel would remain hostile to any kind of Utopianism or attempt to 'design' an ideal state and impose it from above. Social change had to be achieved organically. A reformed state in Germany had to be the outcome of a social movement within a stable political system, not imposed by a foreign army or a benign ruler.

The Industrial Revolution

Hegel followed the social and political developments in England closely, he studied the British political economists such as Adam Smith and James Steuart and subscribed to British journals, and in 1931 wrote a monograph on the English Reform Movement, of which he was very critical. So it is clear that he followed the development of the industrial revolution and its social impact closely. However, in Germany, industrialism was only at an embryonic stage. Hegel regarded factory work as dehumanizing. The artisan and merchant guilds, which Hegel saw as an essential component of governance, were being destroyed by the factory system. Hegel did not live to see the rise of the trade unions, even in England, far less a revolutionary socialist and labour movement such as appeared in the 1840s.

National struggles were endemic in Europe, and Hegel held that any people had the right to violate laws which were imposed on them by an alien power. Again, Hegel believed that every people had a right to self-determination and freedom presupposed preparedness to die for that liberty. Although his contemporaries were apt to use the cry of "slavery!" for any kind of oppression they wished to denounce, Hegel did not see in the self-emancipation of oppressed peoples or African slaves anything resembling the working class overthrowing the bourgeoisie and establishing socialism.

The fundamental difference between Hegel's and Marx's attitudes towards the state arose from the changes that took place in Europe from the fall of the Bourbon monarchy in France in 1830 up to the continent-wide revolutionary movements of 1848. Marx saw the state as an instrument of *one class* against another, whether or not its rule entailed a 'balancing' act. To Marx's contemporaries, the bourgeois state was inherently alien and hostile to the proletariat. Hegel saw the state as essentially universal, even if in a given instance it failed to live up to that. The working class of Hegel's times, chiefly organised in guilds which united masters, journeymen and apprentices in the same organisation, would have seen the state the same way. Hegel held that the poor needed, so far as possible, to be *included*, but it was the responsibility of the elite to lead the reform process.

The poor in early 19th century Germany were a social problem; their condition needed to be ameliorated and they needed to be included in social and political life. But they did not *see themselves* and Hegel did not see them as the agents of revolutionary social change.

This all changed in the 1830s and '40s. The first uprising of a modern proletariat independently of the bourgeoisie occurred in Paris in July 1830. The workers won the streets, but found that they had no voice, and a bourgeois government filled the void. Hegel did live to see this uprising, but he did not recognise in the Parisian mobs the emergence of a new progressive social class. Indeed, such a thing was unimaginable for him.

§3   A Concept is a Form of Practice

If I were to claim that the concept of 'cricket' is a form of social practice, then this would be uncontroversial, as cricket *is* a form of practice, namely a sport. But there is a little more to it than that, even in this uncontroversial case. When people play cricket or even participate as spectators or commentators on the game, the *idea* of cricket is essentially entailed in what they do. For example, an infant who has seen perhaps their older siblings playing cricket and acts out bowling a ball, swinging a bat and running back and forth does not yet quite have the concept of 'cricket' and what the infant doing is just not cricket. To be cricket, a true concept of cricket has to be engaged in the actions of doing it.

Consider someone who spent some years in Denmark and wants to convey to you the concept of *hygge*. Let us suppose that they never asked a Dane to explain it to them in English, but simply observed Danes and how they used the word, and in what circumstances until they were able to use the word appropriately themselves. Rather than making some rough English translations, such as 'cosiness' or 'comfiness' or 'friendliness' they could tell you about the way the word was used by Danes. In other words, the concept could be conveyed by describing the role of the word in practice, when it is and is not appropriate to use the word.

Generally speaking when a word enters the language as the bearer of a new concept (rather than an incidental innovation in terminology), it is solving some problem, and the word is marking a new solution to a problem or a new opportunity or development in social practice. For example, the word 'sexism' entered the English language in the US in 1968, as an extension of the idea of 'racism'. The behaviours designated by the word were not new, but the urge and the possibility for women to come together and publicly fight it was new. Although the word designated male behaviour, its meaning was in the action of those women who acted against it. The new concept was not the object (sexist behaviour by men, which was ancient) but the women's activity to fight sexism, i.e., the subject; though obviously the two sides go together.

So when I say that a concept is a form of practice, I mean it in the sense of the *subject*, the people who act with the concept in mind – the cricketers who know the rules and aims of the game and the women who know sexism as an oppressive behaviour.

What then if the concept is that of a common artefact, such as 'chair'[1]?

A moment's reflection will tell you that a chair can be any of a wide variety of shapes and materials, so it is not a bundle of physical attributes that makes something a 'chair'. Rather it is its 'sittability', its effectiveness in comfortably supporting the human bum. But not quite, an upturned milk crate may, in certain circumstances function as a chair, but it was not manufactured as a chair; it is a *substitute* for a chair. Something that was manufactured as a chair but serves its function very poorly, perhaps collapsing under the weight of a sitter or wobbling because of its uneven legs, is a chair, but a very poor chair, because it does not correspond to its concept. The people who design and make chairs need to have a good concept of what makes a chair, and whoever buys them and places them in suitable locations, such as next to the dining table, but not in a train, needs also to understand the chair in terms of the way it is incorporated in human practices, that is, grasp its concept.

Chairs have only been around since the 16th century as items of workplace and household furniture. Before that chairs were more like thrones and their function was to confer status. Growing industrial strength and a more egalitarian sentiment made it possible for everyone to have a 'throne', and thus arose the modern chair. Now the status conferred by sitting on a chair rather than on the floor or a handy milk crate is taken for granted, but is nonetheless implicit in the use of chairs in contemporary life – imagine inviting a friend around to dinner and have them sit on the floor while you sat in a chair! This status aspect is implicit in all chairs, but so integrated is it in the norms of contemporary society that we are not consciously aware of it. It is part of the concept of 'chair' nonetheless.

Although 'chair' is a concept of a set of practices – from designing and manufacturing chairs, selling them in furniture shops not lumber yards, buying them and placing them next to tables and using them by sitting on them and expecting to be comfortably supported – everyday consciousness takes the word 'chair' to indicate a certain kind of artefact. This practice is called 'objectification'. Hegel calls such objects "thought-determinations" (*Denkbestimmung*, sometimes translated as 'thought-forms', a category which extends to natural objects as well as artefacts. The conviction that a concept is a thing of some kind, that it is what it is independently of human activity, is a 'fetish', a fetish which is necessary for participating in day-to-day life, but nonetheless, a fetish, a superstition.

There is a particular category of such 'thought-determinations' which should be of particular interest to social movement activists, and these are the

---

1   I thank Heikki Ikaheimo for this example, and of which we will have more to say later on.

artefacts which are used to symbolise and mobilise social movements. Let me mention some examples:

Gandhi used the *charkha* – a traditional portable spinning wheel – to represent *swadeshi*, collective self-sufficiency, the concept around which he organised the fight for independence from Britain and in particular the boycott of imported English cloth.

In the early 1990s, the Serbian activists of *Otpor!* fighting against the Milosovic dictatorship used rock music, something which was repressed under the dictatorship, which symbolised freedom for young Serbs.

In January 2018, women of the White Wednesday movement in Iran began wearing white scarves, instead of the traditional black hijab, and wearing them in unconventional ways which did not cover their head, demonstrating their rejection of clerical rule.

Over and above this are all the logos and flags and the numerous 'colour revolutions' which have given scope for sympathisers to improvise endless ways to suggest support for the movement.

So artefacts can be bearers of concepts through their manifold interconnections with human practice. You see a *charkha* and you see a concept – Indian national independence and collective self-sufficiency. Etc.

Words are of course the supreme artefacts and essential bearers of concepts. "Words are the tools of Reason" according to Hegel, just as "the tool is the norm of labour" (1802/1979). But we should not fetishise on words; consider the changes in social life that we have experienced over the past 200 years; would it be reasonable to suggest that this could be understood in terms of changes in language (even though it is all recorded in words), rather than in changes in our technology and forms of social practice supported by that technology? It is surely uncontroversial that culture is transmitted and changed through the artefacts we make and use in our activity. Words have a special place in forming our consciousness of these changes in practice.

§4   A Social Movement is Understood as an Entire Process of Social Change

One of the first things we must learn from Hegel is how to form an adequate concept of 'social movement'. What is usually taken to be a 'social movement' is just one phase in a more extensive process which I usually call a 'project'. A project exhibits the features normally associated with social movements in only *one phase its development,* and it is neither easy nor useful to analytically cut this process up into pieces prior to understanding the whole. Here I will use the term 'social movement' in this broader sense of the *entire* process.

Let me outline what that entire process is.

To begin with, at point zero, so to speak, there is no social movement, there is only a number of people who all occupy some social status or location. But they are not necessarily aware of sharing this status with others. This social status may be being an educated woman, or an African immigrant or a carrier of the BRAC1 gene.

Then something happens which either creates a problem for all the people of this social status or provides an opportunity of some kind. Perhaps only a very few people are aware of this fact or perhaps all of them, but in most cases few of them are aware that the problem or opportunity is one shared with *others* or have an adequate concept of it.

Then someone proposes a concept of the situation they all share, and signifies this concept with a word (probably an existing word imbued with new meaning, or a new word altogether), or some other artefact (such as Gandhi's charkha) and publicises this.

Thanks to this new concept, all the affected or interested people have an understanding of their shared situation and probably some degree of consciousness of being part of a 'group' sharing this situation, and they begin to act in concert in some way. It can also happen that the new concept is *imposed* on a group of people, but in this case the concept objectifies them and cannot become a subject until transformed by the action of those affected and re-appropriated.

New concepts can only arise within institutions where there are *definite norms* which are capable of manifesting contradictions and stimulating the formation of a new concept. Where 'anything goes', there can be no contradiction. Whether the contradiction arises under external pressure or internal critique, once the concept has arisen it can spread into more general usage.

To know the problem does not immediately mean to know the solution. Many different solutions will be tried out one after another. The initial concept is thereby modified; misconceptions are dispelled through bitter experience, more and more adequate concepts are formed, until the problem and solution come together in a simple abstract idea which encapsulates the shared problem in such a manner as to be able to transform their situation.

All going well, next begins a process of institutionalisation. The abstract concept enters general social practice and becomes part of the language. Actions formerly carried out by activists are carried out by institutions – either new institutions (such as a Sex Discrimination Commissioner) or existing institutions are modified (new occupational safety procedures are introduced). Sometimes the activists themselves are appointed to positions in the state apparatus, and even whole activist groups may be co-opted into institutions, such as Aboriginal self-help groups who receive funding for the services they provide.

Through this process the original concept gradually dissolves into everyday discourse and its origin forgotten. There are no longer any special institutions dedicated to dealing with the issue, but the entire society has been transformed. We could say that the social movement has been 'objectified'; as in the beginning, there is no special consciousness of the social movement; it has dissolved into the modified social structure. For example, some people think of restrictions on tobacco marketing as a feature of "government regulation." In fact these regulations are the product of two or three generations of an anti-tobacco social movement which *changed* the concept we have of smoking.

The processes that will be discussed in what is to follow cover this entire life-cycle and a social movement activists needs to be aware of this broader context.

The 'Other' is the Mainstream

Nowadays one quite commonly hears or reads the expression: 'the Other'. 'The Other' originates from the reading of Hegel's master-servant narrative by Alexandre Kojève; on one hand we have the master and on the other hand is the Other. French imperialism was the master, the Algerians were the Other. Simone de Beauvoir adapted the same trope: man was the master and woman was his Other. Nowadays, the Other is taken to be some minority (Muslims, transsexual people, homeless people, ...) denigrated and/or feared in the dominant 'master' culture. This is all very well so far as it goes; it undoubtedly provides certain insights into the reproduction of prejudice and oppression. But it does not help in understanding self-emancipation and social transformation.

In taking the Logic as our central text rather than the *Phenomenology*, the polarity is reversed. The active side (the subject) is the social movement, the group which wants to emancipate itself or otherwise bring about a transformation of social life. The object (the Other) is the existing state of affairs or institution which is the taken-for-granted 'object' which the subject both acts upon and uses.

Our interest is not so much in explaining how oppression reproduces itself but how a subject can emancipate themselves and transform society.

§5   How to Read Hegel and What to Read

I will conclude this introduction with a brief word on reading Hegel. It goes without saying that the more Hegel you can read the better. If you can read

German well, read Hegel in the original German. Otherwise, it is fine to read Hegel in English translation. There will be many occasions when terminological clarification is necessary and may entail reference to the original German. But that is one of the functions of this book.

Recent translations are on the whole superior to old 19th century translations. Personally, I am happy with the most well-known 19th century translation of the *Shorter Logic* by William Wallace because this is basically the same text as that read by thousands of others before me, and I find it advantageous to share the same text. The definitive edition of the *Science of Logic* is the translation by A.V. Miller and this is also the most widely cited translation. Miller's translation of the *Subjective Spirit* is also to be recommended. I use the T.M. Knox translation of *The Philosophy of Right*. Terry Pinkard's very recent translation of the *Phenomenology* is to be highly recommended.

My recommended reading is:
- The Preface to the *Phenomenology*;
- The *Shorter Logic*, i.e., Part One of the *Encyclopædia*, including the Introduction.
- The *Science of Logic*, but do not attempt to read this book from cover to cover. It should be used to further explore material you find in the *Shorter Logic*. The Prefaces and Introduction are of particular interest, and in the course of this book I will direct you to certain particularly lucid passages.
- The *Philosophy of Right*. Hegel's Lectures on *The Philosophy of Right* were recorded in 1817–18 when Hegel could be more frank, before censorship was imposed. But nothing is lost by sticking with *The Philosophy of Right*, the same book which has been read by generations of activists before us.

There are many other books, but if you have read the above you will be well placed to choose whatever suits your particular interests. If Art is your thing, read the *Lectures on Aesthetics*; if Education is your thing, read the *Subjective Spirit*. And so on.

In reading the Logic it is essential to understand Hegel's meaning in *his own terms*. Lay to the side any interpretations or prejudices you may have had about Hegel and just read what he says. Once you gave grasped Hegel's meaning, then you can make interpretations or read secondary literature about the passage. Of course, I am going to usher you into your Hegel reading with this book, but I do urge you, when I direct you to some passage of Hegel, to first lay to the side what I have said about it, and read it in its own terms and try so grasp the argument. Read Hegel slowly, line by line. Then come back to this book or other secondary sources.

At this point, before going on to Part 2, on the Logic, the reader should read the Preface to the *Phenomenology*.

PART 2

The Logic

∵

CHAPTER 6

The Subject Matter of the Logic

Before beginning a detailed reading of the Logic, I want to refresh some basic questions to do with what the Logic is about, and introduce some of Hegel's forms of expression.

§1   The Logic is the Logic of Formations of Consciousness

Let's read how Hegel defines the subject matter of the Logic in the section of the *Science of Logic* entitled "With What must Science Begin?" This essay reflects on the *Phenomenology*, which provides the starting point for the Logic and the whole system.

> There is nothing, nothing in heaven, or in nature or in mind or anywhere else which does not equally contain both immediacy and mediation.
>
> *Science of Logic*, §92

Every transition in the Logic, even its very first concept, Being, or the immediate, is mediated. The *Phenomenology* showed that the beginning of Hegel's philosophy is mediated by the long drawn out process through which consciousness eventually arrives at the system of philosophy, "absolute knowledge." On the other hand, this knowledge is immediate, that is, empirically given objective knowledge, which can be justified in its own terms. Thus the Logic is both mediated and immediate.

So, does the *Phenomenology* provide the 'axioms' on which the Logic is built?

> ... to want the nature of cognition clarified *prior* to the science is to demand that it be considered *outside* the science; *outside* the science this cannot be accomplished.
>
> *Science of Logic*, §92

With the Logic, two different processes are entailed: on the one hand, the derivation or proof of the simple concept from which the Logic will begin, which lies *outside* the Logic, in everyday consciousness, and on the other hand, the exposition of the internal development of that concept itself which forms the *content* of the Logic *scientifically*.

> The beginning is logical in that it is to be made in the element of thought that is free and for itself, in pure knowing. It is mediated because pure knowing is the ultimate, absolute truth of consciousness. The Phenomenology of Spirit is the science of consciousness, and consciousness has for result the Notion[1] of science, i.e. pure knowing. Logic, then, has for its presupposition the science of manifested spirit, which contains and demonstrates the necessity, and so the truth, of the standpoint occupied by pure knowing and of its mediation.
>
> In this science of manifested spirit the beginning is made from empirical, sensuous consciousness and this is immediate knowledge in the strict sense of the word; in that work there is discussed the significance of this immediate knowledge. Other forms of consciousness such as belief in divine truths, inner experience, knowledge through inner revelation, etc., are very ill-fitted to be quoted as examples of immediate knowledge as a little reflection will show.
>
> In the work just mentioned [i.e., *The Phenomenology of Spirit*] immediate consciousness is also the first and that which is immediate in the science itself, and therefore the presupposition; but in logic, the presupposition is that which has proved itself to be the result of that phenomenological consideration – the Idea as pure knowledge.
>
> *Science of Logic,* §93

Despite claims to the contrary, with apparent support from Hegel himself at times, the Logic does *not* begin without presuppositions. The presupposition for the Logic is philosophical consciousness – "the Idea as pure knowledge," the real product of an empirically given history, which knows itself as a product of this history. The Logic is a real product of a real development. The Logic is a real product of people are who capable of philosophical reflection with a cultural development on which to reflect. This is very far from Kant's reliance on Pure Reason being hard-wired into every individual's brain!

Secondly, and related to the point above: "the Logic is the truth of the Phenomenology." That is, Hegel has taken us through the immanent development of consciousness, its *own* internal movement, and in the end consciousness negates itself, and passes over into something eternal, which is its 'truth'. When Hegel says something is 'the truth of' some process, he means: this is what the

---

1   "Notion" is synonymous with "Concept," both being translations of the German *Begriff*.

process turned out to be in the end. In this case, consciousness develops up to the point of absolute knowing ('absolute' because it is secure knowledge, not liable to fall into contradiction with itself when it passes some limit) where it comes to know itself as a necessary process of development, as the work of Spirit, he would say. So its *truth* is the pure essentialities of manifest spirit, the Logic. Putting it another way, the Logic is what turns out to be the "essential phenomenology."[2] We will come across this type of transition later, in the Logic itself.

Thirdly, we see that manifested spirit, of which the Logic is the truth, is a science which refers to an empirical content, manifested spirit, i.e., objectified consciousness. Like any other science, Hegel's *Logic* must have an empirical domain in which its claims can be exhibited and tested. The *Phenomenology* provides this empirical domain. That the narrative presented in the *Phenomenology* is an idealised or notional narrative does not take away from this fact; all sciences have as their object idealised or necessary (as opposed to contingent or accidental) forms of movement. In this sense what the Logic has to deal with is not only mediated, through the development of a science, but also immediate, in that it is given in experience.

The empirical domain in which the subject matter of the Logic is to be validated is consciousness, *objective* consciousness, that is consciousness manifested in the history of social practice and culture. In particular, the Logic is to be the logic of formations of consciousness, or *Gestalten*. These 'projects' (self-conscious systems of social practice – institutions and social movements) are the object domain over which the Logic is validated.

§2   The Logic is the Foundation for a Presuppositionless Philosophy

Now I will defend the opposite thesis: that the Logic is the presuppositionless foundation for a presuppositionless philosophy.

Hegel expends a lot of energy emphasizing that philosophy cannot set off from arbitrary presuppositions or axioms or borrow its premises from another domain. Any finite science being only a part of philosophy, has a beginning

---

2   "This movement of pure essentialities constitutes the nature of scientific rigor per se" §34 of the Preface to the *Phenomenology* in Terry Pinkard's translation. Or "It is in this way that I have tried to expound consciousness in the *Phenomenology of Spirit*. Consciousness is spirit as a concrete knowing, a knowing too, in which externality is involved; but the development of this object, like the development of all natural and spiritual life, rests solely on the nature of the pure essentialities which constitute the content of logic." §10 of the Preface to the *Science of Logic*.

and consequently, must find the content of its subject matter given to it from elsewhere. But philosophy *as a whole* cannot enjoy such a luxury – it must form a *circle*. It is self-construing, and must generate its own beginning. Let's look at this passage:

> Philosophy, if it would be a science, cannot borrow its method from a subordinate science like mathematics, any more than it can remain satisfied with categorical assurances of inner intuition, or employ arguments based on grounds adduced by external reflection. On the contrary, it can be only the *nature of the content itself* which spontaneously develops itself in a scientific method of knowing, since it is at the same time the reflection of the content itself which first posits and *generates* its determinate character.
>
> The understanding *determines*, and holds the determinations fixed; reason is negative and *dialectical*, because it resolves the determinations of the understanding into nothing; it is positive because it generates the universal and comprehends the particular therein.
>
> Science of Logic, First Preface, §§8–9

Note that Hegel contrasts 'understanding' with 'reason'. More on this later, but briefly, for Hegel, 'understanding' means knowing how a process or system works, so to speak, but unlike 'reason' does not see where it is going. 'Understanding' is a necessary first stage in any science: clearly identifying the various categories of things to be found and their relations, etc., but this kind of knowledge is superficial. 'Reason' sees the contradictions present in the categories and sees the science as a finite stage in a process which is going beyond it. The typical stockbroker, for example, understands very well how the Stock Market works, making a living out of buying and selling, but unlike most of the rest of the world seems convinced that stocks will go on rising forever, and he will be the last person to recognise that he is essentially a parasite on the working population. That is, they *understand* the system, but lack the faculty of *Reason*.

Whether and to what extent formations of consciousness really pass away (are "resolved into nothing") as the result of sceptical critique is arguable – often a line of thinking which has been disproved continues on nonetheless. For example, patriarchy is an outmoded system, already thoroughly exposed as irrational and exploitative, but it has not *yet* disappeared.

"It can be only the nature of the content itself" which determines the character of the science. The content here is the logical concept with which the Logic begins – the truth of the *Phenomenology*. The 'pure essentialities' are the principles which *underlie* and generate these appearances, the succession of formations of consciousness. In the case of the *Phenomenology*, Hegel's idea of the underlying dynamics at work in the *Gestalten* is internal sceptical critique of the *Gestalt's* ultimate conception of truth. In the case of the Logic, he will have to demonstrate how the series of logical categories (categories of pure thought) can be generated by internal (immanent) sceptical critique, solely by the nature of the content itself.

The Logic must begin with an empty concept, for if the concept were to have any determinant content, it would not be a beginning: one would have to ask "why *this* content? Where did this content come from?" So the Logic must be developed by beginning with an empty concept – just thought, not thought *of* something else already given, just thought – and then allowing the content to develop through the process of *immanent critique*, critique which at each step, draws only on the concepts derived previously and drawing in nothing from outside.

This method of immanent critique Hegel calls dialectic. Dialectic is negative because its sceptical critique undermines and destroys the given shape of consciousness, showing it to be self-destructive. But dialectic is not only negative but also positive in that it not only negates the original proposition, showing a given concept to be "untrue," but it also reveals a new concept which constitutes the truth of what had gone before. All that is required is to determine a starting point which can be asserted without making any presupposition and importing nothing extraneous that does not arise from the method itself.

A Logic which is a self-generated, presuppositionless science dealing only with the concepts implicit in a contentless initial concept, is itself a formation of consciousness, a *Gestalt*, like those treated in the *Phenomenology*. The claim that it is the pure essentialities of manifest spirit exhibited in the *Phenomenology*, depends on the correct identification of the logical concept with which the Logic is to begin.

§3   The Logic Studies the Inner Contradictions within Concepts

Now at this point it is fair to ask what it means to say that a *concept* is 'internally contradictory' or that it can be shown to be 'untrue'. Surely, in the context of logic, it is only *propositions* which can be true or untrue. Take a concept, 'prosperity' for example: how can we say that 'prosperity' is true or untrue? We can say that prosperity exists here or there, good or bad, but how can the very *concept* itself be true or false?

This is how Hegel expresses it in connection with the concept of 'Being': "Being itself and the special sub-categories of it which follow, as well as those of logic in general, may be looked upon as definitions of the Absolute, or meta-physical definitions of God" (*Enc. Logic* §84). Here "the Absolute" and "God" are effectively synonymous. The Absolute is what is infinite, identical with its concept, never falls into contradiction with itself and cannot be transcended.

Take any concept and put it in place of *x* in the proposition "*x* is the abso-lute." So in the above example, we say: "Prosperity is the absolute" or "Prosper-ity is everything." Now that's a proposition which can be subjected to criticism and tested against reality. This is what Hegel meant by the critique of a *concept*. So to say that a concept is *untrue* simply means that it has proved to be *relative* and not absolute, it has its limits, it is finite, true only up to a certain point, but beyond that point it is false. Pursuit of prosperity is OK up to a point, for a cer-tain level of prosperity is a necessary condition for freedom, but beyond that pursuit of prosperity is bankrupt and self-destructive - untrue. This is what is called a 'Category Logic'.

One example should demonstrate what is meant by 'the truth of' a *social practice* or project. A *Gestalt* is the unity of a way of thinking, forms of activity, and a constellation of material culture. It is an open question what may cause a shape of consciousness, or project, to become internally unsustainable, but it asks whether what people are doing corresponds to what they think they are doing and how they represent what they are doing. Is there dissonance between a concept and the representations and social practices which correspond to it? A social practice is untrue if the actual activity does not correspond to its self-consciousness and self-representation. So if we have a maxim like "Prosperity is absolute," then the truth of this formation of consciousness is tested out in the reality of a form of life organized around the God of Prosperity. In this small example we can see that a vast field for social critique opens up around the concept, as soon as it is treated as something *concrete* in this way. As to what is in fact the truth of prosperity, what transcends the pursuit of prosper-ity, that is a problem for an extensive social-theoretical critique.

So a first approximation to the form of movement represented in the Logic is that Hegel puts up a judgment or a maxim, such as in the form of "*x* is absolute" or "everything is *x*," and subjects it to critique as if it represented some concrete form of life. Nevertheless, corresponding to the basic idea of the *Phenomenol-ogy*, which depends on the thesis that social life is intelligible, the critique of each concept is executed *logically*.

Let us clear up some possible misconceptions. When we're talking about cri-tique of a concept, 'Being' for example, we are not talking about the 'thought of being', or 'Being' as a subjective thought form filed away in a brain cell, or what happens to you when you think of Being, or some such thing. We would be talking about 'Being' as the essential character of a formation of consciousness.

Critique of Being then means critique of the viability and vulnerability to sceptical attack, of a certain life-form. The brilliance of Hegel's discovery here is that he is able to reproduce the character of formations of consciousness through an exposition which is entirely comprehensible as a logical critique of claims for a concept as absolute truth. It's a kind of two part harmony, simultaneously logical and social critique.

§4   The Problem of "Moving Concepts"

A great deal of misunderstanding can arise from reading Hegel through the kaleidoscopic lens of the Kantian subject, and a great deal of mischief also arises from reading the Logic through the kaleidoscopic lens of a Cartesian thought-space. The usual "Introduction to Hegel" includes an exposition of Hegel's Logic as a presuppositionless philosophy; often presuppositionless to the extent that not even Spirit or consciousness is presupposed. This is, as we have seen, in direct contradiction to what Hegel says in a number of key texts, about the connection between *Phenomenology* and *Logic*. Writers can believe that this claim is defensible because they themselves do not see that anything need be presupposed in the existence of concepts, believing that a concept can exist independently of being enacted by people. But *where* do concepts exist? According to René Descartes, in some extensionless thought-space inhabited by thought forms.

Typically the first 3 or 4 categories of the Logic are elaborated (few writers ever go further than the first 3 or 4 categories, beyond just listing them) by claiming that if the reader thinks of a certain concept their mind is drawn to think of another concept, and then another. A person's attention is drawn to a word; the reader then contemplates the word, evidently forming a concept from the word, and the concept "slides into," or "disappears into" or thought (of an individual thinker) "leads itself to" or "becomes" or is "led by its own intrinsic necessity" to contemplate *another* concept.[3] Thus we get a mixture of *concepts which move* and, without any distinction, the *subjective attention* of a thinking person which moves from one concept to another.

And all this without any consideration as to what language the thinker knows and whether in thinking of 'Being' they are an English speaker, or whether the thinker in question has ever studied philosophy, or whether as a student of Husserl or Heidegger or Sartre they may be familiar with a concept of 'Being' quite different from what a student of Hegel might be thinking.

---

3   All these expressions are quoted from Stephen Houlgate's Introduction to Hegel.

And then we are asked to believe that the thinker, in beginning to contemplate the word "Being," B-E-I-N-G, will be led, by necessity through the 204 concepts which constitute the *Science of Logic*, of *necessity*. If Kant is accused of putting too much store in the reliability of Pure Reason, he had nothing on this. It is unlikely that anyone who has had the first two transitions in Hegel's Logic demonstrated to them for the first time, could get further than the third on their own, simply reliant on Kantian "pure reason."

And in what space do these moving concepts move? A puzzling question for even a philosophically trained person, but to talk about how a concept *moves* without settling how it can have a location in the first place is nonsensical. Maybe what is meant by concepts moving is that they change 'shape', but it still remains to explain what would be meant by the 'shape' of a concept – let alone how a concept *becomes* a different concept. And yet almost every book on the Logic will tell you that concepts move, with generally very little explanation as to what is to be understood by a concept and the space in which it exists, to be able to justify such a claim.

It is plausible to say that the attention of a thinker will move from one concept to another. That is at least a plausible claim and indeed, if we think of something long enough, we will tend to be led to think of something else. But word association is not an acceptable method for science, and certainly not for philosophy. We are talking about a philosophical system worked out in the wake of criticism of Descartes, Spinoza, Hume, Kant, Fichte, etc. If we are going to take the *self-reported stream of consciousness* of individuals as the object for science, then we can't call it Logic and it will probably have a great deal of trouble standing up to scrutiny as a branch of psychology too. Stream of consciousness is *not* the object of Hegel's Logic.

To reiterate, Logic is the study of the *pure essentialities* of shapes of consciousness, or *Gestalten*, the objects which were in turn the subject matter of the *Phenomenology*. These *Gestalten* are the normative unity of a way of thinking (or ideology), a way of life (or project or social practice) and a constellation of culture (i.e., language, means of production, etc.). These social practices provide the content for the Logic, in the same way that a formal theory gets its content from intuitions expressed in the form of a series of axioms.

The presuppositions of the Logic are human beings who have come to absolute knowing, that is to say, to Hegelian philosophy, understanding that they are products of and participants in the whole spiritual journey of human kind to self-knowledge, and that the truth of that journey lies in the pure essentialities of this cultural and intellectual history. The Logic is able to present itself in the form of a self-construing method of logical critique, because the historical development of shapes of consciousness is intelligible and can be explicated in its essentialities, by means of what would be in the context, reasonable arguments.

It is now possible to see why the Logic has an important place in the development of Hegel's philosophical system as a whole, and in the development of *each* of the sciences in the *Encyclopædia*. Each science, together with its object, has developed as a part of the unfolding of those same formations of consciousness. All the sciences and social movements are *themselves formations of consciousness* and if the Logic is valid, it ought to give us guidance on the trajectory of each of them under the impact of critical enquiry and on how the various subordinate concepts of a science are derived.

This brings us to a few remarks on the scope and usefulness of the Logic.

§5   The Logic Concerns Real Situations, Not Mathematical Abstractions

What is the difference between Hegel's Logic and the kind of logic which figures in mathematics or the kind of logic implicit in the rules of evidence used in court proceedings?

Hegel's Logic differs from the kind of logic known to positivism and most other forms of philosophical discourse in exactly the way Hegel's understanding of concepts differs from the narrow, formal logical, mathematical conception of concept, which is closely related to set theory and depends on the *attributes of a thing* rather than the thing itself.

In a court of law, the point is to first discover whether a particular *factual* claim is true, and in very general terms, participants will endeavour to establish an agreed or compelling basis in fact, and call upon logic to be able to determine whether a given conclusion can be drawn from those facts. Mathematics is similar, but is not troubled by the need for agreed facts, which is the job of particular sciences, being concerned only with the rules governing consistent sequences of symbolic propositions within a theory beginning from an arbitrary collection of axioms.

Firstly, each of these sciences (jurisprudence and mathematics) constitute a *Gestalt*. They are methods of arriving at truth which recognise certain criteria for reasonable belief, and the scope of questions which may be asked and answers given. As a result of historical and cultural change, as well as crises in the special, historically articulated institutions of which they are a part (legal practice, universities, and so on), these criteria will *change* and be subject to revision and elaboration. It is *this* process of *change* which is the subject of Hegel's Logic: how the legal discourse in the courtrooms of 2000 differs from what existed in 1900, rather than the logic operative in either case. So there is a strong sense in which Hegel's logic is a *meta-logic* in relation to jurisprudence, mathematics, formal logic, natural science, or any other formalized procedure for determining the truth.

Secondly, formal or mathematical logic takes for granted the validity of putting outside of itself the facts and axioms which it uses. Formal thinking, that is to say, thinking with *forms* abstracted from their *content*, is able to do this, because like Kant, it operates with a transcendental subject in this sense: an entity is an *x* with *attributes*. In Aristotlean terms this *x* is called the 'subject', to which various predicates can be attributed, but for modern formal thought, there is *nothing left* when all the attributes have been stripped away and logic operates simply with the dichotomous, Boolean logic of 'has/has not' any given attribute. To the contrary, Hegel's logic is concerned with the *concept itself*, what it essentially *is*. At the same time, Hegelian logic does not see this essence as something *fixed* and stable, but rather in continuous change. The method of considering an object from the point of view of its contingent attributes alone is valid up to a point, but beyond that point it is untrue and fails. It is at that point, when formal logic, within an agreed set of norms breaks down, that dialectical logic must step in.

So finally, it can be seen from the above that the Logic is a meta-theory of science in the sense that it is concerned with the logic entailed in how sciences change what they take to be given without presupposition and what kind of questions and answers they admit.

This passage from the *Science of Logic* expresses something of this kind which is important about the Logic:

> It is only after profounder acquaintance with the other sciences that logic ceases to be for subjective spirit a merely abstract universal and reveals itself as the universal which embraces within itself the wealth of the particular – just as the same proverb, in the mouth of a youth who understands it quite well, does not possess the wide range of meaning which it has in the mind of a man with the experience of a lifetime behind him, for whom the meaning is expressed in all its power. Thus the value of logic is only apprehended when it is preceded by experience of the sciences; it then displays itself to mind as the universal truth, not as a *particular knowledge alongside* other matters and realities, but as the essential being of all these latter.
>
> *Science of Logic*, §71

We can accept that a 13-year-old can be a chess master or a computer whizz, but no-one would accept having a 13-year-old sit on the Appeals Court or lead an army.

In the Introduction to *The Philosophy of Right* Hegel says: "In this treatise we take for granted the scientific procedure of philosophy, which has been set forth in the philosophic logic." (§2ad.) So broad life experience is necessary in order to understand the Logic, but once understood, it sheds light on all other endeavours.

It is not just science. The Logic deals with the Logic underlying the trajectory of any project or social practice that is in some way organized around a shared conception of truth and shared aims, and that's a *very* wide domain.

Very broadly speaking, Hegel's logic differs from formal logic in that it deals with genuinely complex situations, situations which cannot be circumscribed, situations where the constitution of the situation itself is part of the problem, where it is impossible to draw a line between problem and solution, between the object of study and the subject of study, in other words, all genuinely human problems, as opposed to abstract, analytically impoverished, formal, in-group problems.

This is because deduction Hegel's Logic does not rely on the indefinite maintenance of presupposed idealised conditions and idealised objects having a certain set of attributes. Hegel's Logic is based on the *fallibility* of concepts, their *inevitable breakdown*, their tendency to overstep the limits of their applicability.

It's like the difference between a game of chess and the art of (real) war.

CHAPTER 7

The Three Divisions of the Logic: Being, Essence and Notion

There are three divisions of the Logic: Being, Essence and the Notion (or Concept). In this section I will explain the place and content of each of these divisions. This will allow you to get oriented and able to keep the shape of the whole work in mind while working your way through the whole system chapter by chapter. Then, in the four sections to follow I will go through the Logic step by step, before summing up in the final section of Part 2.

Throughout Part 2 I will liberally quote from both versions of the Logic – the *Science of Logic* and the more accessible but less comprehensive *Shorter Logic*. The aim throughout is to prepare readers for reading and appropriating Hegel's ideas for themselves. The § numbers in the *Science of Logic* refer only to the on-line version.

§1   The Starting Point of the Logic: Being

Let us look to the Introduction to the *Science of Logic* to see how Hegel justified beginning the Logic from the concept of PURE BEING.

Firstly, he claims that, as we have already explained, he regards the *Phenomenology* as having produced the basis for the Logic and the concept from which it is to begin:

> The Notion of pure science [i.e., the concept from which pure science is to *begin*], and its deduction is therefore presupposed in the present work in so far as the *Phenomenology of Spirit* is nothing other than the deduction of it.
>
> *Science of Logic*, §51

He claimed that the *Phenomenology of Spirit* had created the presuppositions for a system of philosophy based on the concept of *pure knowledge*. "Absolute knowledge," the concluding chapter of the *Phenomenology*, is the fully worked out and concrete concept of the historical starting point, which was simply "pure being," i.e., pure knowledge, a starting point which turned out to be internally contradictory.

"Pure knowledge" means not knowledge *of* any particular thing, but *pure* knowledge, knowledge *as such*, that is, Logic. He claimed that the concept of Logic "cannot be justified in any other way than by this emergence in consciousness" (*Science of Logic*, §50).

> What logic is cannot be stated beforehand, rather does this knowledge of what it is first emerge as the final outcome and consummation of the whole exposition. [It can only be justified] by the aid of some reasoned and historical explanations and reflections to make more accessible to ordinary thinking the point of view from which this science is to be considered.
>
> *Science of Logic*, §34

The reference to "ordinary thinking" is not gratuitous.

> The definition with which any science makes an absolute beginning cannot contain anything other than the precise and correct expression of what is *imagined* to be the *accepted and familiar* subject matter and aim of the science.
>
> *Science of Logic*, §50

"Pure Being" is not a concept generated by the Logic and we should not expect the Logic to begin with a definition of 'Being'. Hegel will only give "precise and correct expression" to what is meant by the term in philosophy. But he is not or claiming that this term can be deduced scientifically – his claim is that it has already been posited objectively *by the history of philosophy itself.*

We read in the section of the *Shorter Logic* on Pure Being:

> Logic begins where the proper history of philosophy begins. Philosophy began in the Eleatic school, especially with Parmenides [b. 515BCE]. Parmenides, who conceives the absolute as Being, says that 'Being alone is and Nothing is not'. Such was the true starting-point of philosophy, which is always knowledge by thought: and here for the first time we find pure thought seized and made an object to itself.
>
> *Enc. Logic*, §86

In other words, historically, philosophy began with the concept of Pure Being, and the *Phenomenology* has shown how this concept developed in the history of philosophy to the point of 'absolute knowledge' – a *concrete* concept of Pure Being, while at the beginning, before there was any prior philosophical discourse which could be sublated into the concept, 'Pure Being' could only be a bare, empty abstract concept. But Absolute Knowledge knows itself to be the product of what was unfolded out of the concept of "Pure Being."

"Pure Being" is this bare, empty abstract concept. We can say that *something* is, but that 'something' entails a particular content. Pure Being is simply the 'is'.

§2   Being is the Concept In-Itself, Not yet Conscious of Itself

So far as possible you need to put out of your mind for the moment, any pre-conceptions you have derived from philosophical study about the meaning of the word 'Being', and the same applies to any other of the words you come to as we progress through the Logic. Whatever you may have learnt from the Marxists, Phenomenologists, Existentialists, Psychoanalysts or Analytical Philosophers, the subject matter of these theories is quite different from that of Hegel's Logic and it can be very confusing if you try to follow Hegel's argument with concepts belonging to these ideologies in mind.

In the days when Hegel became a professor, professors of philosophy were required to present a Logic, a Metaphysics, a Philosophy of Nature and each of the other classical disciplines. 'Ontology' is the study of Being, that is, theories about the kinds of thing which can exist and the nature of existence, was normally seen as a sub-discipline of Metaphysics. The series of lectures that Hegel developed for his Ontology became what we now know as his 'Doctrine of Being' (*Die Lehre vom Sein*), the first book of the Logic. Hegel replaced Ontology with Logic.

I have already explained that Hegel saw Logic as the truth of the *Phenomenology*, and that the Logic expresses the pure essentialities of the Phenomenology, that is, the truth of manifest spirit. Further, we know that for the Logic he is looking for a concept which presupposes nothing outside of itself, a concept which imports no content from outside, rests upon no axioms. One can't help but be reminded of Descartes' search for a proposition whose truth and certainty rests on nothing else, and is in that sense, presuppositionless. In fact, Descartes' solution ('I think therefore I am') fails because he presupposed the Ego ("I think ..."), which is a defective foundation for a scientific philosophy.

Hegel's solution is different because he has already, in the *Phenomenology*, elaborated consciousness as something empirically given, so he does not look for his starting point in inward, personal contemplation, but rather in manifest spirit. Further, he is not searching for *certainty*, but on the contrary, he already knows that truth issues from *falsity*.

The outcome of Hegel's search for a starting point for his philosophy is Ontology, but instead of dogmatically setting out with a list of the various kinds of things which can be deemed to be, he conducted a logical critique of the *concept of Being* itself, producing a dialectical unfolding of the contents of the concept of Being.

I should mention here as an aside that all Hegel's major works have the same structure: he identifies the simple concept or notion which marks the unconditioned starting point for the given science, and then he applies the method, the model for which is given in the Logic, in order to elaborate what is implicit in the given concept; he develops "the peculiar internal development of the thing itself."

- In the case of the Philosophy of Nature, he begins from the concept of *Space*, and claims to unfold the philosophy of Nature through critique of the concept of Space.
- The truth of Nature is *Spirit*, which appears in the form of *Soul*, the starting point of the Subjective Spirit.
- The truth of Subjective Spirit is *Freedom*, which is in turn the starting point for *The Philosophy of Right*, which takes the form of a logical critique of the concept of Freedom, the simplest form of which is *Property*.
- The whole *Encyclopædia*, which began with Being, winds up back at Being again, but instead of immediate Being, the entire experience of Spirit is sublated into Being.

This is how Hegel conceives of philosophy as a "circle of circles."

The real subject matter of the Logic is concepts, but the Logic begins with a critique of Being – the Concept 'in itself', that is, yet to be 'unfolded', its content still implicit. The Doctrine of the Notion (or 'Concept') is the third book of the Logic, the Concept *for* itself. Between Being and the Concept is the Doctrine of Essence, the genesis of the Concept.

This concept of 'in itself' comes from Kantian philosophy. It means what the thing is independently of and prior to our knowledge of it. Being is the Concept 'in itself'. We are talking about shapes of consciousness, so we mean the concept under conditions where the shape of consciousness has not *yet* unfolded and become conscious of itself. The 'yet' implies of course that should the shape of conscious which is 'in itself' further develop, then it may become *self-conscious*. But it is not *yet* self-conscious.

So we have something possibly contradictory here: a shape of consciousness which is not conscious of itself, but may become so. So this is an *observer* perspective, because if we are talking about a shape of consciousness which is not self-conscious, then the only terms we have in order to describe it are observer terms.

But what does it amount to? It is an idea or a form of social practice or a project which cannot yet even be described as emergent. People are acting in a certain way, but they are not conscious of acting in any such particular way. So we have for example, people who have been kicked off their land and have found a living by selling their labour by the hour, but they still think of themselves as peasants who have fallen on hard times perhaps, but they have no concept of themselves as proletarians.

So this is what Being is, and we will see presently that Hegel is able to demonstrate the nature of Being by a critique of this concept of Being. This critique tracks the way the actors in such a non-movement become self-conscious and begin to act collectively.

If there is to be some thing amidst the infinite coming and going, the chaos of existence, the simplest actual thing that can be is a QUALITY, something that *persists amidst change*. And if we ask what it is that can change while the thing remains of the same quality, what changes while the thing remains what it is, then this is what we call QUANTITY.

You can be 'hard up' and as inflation eats away at the purchasing power of your wages you get *more* hard up (i.e. there is a quantitative change, but the quality – 'hard up' still remains the same). That's the difference between Quality and Quantity.

But something cannot undergo quantitative change indefinitely and remain still what it is, still retain the same quality; at some point, a quantitative change amounts to a change in Quality, and this Quantitative change which amounts to a Qualitative change, the unity of Quality and Quantity, we call the MEASURE of the thing. If the real value of your wages falls beyond a certain point, then you are not just hard up, but destitute, and 'purchasing power' is a meaningless term for you. Measure means the combination of Quality and Quantity and its limits.

Thus there are three grades of Being: Quality, Quantity and Measure. We apply these categories to things that we regard as objects, the business of the positivist sociologist, the observer. Even a participant in a not-yet-emergent social change or social group, has to play the role of sociologist to be conscious of it. We can have a sociological attitude towards ourselves, without being self-conscious – like the pupil who explains his failure learn to read by observing that 25% of children leave school illiterate.

So unlike with Kant, the thing-in-itself is not existent in some yonder, beyond the limits of knowledge, but rather is something which is *not yet* self-conscious. There is no hard and fast line between appearance and the thing-in-itself. What is in-itself today, may make its appearance tomorrow. What the sociologist describes today, may speak for itself tomorrow.

Like what American feminist Betty Friedan (1963) called "the problem that has no name."

So that's Being, existence which is *in itself*, not yet self-conscious. We will see below how Hegel goes about demonstrating the dynamics of a movement which is in itself, through an immanent critique of the concept of Being.

§3   Essence is Reflection

Next we come to the Doctrine of Essence. 'Essence' for Hegel is not what it means for other people. When feminists talk about "essentialism" for example, this refers to the belief that women differ from men because of what is in their biological nature. Nor is it the same as what the ancient philosophers debated as the "essence" of this or that thing as opposed to what was contingent or inessential (Although Hegel also uses the word in this way, too, more often Hegel would refer to this as the *concept* of the thing). For Hegel, Essence is the *process* of "peeling the layers off the onion," of looking behind appearance, of probing reality, but in no way did Hegel think that there was some fixed *end point* to that process. Essence is just that *process* of probing the in-itself, testing out appearances and bringing to light what is *behind* appearances.

Essence is reflection. So if we have something going on in the world, maybe or maybe not, some emergent project, some emergent new form of social practice, or some new thought that is doing the rounds, maybe not yet corresponding to any apparent change in social practice, some new art form, some detectable change in fashion, then this may come to light in terms of unexplained events, statistical observations, a press report perhaps, and people try to make sense of it, people reflect on it. But this process of trying to make sense of experiences is different from the observer standpoint represented in Being. There is a struggle to explain things, to make sense of observations, to find solutions to a social problem. This is the birth process of a social movement, the emergence of self-consciousness. And this is what Essence is about.

When people reflect on things, they do so only in terms of *what they already know*. So reflection is an appropriate term. In German, Essence is *Wesen*, meaning "the was." It is Being *now*, but reflected in the mirror of *old* concepts. It's like what Marx was talking about in the "Eighteenth Brumaire of Louis Bonaparte":

> The tradition of all dead generations weighs like a nightmare on the brains of the living. And just as they seem to be occupied with revolutionising themselves and things, creating something that did not exist before, precisely in such epochs of revolutionary crisis they anxiously conjure up

the spirits of the past to their service, borrowing from them names, battle slogans, and costumes in order to present this new scene in world history in time-honoured disguise and borrowed language.

18th Brumaire, I

So Essence is a process, which begins with the simplest kind of reflection on quantitative and qualitative changes, the discovery of differences and eventually leads up to a new concept, an adequate concept befitting a unique form of social practice. The final emergence of the new concept is a kind of leap; it can't be given by any kind of formula because the notion which arises out of this process is the result of reflecting what is new in an *old mirror*. But Hegel outlines the Logical stages through which the genesis of a new concept passes, broadly a series of counterposed propositions, a contradictory struggle of Fors and Againsts, an 'on the one hand and on the other hand'. In the course of its genesis, the new phenomenon, if such it proves to be, penetrates and sheds light on everything else, every other aspect of life, summoning it up for an opinion on the matter.

Essence is that whole phase in the development of a science which sets off from a mass of measurements – quantitative/qualitative data – and reflects on it, trying to find the patterns, dig out the forces at work, find out what's going on behind the data. Being, by contrast, is the process of collecting all that data. It is in Essence that science discovers, by *critical reflection* on the data, that the data is distorted reflections in an old mirror.

Essence is that whole phase in the development of a social movement which begins from the first expressions of dissatisfaction or outrage, through marches and protests, lobbying, formation of various types of organisation, the formulation of various demands, etc. prior to that 'breakthrough' which signals the first signs of real success. In other words, it is the growth of *self-consciousness* in what was formerly merely a 'social problem'.

The grades of Essence are as follows.

Firstly, we have Reflection, or Reflection into Self. The process of Reflection is described as the dialectic of MATTER AND FORM. This means that at first a quantitative-qualitative change which oversteps the bounds of Measure and announces itself as a new Thing; the question is: is this a new Form of the same material or a completely new kind of material? Are the daily demonstrations in Belgrade just further expressions of discontent or is this an organized campaign in preparation for a coup, or ...?

At bottom, Form and Matter are the same thing. As a form of self-consciousness this is the dilemma as to whether you are just doing the same old thing in a new way, or whether this is a new thing showing itself in the shape of an old thing. 'A matter' means a substrate that underlies different forms. So is this a different *kind* of matter, or it can be reduced to the same old matter in a different form? Cosmology is currently wrestling with the problem of 'dark matter': is 'dark matter' a new kind of matter, responding to gravity but not radiation? or do the laws of gravity and/or dynamics need tweaking?

The second division of Essence is APPEARANCE. Appearance is the dialectic of *Form and Content*. This can be seen as the struggle of the new content to find a form adequate to itself; it is manifested in a succession of forms, each bringing forward new content and ultimately proving to be inadequate to its content and demanding a new form.

The third division of Essence is ACTUALITY, which is the dialectic of *Cause and Effect*. A phenomenon arises as the effect of something, but then it is also in its turn, the cause of things. Each effect is also a cause, just as much as every cause is also an effect. The cause-effect chain extends out everywhere in all directions until it feeds back on itself, this culminates in the notion of Reciprocity, that everything together forms a complex of mutually causing effects all inseparable from one another. You do something and get a reaction, and as often as not the same problem pops up in a new form; you modify your policy accordingly. Policy-making is now integrally tied up with the response of the wider public – each is both cause and effect, and policy becomes more and more complex, trying to plug holes in the dyke. But this state of affairs still remains a form of *reflection*; even the infinite network of cause and effect, and the increasing adequacy of form and content, do not yet constitute a *notion* of the problem or issue.

This is the process of a new type of self-consciousness struggling to find itself, so to speak, still testing out all the old categories, trying to find a fit. The process of genesis is always the struggle between opposing propositions, between compromise and radicalism, between protest and direct action, etc.

There is an essential two-ness to Essence. For example, Empiricism and Rationalism are two opposite currents, characteristic of just a certain period in the history of philosophy; the opposition never entirely goes away; to this very day a new problem in science will find itself rationalist and its empiricist proponents. The struggle between Empiricism and Rationalism was overtaken by the struggle between Dogmatism and Scepticism, which moved into the limelight, pushing the struggle between Rationalism and Empiricism into the background. That's the nature of Essence: a series of oppositions which persist, but as one moves into the limelight it pushes others to backstage. It is the genesis of a Notion out of its abstract Being. It is the truth of Being; it is what is essential in the flow of Being, stripped of what is inessential.

§4   The Notion is the Concept Conscious of Itself

The third part of the Logic is the Doctrine of the Notion, sometimes called 'the Concept Logic'.

At this point we need take note of how Hegel uses the word 'abstract'. By 'abstract' Hegel means undeveloped, lacking in connections with other things, poor in content, formal and so on, as opposed to 'concrete', which means mature, developed, having many nuances and connections with other concepts, rich in content. He does *not* use the words abstract and concrete to indicate something like the difference between mental and material, or any such thing. The *outcome* of a process of development is *concrete*, but the embryo of a process is *abstract*. Essence goes from abstract Being to concrete Concept. This will be fully discussed in 11§1 below.

The Doctrine of the Notion begins with an *abstract* notion, and the process of the Notion is that it gets more and more *concrete*.

Think of the Notion as a new idea, like at some point in 1968, somewhere in the US, a woman reflecting on the relation between the position of women and the position of African Americans, coined the word 'sexism'. This was a new idea, in everything that had gone before since people like Mary Wollstone-craft talked about the impact of gender roles on women in the 18th century, this idea had been in gestation, but it hadn't quite crystallized – what a vast and complex issue was captured in just one word!

Or take Einstein's Special Theory of Relativity; when Einstein proposed it in 1905, it was a complete break from anything that had been talked of before, and resolved problems that physicists had been facing up till then, but it also raised innumerable new problems that are still being worked through.

These are examples of an abstract Notion – 'sexism', 'Special Relativity' – new projects, simple ideas that correspond to a new shape of consciousness, a new form of social practice along with its own language, symbolism and self-consciousness.

The Genesis of the Notion

There is not a gradual shaping of this new abstract concept in Essence; the Concept comes as a complete break. It is like the judgment of Solomon, settling the argument with something that come out of left field. It is a breakthrough, a new connection, which launches a new science, or a new social movement out of the confusion and difficulties which preceded it.

The Notion is the unity of Being and Essence, because it makes sense of the original observations, the facts of the matter, as well as all the disputes and alternative explanations of the facts. A satisfactory solution to a complex problem must do that: not only fit all the facts of the case, but also show why all the alternative theories and counter-theories which have been put forward to explain the facts fail.

In that sense it is a negation of the negation, and immediate perception (i.e., Being) can then be reconstructed on the basis of the new conception.

The Notion is the truth of Essence, in that it is what emerges as the final conclusion which settles the series of disputes which make up Essence. The Notion, the *concept* of the thing, comes closer to what would normally be meant by the 'essence of a thing'; Hegel uses the word 'essence' for the whole process, and the truth of that process of Essence, he calls the Notion (or Concept).

Being and Essence, which are together what Hegel calls 'The Objective Logic', make up the *genesis* of the 'Subjective Logic', which is the Doctrine of the Notion.

The Subject

The first section of the Notion is Subjectivity, or the Subject. And here for the first time we get a glimpse of Hegel's conception of the subject: it is not an individual person, but a simple element of consciousness arising from social practices which implicate the whole community, reflected in language, the whole social division of labour and so on. (See §17.1 for the various usage of 'subject' across Hegel's works.)

In a sense, for Hegel, there is only *one* concept. But that *one* concept, the Absolute Idea, is nothing more than the outcome of a whole, long-drawn-out historical process, a process in which different individual concepts are posited at first as abstract notions, and then enter into a process of concretisation in which they *merge* with every other practice or concept, taking on all the implications of their own existence. The Absolute Idea, the final product, is the result of the mutual concretisation of all the abstract notions, the objectification of each one on every other, each of them merely a 'corollary' or 'special form' of the Absolute Idea.

In this conception, issues come up about Hegel having a master narrative, about totalising everything, and of practicing a kind of philosophical colonialism. To get Hegel's whole system, then you do have to push this idea through to the extreme so you get the Absolute Idea externalizing itself as Nature and Spirit proving to be the truth of Nature and so on, all of which is a kind of philosophical theology. But we can get all we need out of Hegel's Logic without swallowing the Absolute Idea. The Absolute Idea can be taken as a kind of hypothetical end point, a kind of Utopia which can be used as a signpost, but should not be taken as something existent.

The first section of the Notion, the Subject, is very complex and very important. Think of it for the moment in terms of the pure essentialities of a single *unit* or 'molecule' of a shape of consciousness.

The Structure of the Subject

The structure of the Subject is Individual-Universal-Particular, which are referred to as *moments* of the Notion. That is, the subject entails a specific, all-sided relation between the consciousness of finite, *individual* acts, the *particular* on-going activities of which the acts are a part, and the *universal*, material products, artefacts and symbols through which the Subject is represented and which carry the concept into future generations.

The divisions of the Subject are the Notion, the Judgment (which is a connection between two moments) and the Syllogism (in which a judgment is mediated by one of the three moments).

The Object

The process of the Doctrine of the Notion is the abstract notion becoming more and more concrete. This process of concretisation takes place through *objectification* of subjectivity, that is, through the subject-object relation. The first thing to grasp about the Object, which is the second division of the Doctrine of the Notion, is that the Object may be other subjects, subjects which are objects in relation to the Subject or subjects which have become thoroughly objectified. Objectification is not limited to the construction of material objects or texts; it's a bit like 'mainstreaming', or institutionalising the Subject. The process of development of the Subject is a striving to transform the Object according to its own image, but in the process the Subject itself is changed and in the process of objectification becomes a part of the living whole of the community.

The Structure of the Object

The subject-object relation goes through three stages, the *mechanical* relation in which the subject and object are indifferent to one another and impact one another externally, the *chemical* relation, in which there is an affinity between subject and object, and the object presents itself as processes rather than things. The third division of the Object is *Teleology* (or Organism), where the subject-object relation becomes a life process in which each is to the other both a means and an end. In Organism, each element is like the organs of an organism: it cannot live other than as a part of the organism and the organism cannot live without all its organs – not just affinity, but all-round interdependence like the components of an ecosystem.

The Idea

The unity of Subject and Object, the third and last grade of the Doctrine of the Notion, is called the Idea. The Idea is the whole community reconstructed as an intelligible whole, the summation of the pure essentialities of a complete historical form of life. It is the logical representation of Spirit, or of the development and life of an *entire community*, in the form of a concrete concept.

Again, it is not necessary to swallow this idea whole. If you don't accept that a community, at any stage in history whatsoever, can be encompassed in a single concept, then this doesn't invalidate the whole of the Logic, of which the Absolute Idea is the end point. Every nation or community is a whole, even if it is also riven with differences and conflicts.

In this section, I have given a brief summary of the series of concepts making up the Logic. To complete this initial review, let us make a couple of points of overview before we start going through these concepts one step at a time.

§5   Being and Essence Constitute the Genesis of the Notion

The first point to consider is the difference between the two "Volumes" of the Logic: Volume One: Objective Logic – Being and Essence, and Volume Two: the Subjective Logic, the Notion. The Objective Logic is the genesis of the Subjective Logic, genesis in the sense of being the process leading to the birth of the Notion. So the Objective Logic logically precedes the Subjective Logic, it is the objective (i.e., not yet self-conscious) formative process which precedes the birth of the Notion as a self-conscious abstract notion, its pre-history. On the other hand, the Subjective Logic is the process of development of the Subject itself, that is, its successive concretisation, beginning from the first simple, undeveloped embryo of a new science or social movement or project or whatever to the transformation of science as a whole or the whole community.

At the same time, each of the three books of the Logic itself constitutes a distinct science – Ontology, the science of Being; Essence, the science of Reflection; and finally the science of the Concept. Like the Logic as a whole, each book begins with a simple, abstract concept and unfolds the content from that conception, concluding with a concrete concept of the whole, and throwing up a problem, contradiction, 'loose end' or barrier, which forms the starting point for the next 'circle'.

This *unfolding* of what is *in* a conception, is quite distinct from the process of *genesis* which led up to the creative leap in which the conception is born. Once the situation has produced a conception, it is relatively unimportant how it came about. So this is a very important corrective to the conception of

Hegel as an historical thinker. Hegel did not commit the genetic fallacy. It is possible to understand the various conflicting forces which lay behind a thing coming into being, but the scientific study of *the thing itself* means to grasp it as a *concept* (which a study of its historical origins contributes to but is not equal to) and then to determine what follows from, or unfolds from the concept. For example, Hegel says "Although the state may originate in violence, it does not rest on it; violence, in producing the state, has bought into existence only what is justified in and for itself, namely, laws and a constitution" (*Subjective Spirit*, 432n).

So the starting point of a science is the concept which forms the abstract subject matter of the science. This is worth mentioning because there is a widespread fallacy about the relation between Marx's *Capital* and Hegel's *Logic*. Some writers have put *Capital* up against the *Logic*, and in an effort to match them, and start by equating the commodity relation with Being, on the basis that the commodity relation is the "simplest relation" or on the basis that the commodity relation is immediate. But the first thing to be done in a science, according to Hegel (and Marx followed Hegel in this), is to form a *concept of the subject*, the simplest possible relation whose *unfolding* produces the relevant science. In the case of *Capital*, this abstract notion, the *germ* of capital, is the commodity. In the case of *The Philosophy of Right*, it was the relation of Abstract Right, that is *private property*. The problem of the *origins* of value or of the commodity relation is a different question, and Marx demonstrates his familiarity with the Doctrine of Essence in the third section of Chapter One, where the money-form is shown to emerge out of a series of relations constituting historically articulated resolutions of the problem of realizing an expanded division of labour. See Chapter 21 for more on this.

The Objective Logic and the Subjective Logic *both* begin from a kind of simplicity. In the case of the Objective Logic, the simple starting point is *unreflective immediacy*, which immediately gives way to a new immediacy. In the case of the Subjective Logic, the simple starting point is an idea, an *abstract concept*, a relation which is the outcome of a long process of gestation, but once formed remains the concept of the science, initially abstract, developing towards a *concrete* concept. In this process of concretisation involves interacting with many *other* concepts as well as its own internal development.

Finally, although Hegel presents all these categories in the only way possible, that is, as a linear series of concepts, it is rarely the case that the formation and development of a concept takes place in a sequential way like that. A new concept may emerge and begin to concretise itself, but then come under attack by a new concept. What looked like a process of development, belonging in the second division of the Concept Logic, is suddenly thrown back into a typical moment in the Doctrine of Essence. This means that the Logic cannot and must not be viewed as a *schema*. The point is to understand each concept in its own terms and let the nature of the subject matter itself determine the movement of concepts. More on this in 15§6 below.

§6   Each Division has a Distinct Form of Movement or Development

Each of the three books of the Logic constitutes a self-standing science, beginning with an abstract concept, and unfolding what is contained in that notion. The three sciences are the science of Being, the science of Reflection and the science of the Concept. Each of these three sciences manifests a *distinct form of movement* (Fig. 1).

In Being, the form of movement is *seriality*. That is, a concept passes away and has no more validity, it is then replaced by another, which in turn passes away. It's just one damn thing after another, a transition from one to the next to the next.

In the sphere of Being, when somewhat becomes another, the somewhat has vanished

In Being, everything is immediate

In the passage of different into different in Essence, the different does not vanish: the different terms remain in their relation

In Essence, everything is relative

The movement of the Concept is development: by which that only is explicit which is already implicitly present

The movement of the Concept is no longer either a transition into, or a reflection on something else, but **Development**

FIGURE 1   Forms of movement in the Logic

In Essence, in the passage from one relation to another, the former relation does not pass away but remains, although pushed to the background, so the form of movement is *diversity*.

In the Notion, the movement is *development*, with each new relation incorporated into the concept and all the former relations merged with it.

Hegel puts it this way in the *Shorter Logic*:

> The onward movement of the notion is no longer either a transition into, or a reflection on something else, but DEVELOPMENT. For in the notion, the elements distinguished are without more ado at the same time declared to be identical with one another and with the whole, and the specific character of each is a free being of the whole notion.
>
> Transition into something else is the dialectical process within the range of Being: reflection (bringing something else into light), in the range of Essence. The movement of the Notion is development: by which that only is explicit which is already implicitly present.
>
> *Enc. Logic*, §161

In each Book, there are different forms of *reference* between the opposites. Hegel describes the difference between Essence and Being thus:

> In the sphere of Essence one category does not pass into another, but refers to another merely. In Being, the form of reference is purely due to our reflection on what takes place: but it is the special and proper characteristic of Essence. In the sphere of Being, when somewhat becomes another, the somewhat has vanished. Not so in Essence: here there is no real other, but only DIVERSITY, reference of the one to *its* other. The transition of Essence is therefore at the same time no transition: for in the passage of different into different, the different does not vanish: the different terms remain in their relation. ...
>
> In the sphere of Being the reference of one term to another is only implicit; in Essence on the contrary it is explicit. And this in general is the distinction between the forms of Being and Essence: in Being everything is immediate, in Essence everything is relative.
>
> *Enc. Logic*, §111n.

Observe that Being has the nature of 'one-ness', Essence has the nature of 'two-ness' and the concept has the nature of 'three-ness'.

Each of Hegel's books - including the three books making up each of the Philosophy of Nature, the Subject Spirit and *The Philosophy of Right* – has its distinct and characteristic form of movement. I will explain these forms of motion in the appropriate place in each case. But beware: just because you have understood the first few moments of the Logic, this does *not* mean that you understand the dialectic, which proves to have many distinct forms of movement.

At this stage, the reader should be able to read the two Prefaces and Introduction to the *Science of Logic*, and/or the Introduction and the Preliminary Notion of the *Shorter Logic*, that is, §§1 to 25.

CHAPTER 8

The Doctrine of Being, or Ontology

§1   "Being is the Absolute" Marks the Beginning of Philosophy

Pure Being for Hegel is the pure essentiality of a formation of consciousness (such as a social movement) which is as yet unself-conscious, unaware of itself. To grasp this as an object in order to determine its internal dynamics, Hegel must *enter into it* so as to be able to execute an immanent critique. But how can he do this if Pure Being represents such a formation of consciousness, standing at the very beginning of the development of self-consciousness? The history of philosophy provides the key to this kind of critique.

Philosophy is a part of a formation of consciousness (an historical community) which produces concepts which are responsive to logical critique as well as voicing a conception of the Absolute proper to the given formation of consciousness. Consequently, the history of philosophy manifests the same series of concepts which he required for the Logic. However, history is subject to contingencies and externalities and even if a social formation exactly corresponded to this pure essentiality, no real philosopher is going to perfectly express the essential spirit of their times. Though Logic does have an empirical domain in which it can be validated it is not an empirical science. The progression of concepts from one philosophical school to another is *intelligible*, and it is the job of the historian of philosophy to trace this with a critical examination of each stage in that progression.

This paragraph from the Doctrine of Being in the *Shorter Logic* illustrates how Hegel saw the relation between the real history of philosophy and the purely essentialities of the unfolding of the Idea, i.e., the Logic:

> In the history of philosophy the different stages of the logical idea assume the shape of successive systems, each based on a particular definition of the Absolute. As the logical Idea is seen to unfold itself in a process from the abstract to the concrete, so in the history of philosophy the earliest systems are the most abstract, and thus at the same time the poorest. The relation too of the earlier to the later systems of philosophy is much like the relation of the corresponding stages of the logical Idea: in other words, the earlier are preserved in the later: but subordinated and submerged. This is the true meaning of a much misunderstood phenomenon in the history of philosophy – the refutation of one system by

another, of an earlier by a later. Most commonly the refutation is taken in a purely negative sense to mean that the system refuted has ceased to count for anything, has been set aside and done for. Were it so, the history of philosophy would be, of all studies, most saddening, displaying, as it does, the refutation of every system which time has brought forth. Now although it may be admitted that every philosophy has been refuted, it must be in an equal degree maintained that no philosophy has been refuted. And that in two ways. For first, every philosophy that deserves the name always embodies the Idea: and secondly, every system represents one particular factor or particular stage in the evolution of the Idea. The refutation of a philosophy, therefore, only means that its barriers are crossed, and its special principle reduced to a factor in the completer principle that follows.

Thus the history of philosophy, in its true meaning, deals not with a past, but with an eternal and veritable present: and, in its results, resembles not a museum of the aberrations of the human intellect, but a Pantheon of godlike figures. These figures of gods are the various stages of the Idea, as they come forward one after another in dialectical development.

To the historian of philosophy it belongs to point out more precisely how far the gradual evolution of his theme coincides with, or swerves from, the dialectical unfolding of the pure logical Idea. It is sufficient to mention here, that logic begins where the proper history of philosophy begins. Philosophy began in the Eleatic school, especially with Parmenides. Parmenides, who conceives the absolute as Being, says that 'Being alone is and Nothing is not'. Such was the true starting point of philosophy, which is always knowledge by thought: and here for the first time we find pure thought seized and made an object to itself.

Enc. Logic, §86n.

Now of course we cannot have the same understanding of Being as did Parmenides, and that is not really the point. We can determine the concept of Pure Being precisely in the sense *necessary* to make the starting point of philosophy, a concept which requires a thinker, capable of philosophical thought, to think rigorously the first concept of philosophy which is utterly abstract in the sense that it contains nothing introduced from outside, from 'before philosophy' and stands at the very beginning of philosophy.

What Hegel needs is not so much a real history as an *idealised* history. But in the same sense that *any* science sets out to determine the *necessary* movement, logic goes hand in hand with empirical observation, thought experiment and reasoning, as Hegel explained in the foregoing quote.

§2   Being, Nothing and Determinate Being

The concept of Pure Being we need, then, is that concept which expresses (that something) *is*, without any qualification, without attributing any quality, any here and now, just "pure being," to just *be*. So in the terms of philosophy we are looking for the conception of the Absolute as just Being, not being anything in particular, just Being. A *capacity for philosophical thought* is required for this concept, because it is the ultimate abstraction, and the capacity for abstraction presupposes a certain development of society, so in that sense there is a presupposition. But the concept which forms the beginning of the Logic, and consequently, forms the subject matter of the Logic, is the concept of being utterly *indeterminate*.

After having demonstrated that a beginning cannot be made by the thought *of* anything, be that an intuition or God or certainty, or a 'clear idea' or whatever, Hegel explains:

> The beginning cannot be made with anything concrete, anything containing a relation *within itself.* For such presupposes an internal process of mediation and transition of which the concrete, now become simple, would be the result. But the beginning ought not itself to be already a first *and* an other; for anything which is in its own self a first *and* an other implies that an advance has already been made. Consequently, that which constitutes the beginning, the beginning itself, is to be taken as something unanalysable, taken in its simple, unfilled immediacy, and therefore *as being,* as the completely empty being.
>
> *Science of Logic,* §114

So the Logic begins with the claim that "Being is Absolute." But as soon as we considers this claim, and clarify that what is meant by 'Being' is a concept utterly without determination, then we see that we are asked to think an empty concept; so *ipso facto*, we are driven to the conclusion that Being is NOTHING. This is the first and classic example of this process of sceptical critique. If Pure Being is the Absolute, then the Absolute is Nothing.

Hegel claims that philosophy proper began with Parmenides. Thales, who was alive about 140 years before Parmenides, could have claimed that honour, but the very early philosophers of that time were still tied up with conceptions which are not yet scientific, ideas about the priority of Earth, Fire, Water or Air, and so on. But philosophy proper began with Parmenides. According to Parmenides (c. 500 BCE):

> 'Thought, and that on account of which thought is, are the same. For not without that which is, in which it expresses itself, wilt thou find Thought, seeing that it is nothing and will be nothing outside of that which is.' [and Hegel comments] That is the main point. Thought produces itself, and what is produced is a Thought. Thought is thus identical with Being, for there is nothing beside Being, this great affirmation.
>
> HEGEL, *History of Philosophy*, D1

And according to Hegel, Being 'passes over to' Nothing. Hegel associates the claim that God is Nothing with Buddhism. In his history of philosophy he can't really pin a philosophy of Nothing on Pythagorus, for whom the Absolute was the *One*, or any Greek philosopher of the appropriate time. So the history of Greek philosophy did not quite follow the sequence suggested in the Doctrine of Being.

However, if the truth of Being is Nothing, and as Heraclitus showed Nothing *is something*, then the destruction of Being has led in fact to something, and this insight can be summed up in the maxim: "Everything is BECOMING" or "Becoming is Absolute": Here is how Hegel describes Heraclitus, drawing on the reports of Aristotle:

> For Heraclitus says: 'Everything is in a state of flux; nothing subsists nor does it ever remain the same'. And Plato further says of Heraclitus: 'He compares things to the current of a river: no one can go twice into the same stream', for it flows on and other water is disturbed. Aristotle tells us that his successors even said 'it could not once be entered', for it changed directly; what is, is not again. Aristotle goes on to say that Heraclitus declares that 'there is only one that remains, and from out of this all else is formed; all except this one is not enduring'. This universal principle is better characterized as *Becoming*, the truth of Being.
>
> *History of Philosophy*, D1

But if Becoming is absolute, *something* must be becoming, so everything is a determinate being, not some abstraction or just a flow, but a determinate being, or "DETERMINATE BEING is Absolute," or: "Everything is *some* thing."

Being is being, and nothing is nothing, only in their contradistinction from each other; but in their truth, in their unity, they have vanished as these determinations and are now something else. Being and nothing are the same; *but just because they are the same they are no longer being and nothing,* but now have a different significance. In becoming they were coming-to-be and ceasing-to-be; in determinate being, a differently de-termined unity, they are again differently determined moments.

    Science of Logic, §187

So here we have the succession of the first four concepts of the Logic: Being, Nothing, Becoming, Determinate Being (*Dasein*).

Determinate Being (or Being something) turns out to be some Quality, and Quality constitutes the first main subdivision of the Doctrine of Being.

I will not continue the theme of naming the different philosophers who Hegel associates with the different categories of the Logic, because the con-nection gets more and more tenuous as the narrative goes on. Really, Hegel has abstracted the logic from a study of a large number of projects, or concepts, and the real history of philosophy bears only a distant relation to the course of the Logic from here on.

The Logic is really not an idealised history of *philosophy*; it is a formation in itself, the pure essentialities of the history of *all* formations of consciousness.

§3   Quality, Quantity and Measure

These first moments of the Logic: Being, Nothing, Becoming and Determinate Being belong to the category of QUALITY:

Quality may be described as the determinate mode immediate and iden-tical with Being – as distinguished from Quantity (to come afterwards), which, although a mode of Being, is no longer immediately identical with Being, but a mode indifferent and external to it. A something is what it is in virtue of its quality, and losing its quality it ceases to be what it is.

    Enc. Logic, §90n.

Contrariwise, a something can change its quantity and still be what it is. The dialectic of Quantity and Quality, involves the *Limit* and takes us to the cat-egory of *Measure.*

Everything is in perpetual change; but through all this change don't we also have constancy? or is this constancy an illusion? Hegel says that an existent thing is first of all a Quality. If that Quality of a thing changes beyond some point, then it's not the same thing any longer – a 'qualitative' change has taken place.

The LIMIT is the first conception of this boundary between something being what it is or not. "Through the limit something is what it is, and in the limit it has its quality," (*Science of Logic*, §246) but this limit is the *principle* of the thing, which it therefore *shares* with the other thing for which it is also a limit – the negation of the negation of the limit. So through the limit they share, two things show themselves to be *in principle* one and the same thing.

Things can change, and yet we say that they remain what they are, just more or less of what they were before and remain so. This aspect of a thing which can change, but does not thereby constitute a change in its substratum (the Quality), we call QUANTITY. So for example, if we are considering whether or not something is a fish, we might consider all sorts of predicates which can be attributed to the thing, such as size, shape, colour, weight, habitat, mode of movement, and so on, and no matter how these things may vary, they would not cause us to deny or confirm that we have a fish; it would just be a large fish, or a round fish, or whatever. All these attributes are Quantities. On the other hand, there may be predicates which can be attributed to the thing such that if they are changed then this will cause us to deny that we have a fish. Attributes like having scales, gills, a backbone, and so on, are not things which an animal can have more or less of; take away a fish's gills and it could no longer be called a fish. These attributes are Qualities.

Now there are limits to this distinction between Quantity and Quality. We find that if we vary the size of something, or the degree of its adaptation to breathing air – all Quantities – beyond a Limit, then what were formerly seen as solely variations in Quantity and not touching the very nature of the thing itself, become transformed into Qualitative changes, and this is the famous transformation of Quantity into Quality.

MEASURE is defined as the unity of Quantity and Quality: something remains what it is up to a certain Measure, but beyond that Quantity becomes Quality; that is the measure of a thing: just so much of such a quality.

A social practice of some kind may come to notice, for example, universities have observed over a period of time that more and more students do more and more paid employment. Surely beyond a certain point being a (full-time) university student loses the meaning it used to have and universities have to start redesigning their courses, their campus services, their arrangements for contact with staff and so on. But some *Measure* is needed before a decision is made to radically reconceive the idea of the university. The limit is key. How can a 'student doing part-time work', as opposed to a 'worker doing part-time study', be defined? What should be counted? These questions of measure have to be answered before we can start to think about whether something needs to be done and what.

308 pages of the *Science of Logic* are devoted to the Doctrine of Being, 36% of the entire book. Here I am devoting only about 10 pages to Being. This is, I think, reflective of the relative importance of this section of the Logic for people interested in social movements rather than Logic as such. Without going into the vast passages on natural science and mathematics in this part of the Logic, there are a couple of critiques which have eternal relevance.

The first of these is Hegel's critique of the Newtonian concept of *force*. He points out that the discovery of so-called new forces, was nothing more than a *reduction* of the reality of a thing to that of another thing as if this solved some problem. This is what Hegel calls something 'having its being in another'. Like for example explaining the rise in the population of the cities by reference to the attractive force of the cities. This explains nothing. He also critiques the popular notion of *attraction and repulsion*; these are simply *forms of motion* constituted by acceleration towards a point, so as to define a new forces. 'Centrifugal force' is the classic example of this, universally recognised as an illusion produced by the acceleration entailed in uniform movement in a circle or ellipse; it is a non-solution of the problem.

A modern day example of this positivistic pseudo-science would be Francis Fukuyama's discovery of a 'drive to recognition', supposedly located in the human soul which drives people to do all sorts of things in search of 'recognition'. All the Freudian inventions come under the same rubric.

§4   In the Sphere of Being it's Just One Damn Thing After Another

So, in summary, the Doctrine of Being can only go as far as sorting objects according to their attributes. This is because in the Doctrine of Being we have an *observer perspective* – there is no self-consciousness in the formation of the object. Attributes are *inessential* however; subjects may take or leave attributes and still be what they are. As far as we can go is Measure; that is to say, for any given object, we have its measure, between this and that size, this or that colour, to be found in the following parts of the world, and so on and so forth. This is the measure of things and it is as far as we can go with Being. The culmination of the Doctrine of Being and Measure is a complete, objective, quantitative and qualitative description of the object.

To go beyond this requires some reflection: what are the essential features as opposed to the inessential features? what is real and what is only apparent?

Importantly, what is in the eye of the beholder and what is genuinely objective? In the Doctrine of Being, prior to and independently of reflection, we cannot answer these questions. This is the stuff of opinion polls, statistical correlations, sociological surveys and pseudo-scientific quantitative research – science which never tries to get beyond this, to the *essence* of the thing, science which is never able to grasp the thing immanently, in its own terms.

'Pure Being' is the category even before all this Quality, Quantity and Measure arise – it's not even qualities and quantities. But throughout the Doctrine of Being, Being remains just the object of study, and in no sense conscious of itself as something.

That is why in the sphere of Being, it's always just one damn thing after another. You can take an opinion poll every day, and all you get is the government's approval rating for today, the next day, the next day, and so on. Just one damn thing after another. Explanations are just not part of the Doctrine of Being – they arise from reflection. To get any more than that, you have to have some theory about what is going on, and that is not given in your "observations," in your Measures.

Working in the sphere of Being, *the point is* lack of reflection – we strive to be objective and to *not* introduce our preconceptions into measurements. But of course that is always *asking the impossible*, Quantities and Qualities are always theory-laden, and that is what takes us to the Doctrine of Essence. We come to realise that our 'data' is already theory-laden thanks to the categories by means of which we perceive it.

In terms of the development of formations of consciousness, in the sphere of Being we are talking about social practices, forms of representation, lines of thought or projects which are happening, but they are happening under obsolete headings or under yet-to-be-coined names, so to speak. People are just trying to manage their lives, and have no thought (to continue the above example) of the nature of full-time university study, the kind of social conditions which are implicit in it or the reasons for its demise.

§5   Social Movements Do Not Exist Until They Realise It

Sociology or Dialectics?

Daniel Pinos came from a family of refugee Spanish anarchists, but as a 15-year-old pupil at the lycée technique in Lyon, the only social movements he knew were those he heard his father reminiscing about after dinner (Abidor 2018). When, in May 1968, a general assembly of students at his college voted to go on strike in solidarity with the factory workers he cried: "*Merde! Nous existons!*" Up to that point, even though all the pupils at the Villefranche-sur-Saône school were in the same social position, a position which they shared with millions of young French people at that moment, none of them were aware of it. Daniel had been reading the newspapers and he had read about events at Nanterre and in the Latin Quarter, but he was not a part of it. From the standpoint of the real events reported in the French newspapers, and from their own point of view, they did not exist. Suddenly, in a moment, *we* existed! Pure Being is about the moment *before* the pupils at school voted to act. All the conditions were present, and could have been measured by an astute sociologist. But as a matter of fact, prior to about 21 March, *no-one* in France knew what was about to manifest itself, let alone teenagers attending the lycée technique in Lyon.

Daniel's cry of "*Merde!*" captures the *leap* which marks the transition from Being to Essence.

Things and Processes

Engels summed up Hegel's contribution thus:

> "This new German philosophy culminated in the Hegelian system. In this system – and herein is its great merit – for the first time the whole world, natural, historical, intellectual, is represented as a process – i.e., as in constant motion, change, transformation, development; and the attempt is made to trace out the internal connection that makes a continuous whole of all this movement and development. From this point of view, the history of mankind no longer appeared as a wild whirl of senseless deeds of violence, all equally condemnable at the judgment seat of mature philosophic reason and which are best forgotten as quickly as possible, but as the process of evolution of man himself. It was now the task of the intellect to follow the gradual march of this process through all its devious ways, and to trace out the inner law running through all its apparently accidental phenomena."
>
> ENGELS, 1880, §II

In the Doctrine of Being, we are still in that necessary first stage of both the development of a scientific understanding of a phenomenon, and of the self-consciousness of the social processes and movements themselves – "a wild whirl of senseless deeds." Engels' description of the state of the human sciences prior to Hegel captures the nature of Being perfectly.

Note however that this means that while it is often said that we need to see the world as processes and not objects or things this cannot be done forthwith, so to speak. You first have to collect your data, sort observations into categories, count things, compare things, and so on ... and then *reflect* on what you have before you.

This is the same kind of process that the actors in a social movement go through when they first identify themselves as part of a social movement. They know the various aspects of their situation, but at a certain moment, this becomes *something*. But what that something is, changes.

As a matter of fact, to understand the world as made up of processes "in constant motion, change, transformation, development" goes only part of the way there, as we will see later on.

At this stage the reader should be able to read and understand the Doctrine of Being – §§84 to 111 of the *Shorter Logic*.

CHAPTER 9

The Doctrine of Essence: Mediation or the Truth of Being

§1   Identity, Difference, Diversity, Opposition, Contradiction and Ground

Hegel says that the Doctrine of Essence is the most difficult part of the Logic; it could be argued that in fact the Third Book (the Doctrine of the Notion) is more difficult, but in my view the Second Book (the Doctrine of Essence) is the most enjoyable and everyone will be able to relate this part of the Logic to real issues in social life. You will also find that some relations found here are recapitulated in the Third Book.

Essence is about a new formation of consciousness or form of social practice becoming self-conscious. It is all about those phases in the emergence of a social movement when people know that they exist, but have not yet quite figured out who they are, and are still searching for identity. What is given in the sphere of Being is just as it is, but with more and more reflection, diversity comes to light, contradictory explanations present themselves, responses to the situation repeatedly prove to be unrealistic or self-defeating, and are shown to have been based on wrong conceptions of the situation. Essence deals with the whole range of logical forms that are tested out during this complex and contradictory process of an emergent form of social practice arriving at an adequate, practical conception of itself.

The very first moments of Essence, called the moments of Reflection, are maxims which express those first glimpses of the self-consciousness of a social practice.

The first moment of reflection is Identity:

> The maxim of IDENTITY, reads: Everything is identical with itself, A = A: and negatively, A cannot at the same time be A and Not-A.
> *Enc. Logic*, §115

This is like when a group of people come together for the first time, and you will often hear people say things like: "We're all here for the same reason," or "We all know why we're here," and amongst those who study group dynamics this is sometimes called the stage of politeness, because everyone is at pains to avoid difference and celebrate common cause. It can be likened to the first stages of the Women's Movement when women emphasized the idea that all women suffered from the same problems, and obliterated differences of class, ethnicity and so on.

Not only is this maxim easily subject to critique, but in any emergent formation of consciousness, it invariably *is* subject to critique. As part of the very celebration of identity, people celebrate the Diversity of people who have been brought together under the same measure. Hegel observes:

> Maxim of DIVERSITY: To ask 'How Identity comes to *Difference*' assumes that Identity as mere abstract Identity is something of itself, and DIFFERENCE also something else equally independent ... Diversity has, like Identity, been transformed into a maxim: 'Everything is various or different': or 'There are no two things completely like each other'.
> *Enc. Logic*, §116n.

So the essential identity of the group is expressed in their diversity, but the essence of this diversity invariably turns out to be Difference. "We are such a diverse group, all interested in the same problem, and we will all be able to contribute in our own way," people might say. This often turns out to be wishful thinking.

Essential difference means OPPOSITION. This is reminiscent of that phase in the Women's Movement which underlay the emergence of so-called Third Wave feminism, that not only are women diverse and different, but some women have interests *opposed* to those of other women. This is also associated with the stage when differences in an emergent social movement begin to take on the form of opposing groups and perspectives.

Essential opposition arises from the bringing together of the opposition with the original identity – not just ships in different oceans, but CONTRADICTION. If we are all fighting for the same thing, but we have opposite claims, then this has to be resolved. Contradiction is different from opposing views on a matter because the opposite poles of contradiction are *incompatible*, and a *power struggle* must ensue.

Essential contradiction is Ground, and Hegel explains:

> The maxim of GROUND runs thus: Everything has its Sufficient Ground: that is, the true essentiality of any thing is not the predication of it as identical with itself, or as different (various), or merely positive, or merely

negative, but as having its Being in an other, which, being the self-same, is its essence.

Enc. Logic, §121

The Contradiction has its Ground. Contradiction must be resolved if the project is to continue towards a concept of itself, and both sides of the contradiction must bring forward the *Grounds* of their position and argue their case and seek common ground. In this way the essential Ground of the contradiction itself can be brought to light, both theses be affirmed, and form the basis for a provisional self-definition of the Thing – a genuine basis for unity, if there is one. This is a really productive phase of Essence.

One of the truisms of this kind of work is that as a campaign grows it not only passes through these various stages, which have been categorized differently by different theorists, but at every meeting, or every time a new person joins, the whole process has to be *recapitulated*, even if in a telescoped form. The same is true of how we should read Hegel's *Logic*. The processes are elaborated in the *Logic* one after the other, but in the development of a formation of consciousness, all these processes are continuing one inside the other, compounding each other, rather than just succeeding one after another.

Another point about Reflection which is worth recalling at this point. When a social formation reflects on itself, we have what is newly emergent in the sphere of Being reflected in the categories and ideas of an earlier moment. That is why the result is contradictory, and because the process of Being continues and compounds itself, these contradictions continue – the continual movement from identity to essential identity, from diversity to essential diversity, from difference to essential difference and from contradiction to the essence of contradiction which is ground, and form the 'driving force' of the phase of Essence.

The moments of Reflection culminate in EXISTENCE – as when Daniel Pinos calls out: "*Merde! Nous existons!*" This is how the leap from Being to Essence takes place, with the emergence of something new.

§2   The Thing: The Dialectic of Matter and Form

The moments of Reflection are the basic form of reflection which generates the contradictions to be resolved in the process of Essence and the formation of a new Concept. The first stage of Essence, Reflection, is also called the Thing, which is the dialectic of *Matter and Form*.

The Thing is the first attempt at self-definition as a distinct entity with various properties and not just another one like we've had before. According to a trend of the times when Hegel was writing, self-subsistent qualities were referred to as MATTERS, and this provides the opportunity for Hegel to present a critique of the positivistic practice of discovering new Matters.

An example. From 1667 until the late 18th century, the dominant scientific theory of heat was the phlogiston theory. Phlogiston was the *matter* of heat, that is, heat was a material with negative density which flowed into a body when it was warmed by a fire, and drained out of it when the body cooled (explaining why the products of combustion, including the smoke, weigh more than the original material). After this we had electrical and magnetic *flux, ether* that carried light waves, and so on. This process of inventing Matters, as a pretence of having explained some phenomenon, ought not to be just dismissed; 'discovery' of a matter may be a legitimate step in the understanding of a phenomenon. We have a continual procession of genes which explain human behaviour, newly discovered syndromes with unknown aetiology which explain social problems, an unending series of subatomic particles which rationalize practices in the domain of experimental physics and the discovery of substances in the brain which 'explain' social behaviour on the basis of neurobiology.

The point Hegel is making here is this: saying that heat is caused by the loss of phlogiston or that the increase in suicide is due to the spread of depression *explain nothing*. But the *naming* of a new syndrome or new matter or whatever, is a *step towards* the development of an adequate concept of the thing. Further reflection on supposed differences located in different Matters, will eventually resolve into a *practical* distinction.

From here, Hegel enters into a critique of the notion of Matter itself.

> Matter, being the immediate unity of existence with itself, is also indifferent towards specific character. Hence the numerous diverse matters coalesce into the one *Matter*, or into existence under the reflective characteristic of identity. In contrast to this one Matter these distinct properties and their external relation which they have to one another in the thing, constitute the *Form* – the reflective category of difference, but a difference which exists and is a totality.
>
> This one featureless Matter is also the same as the Thing-in-itself was.
>
> *Enc. Logic*, §128

In other words, the logic of the discovery of Matters is that at various points, Matters are resolved into Forms of one and the same Matter, and this process continues to the point where everything is just a form of one and the same abstract, indifferent Matter, just like the Thing-in-Itself of Kantian philosophy, beyond and outside experience, just a blank substratum of existence. Matter is a philosophical abstraction representing everything that is outside of and independent of thought, just like the Thing-in-itself; it can *explain* nothing because it is a nothing. It is Pure Being.

This brings us to Appearance which Hegel identifies with the Kantian Philosophy.

§3   Appearance: The Dialectic of Content and Form

The second division of the Doctrine of Essence is APPEARANCE, which is the dialectic of *Form* and *Content*. The claim of Kantianism is that Appearance is absolutely separated from the Thing-in-Itself. Hegel's aim is to refute this and show how the Thing-in-Itself is given in Appearance – there is a continual movement from the Thing-in-Itself into Appearance and no hard and fast line between appearance and the thing-in-itself.

> The Essence must appear or shine forth. Its shining or reflection in it is the suspension and translation of it to immediacy, which, while as reflection-into-self it is matter or subsistence, is also form, reflection-on-something-else, a subsistence which sets itself aside. To show or shine is the characteristic by which essence is distinguished from Being – by which it is essence; and it is this show which, when it is developed, shows itself, and is Appearance. Essence accordingly is not something beyond or behind appearance, but – just because it is the essence which exists – the existence is *Appearance*.
>
> Enc. Logic, §131

The point is that Appearance is objective too, just as much as the content of Reflection is objective, and Hegel says that Kant's mistake was to put Appearance solely on the subjective side. But Existence and Appearance are stages in the self-determination of a formation of consciousness.

Appearance for Hegel is the domain of *laws*; so, in the flux of things, as they enter Essence as reflected Beings, as a continual flux of *Existence* (the first division of Appearance), Appearance is what remains stable in that flux. Appearance is the *correlation* or the relation of essential Existence. It is not just a subjective process. The appearance of a new social movement is marked by the recognition by the participants that their issue is a *real issue*, not just a matter of their feelings having been hurt, or their having been offended, or other such dismissive characterisations.

Hegel describes Appearance as the dialectic of Form and Content, the transformation of form into content and vice versa, the repulsion of form by content, and the search of a content for its adequate form:

> Form and content are a pair of terms frequently employed by the reflec-
> tive understanding, especially with a habit of looking on the content as
> the essential and independent, the form on the contrary as the unessen-
> tial and dependent.
>
> *Enc. Logic*, §133n.

Every content must have a form, every form must have a content, but form and content may be at odds with one another. Like a campaign against the harm-ful effects of drugs which takes the form of a 'war on drugs'. So it is certainly wrong to say that form is indifferent to its content or that content is indifferent to form. When a content and its form come into conflict with one another, then we can see their reciprocal *revulsion*. Like a person who is promoted to a job for which they are not really fit – a kind of explosion can result. In order for the content to show itself, it has to find a form in which it is adequately expressed, for it is form that appears; but neither form nor content is more or less essential than the other. The search of a content for an adequate form and the struggle for a content to realize itself in an appropriate form, brings us to *Actuality*.

What we are looking at here is a new project or form of social practice find-ing a form in which it can be conscious of itself. A content must exist in *some* form, so if we are looking at an emergent social practice that is only begin-ning to reflect on itself, and for which there is as yet no adequate concept, then so long as an adequate form has not been found for it, the relevant shape of consciousness will be mistaken for something else, that is, be expressed in a false form, and as a result, will be distorted, misunderstood and probably counterproductive. If we are dealing with a reality, the content will shed an inadequate form, and go on shedding forms, until a form adequate to the content is arrived at. The content then appears. The way Hegel looks at this is that the Content has found its true Form. The sceptic could say that the con-tent which lies behind the form at any given moment is unknown and inac-cessible. But content *without* a form is meaningless; the dialectic of content and form is a process, and content shows itself in form. When we see that the content is itself active, and that the relation between form and content is not an arbitrary or subjective one, but that the content ultimately shows itself in some form, then the line between existence and appearance is bro-ken down. Existence passes into Appearance and Content passes into Form, continuously.

The content is accessible only through the form in which it is manifested. Appearance is the correlation of form and content, because at any given mo-ment, content and form are not identical. This is the analysis which Hegel makes of what is called *law*. The formulation of a law indicates on the one hand that we haven't got to the content, but on the other hand, we can describe the way the content is manifested. That's why the dialectic of form and content is described as the 'world of appearances'.

§4   Actuality: The Dialectic of Cause and Effect, Reciprocity

The third and last division of Essence is Actuality. Actuality is the dialectic of Cause and Effect, and its subdivisions are SUBSTANCE, Causality and Reciprocity. In this stage, the emergent shape of consciousness is still yet to find an adequate Notion of itself, but is becoming more and more concrete, implicating every aspect of social life. In this section of the Logic, Hegel uses the opportunity to make a critique of a range of misconceptions to do with Freedom and Necessity, Blind Necessity, Free Will, the maxim that "Anything is possible," Causality and so on.

In Actuality, Essence and Existence have become identical and this identity is immediate. Every aspect of Being has been incorporated in Reflection, and is part of the picture, so to speak – all the myriad of things and events around us, everything which is existent, is intelligible. Hegel argues against the counterposing of the Ideal and the Actual. He conceives of Actuality, not as senseless and unintelligible, and the opposite of the ideal, but on the contrary, *everything that is actual, must* in that measure be rational, that is to say, *intelligible*. This conception of the world as indefinitely complex contingencies, which are nevertheless intelligible, is summed up in the maxim "All that is real is rational; all that is rational is real" (*Philosophy of Right*, Preface). The converse of this maxim is the dictum: "*All that exists deserves to perish*," (Goethe, *Faust*) for not everything that *exists* is rational, and those elements of reality which have no basis in Reason, he says, sooner or later pass will away. He calls this conception: infinitely *intelligible reality* – Substance, and he sees Spinoza, who sees God as an infinite chain of causality, as the philosopher of Substance.

This myriad of relations manifested in Actuality as Substance, is made sense of by the relation of Cause and Effect, which Hegel sees as a limited point of view which science must transcend. In Hegel's view, to say that something is caused by something else, is to say that is has its being in another, and therefore fails to capture the concept of the thing itself, because the question of its existence has been simply moved to something else, its *cause* and its conditions.

An emergent social movement concretizes itself through all of its actions having some effect in the world, and ricocheting back on itself, through the reactions of others – action and reaction. This is how an emergent movement gains a more objective understanding of itself.

However, the relation of Causality sets up an infinite regress, and the chain of cause to effect, which in turn becomes cause, etc., etc., which eventually bends back on itself. A social problem can turn out to be *a cause of itself*, or a remedy can turn out to eradicate the conditions of its own efficacy. There seems to be no proper starting point, everything is the cause of something else and the effect of something else.

This conclusion, that a certain set of circumstances do not have any one of those circumstances as the cause of the others, but all together constitute a re-ciprocal relation of causation, is called *Reciprocity*. Reciprocity is often regard-ed as the end of the investigation. If poverty is the cause of unemployment, urban decay, poor health and dysfunctional schools, each of which is in turn the cause of unemployable workers, bringing up unruly children in a decaying neighbourhood, endlessly extending the 'cycle of disadvantage', then there is nothing more to be said. To finger any one point in this complex as the cause would be foolish; so says Reciprocity. Hegel exemplifies this with the question of the nature of the Spartans:

> To make, for example, the manners of the Spartans the cause of their constitution and their constitution conversely the cause of their man-ners, may no doubt be in a way correct. But, as we have comprehended neither the manners nor the constitution of the nation, the result of such reflections can never be final or satisfactory. The satisfactory point will be reached only when these two, as well as all other, special aspects of Spartan life and Spartan history are seen to be founded in this notion.
> *Shorter Logic*, §156n.

This failure of Reciprocity leads us to the doorstep of the Notion. Only by grasping Actuality and the infinite network of cause and effect under an ad-equate Notion which captures, 'in a nutshell', so to speak, what is going on, can the basis for a real science be created. Otherwise we remain mired in the conundrums of Reciprocity.

Free Will

Let's look at how Hegel deals with the notion of Free Will.

> When more narrowly examined, free choice is seen to be a contradiction, to this extent, that its form and content stand in antithesis. The matter of choice is given, and known as a content dependent not on the will itself, but on outward circumstances. In reference to such a given content, free-dom lies only in the form of choosing, which, as it is only a freedom in

form, may consequently be regarded as freedom only in supposition. On an ultimate analysis it will be seen that the same outwardness of circumstances, on which is founded the content that the will finds to its hand, can alone account for the will giving its decision for the one and not the other of the two alternatives.

> *Enc. Logic*, §145n.

The narrow view of free will, associated with this stage in the development of the idea, is that of making a decision between this or that option, but misses the question of where the *options* come from leaving to the supposedly free will only the task of figuring out which of the given options is the better. So Free Will turns out to be an illusion, but only because of the limited terms, that is of Decision Theory, in which it is conceived. (See "Hegel's theory of action, Part 2" below for more on this).

Freedom and Necessity

This brings us to the notion of "freedom and necessity." The following observation prefigures Hegel's views on the State.

> A good man is aware that the tenor of his conduct is essentially obligatory and necessary. But this consciousness is so far from making any abatement from his freedom, that without it, real and reasonable freedom could not be distinguished from arbitrary choice – a freedom which has no reality and is merely potential. A criminal, when punished, may look upon his punishment as a restriction of his freedom. Really, the punishment is not a foreign constraint to which he is subjected, but the manifestation of his own act. In short, man is most independent when he knows himself to be determined by the absolute idea throughout.
>
> *Enc. Logic*, §158n.

Which leads to the famous aphorism about Freedom and Necessity, that Freedom is the understanding of Necessity, or that "Freedom is the truth of Necessity."

Freedom in fact essentially *depends on* Necessity. The truth of Substance is the Notion, Freedom concrete and positive. In a realm of arbitrariness and irrational contingency, there could be no freedom at all.

> Necessity indeed, *qua* necessity, is far from being freedom: yet freedom presupposes necessity, and contains it as an unsubstantial element in itself.
>
> *Enc. Logic*, §158n.

§5   Development is the Struggle of Opposites Which do not Disappear

Before completing this section, we should reflect on the form of movement in Essence (Fig. 2). What we see throughout Essence is pairs of opposing determinations: Matter and Form, Form and Content, Existence and Essence, Positive and Negative, Likeness and Unlikeness, Whole and Parts, Inward and Outward, Possibility and Contingency, Freedom and Necessity, Cause and Effect, only some of which we have touched on here. The successive concretisation of

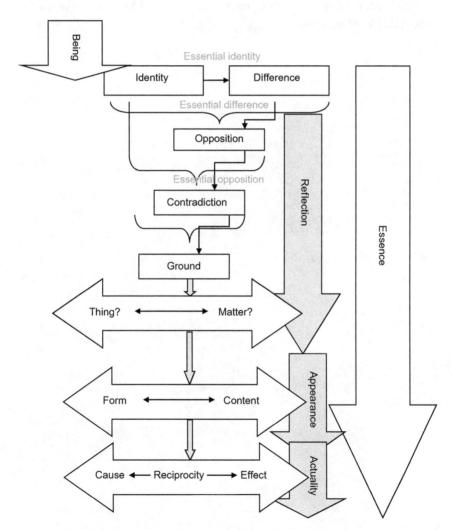

FIGURE 2   The structure of Essence

the growing self-consciousness of a project takes place through this succession of opposing determinations. In each case the opposition between them is made relative, as the counterposing of the opposite determinations leads to a deeper conception which comprehends the opposition within its new terms. So the opposing determinations do not disappear, but continue and in specific circumstances may come to the fore again. But in the process of Essence, we see a succession of polar oppositions, and as each opposition is sublated, their opposition is relativised and pushed into the background by new axes of polarisation.

The reader should be ready to read the Doctrine of Essence in the *Shorter Logic*, that is, §§112 to 159.

CHAPTER 10

The Subjective Notion: Universal, Individual and Particular

§1   The Whole is Reconstructed by Rising from the Abstract to Concrete

In the foregoing divisions of the Logic, we have seen how a new idea gradually takes shape, finds a form adequate to its content and a place for itself in the wider social formation. This new simple concept was thrown up as the solution to all the contradictions disclosed in Essence, like Alexander cutting the Gordian Knot or the notion of 'sexism' which suddenly appeared in 1968 after millennia of patriarchy. The outcome of this process is an essentially *abstract concept*. It is merely 'abstract' because it is undeveloped and lacking connections with other concepts – it's the new kid on the block so to speak.

The next phase of the Logic, the Doctrine of the Notion, details how the concept becomes *concrete* – a fully worked out concept embedded in and transforming all aspects of the social formation of which it is a part.

But this story is not entirely the story of a *single* concept, because the process of concretisation entails the merging of the concept with *other* concepts, and ultimately the interpenetration and mutual transformation of *all* the concepts found in a social formation. All these other concepts are themselves independently products of the same kind of development. So, as was explained above, the Logic cannot be seen as a linear narrative involving a single actor. The flux of Qualities in Being is continuously reflected in Essence, stimulating the genesis of emergent concepts. And likewise, when the Subject (the first abstract form of the Concept) encounters the Object (the existing community), it encounters all the already-existing concepts making up the social formation – the products of earlier development, and as it matures it encounters further newly emergent concepts.

This means that a whole social formation is seen as an aggregate of many different concepts, each having their own process of gestation, all merging with each other in complex ways. A society is thus seen as a 'work in progress', the living product of all the social movements of its past and present, but which nonetheless form a unity through their mutual interaction. Science, to take another example, is an aggregate of all the separate sciences, each having their own history, but at different times different sciences have taken the leading position and transformed others by their influence, the divisions between the sciences has been continuously reworked, exchanging form and content, mutually transforming each other, so that Science becomes an organic whole, inseparable from any of its parts, which in turn exist only as moments of the whole.

A country's legal system is the residue of all the social movements in the past, which have registered their demands in the form of legal rights.

So, by tracing the entire development of a single abstract concept, Hegel gives us a way of conceptualising a complex, multi-sided, concrete whole, a whole which has a unity of its own and is in continuous change and development.

There are two sides to the development of a concept: there is the *inner* development of the concept itself (the internal structure of a movement or institution, its rules and principles, etc.), and on the other hand, the development of its relations with *other* concepts and their mutual transformation. The first aspect is called 'Subjectivity', and the second aspect Hegel calls 'The Object'. The third phase of the Doctrine of the Notion is 'the Idea', which is a Subject-Object, and represents the development of the social formation as a whole having particular regard to the Subject.

Self-evidently, these three moments cannot be conceived of as happening sequentially, but on the contrary, happen simultaneously. Nonetheless, there is a logical relation between the three phases which allow us to first consider 'Subjectivity', which will be the topic of the remainder of this section. The Object and the Idea will be dealt with in each of the following sections respectively.

§2   The Subject is What is Active

Subjectivity, or the Subject, is here presented as a *logical* category. It is not possible to give a definition of what the Subject is forthwith, but it will be made clear presently. The Subject here is not Aristotle's subject as the substrate underlying attributes, and nor is it the Kantian 'transcendental subject' or the post-structuralist subject who is 'subjected' to some social position – though there are elements of all of these to be found in Hegel's conception. Further, Hegel also uses 'subject' in two distinct meanings in *The Philosophy of Right*, so we can't unambiguously define "Hegel's concept of the Subject."

Any thing, any process or social practice which is part of a culture or social formation originates as a solution to some problem, aporia or contradiction which otherwise existed in the social formation. The social formation is transformed by a social practice which takes as its object the resolution of this contradiction. Such a social practice entails individual people taking actions all oriented in some way by a symbol, word or artefact of some kind. Over time, the guiding concept becomes more concrete, but it is that first conception, the abstract concept, which is the *active* element transforming the social formation while itself being subject to change. As an archetypal concept it represents the whole developed social practice. The process of Essence can be seen as "ferreting out" this concept, which once brought to light does its own work, so to speak. Although the Subject has acquired its necessity from its genesis, everything that is 'unfolded' from it by immanent critique is implicit within the abstract concept.

The abstract concept is the key to understanding the *whole* of the formation of consciousness or social practice which unfolds from it. It can be seen as a 'unit of analysis' of the whole formation of consciousness, that is, that the whole is made up of many such abstract concepts (like the cell of an organism).

In this case, the relevant formation of consciousness is the Science of Logic. By an analysis of the problems in the history of philosophy, Hegel concluded that the solution to the crisis facing philosophy was this conception of the Concept. Hegel's conception of the abstract concept was the 'key' which unlocked a whole range of problems and stimulated a 'paradigm shift'. Thus, the Logic provides a model for the resolution of crises in all formations of consciousness. So *this* section of the Logic, in which Hegel analyses what the concept *is*, is a crucial one, and it is hardly surprising that it cannot be summed up in a few words.

The *abstract notion*, or Subject, is the first concept of the Doctrine of the Notion, which develops up to the Idea, a whole concrete form of life. This first abstract concept which constitutes the starting point for a science is of crucial significance for Hegel. Once the starting point is found, the whole of the science then unfolds itself by immanent critique. The abstract concept therefore constitutes the whole which is reconstructed from it. The Logic forms the model for this method. In this case, the abstract notion or subject forms the starting point of the science of the Idea – the conception of an entire social formation as a 'formation of consciousness'.

§3   The Subject is the Truth of Being and Essence

It might perhaps seem that, in order to state the Notion of an object, the logical element were presupposed and that therefore this could not in turn have something else for its presupposition, nor be deduced; just as in geometry logical propositions as applied to magnitude and employed in that science, are premised in the form of *axioms*, determinations of cognition that *have not been and cannot be deduced.*

Now although it is true that the Notion is to be regarded, not merely as a subjective presupposition but as the *absolute foundation*, yet it can be so only in so far as it has *made* itself the foundation. Abstract immediacy is no doubt a *first*; yet in so far as it is abstract it is, on the contrary mediated, and therefore if it is to be grasped in its truth its foundation must first be sought. Hence this foundation, though indeed an immediate, must have made itself immediate through the sublation of mediation.

> *Science of Logic*, §1279

The Abstract Notion is itself the germ or prototype or *Urphänomen* or embryo of a developed, concrete formation, an entire science or more generally a formation of consciousness. But the abstract concept does have an internal structure: it is the unity of the individual, particular and universal. I will explain this in §4 below, but note at this point that this conception differs from the ancient concept which was simply universal, and the modern, positivist concept which is exhausted by its essential attributes.[1]

Hegel says:

> Thus *the Notion is the truth of Being and Essence*, inasmuch as the shining or show of self-reflection is itself at the same time independent immediacy, and this being of a different actuality is immediately only a shining or show on itself.
>
> *Enc. Logic*, §159

The pre-history of a new concept is a series of failed projects, false dawns and disappointments, efforts of an emergent form of social practice to understand itself and find a form in which its content can be fruitfully developed. Eventually this process gives birth to something that *does not pass away*, something permanent, something which does not flee at the first sign of enemy fire or disintegrate in internal dissension, but actually absorbs fire and grows stronger from internal debate. Its material is gathered from reflection, so in that sense it is the truth of Essence.

The Notion is the truth of Being in a double sense, since Essence is already the truth of Being. But also, as the reflected form of Being which does not pass

---

1   See the first chapter of my book: "Concepts. A Critical Approach" for the variety of ways the positivist account of concepts has been developed.

away and proves to be persistent, it is in that sense the truth of Being, it's what Being turned out to be and continues to prove so.

The Notion is both immediate and mediated. It is mediated because it is the outcome of a protracted process of reflection and is itself a form of reflection, but it is also given sensuously and immediately.

The new Notion is perceived in the same way as any other thing, *sensuously*, but it is perceived not by contemplation, but in a *practical* context. We live (predominantly) in a 'second nature' made up of artefacts. Every thing in this humanised world interconnects with other things, finds its use in relation to other things and through the cooperative activity of people using elements of the culture, all of them are given to us immediately, in sensation. The norms, or ideals, which motivate these activities are implicit in the activities and constitute what can be seen as 'objective mind' In this sense, the Notion is a *product of thought*, and is subject to *logical* analysis. A new concept is a new constellation of ideals and norms which in some way responds to the problems which have arisen in practical, social life.

Subjectivity throws Being into a new light. It is not that what was only sensuous perception becomes conceptual, Being is *always theory laden*. There is no such thing as Pure Being, that is, immediacy which is not also at the same time mediated. But Subjectivity throws Being into a new light. Being is the same but not the same. Likewise, Subjectivity makes sense of the contradictory series of determinations in Essence and has sublated into itself all the contradictions that led up to its emergence.

§4   The Concept is the Identity of the Individual, Universal and Particular

Introduction

In the simplest terms:

- the universal (U) is what makes a thing or some action part of an entire genus, community or formation of consciousness, which it therefore shares with all the others. The universal is in principle imperishable, even if it is subject to change;
- the individual (I) is a single concrete thing or action which has only a transitory existence. It is concrete because there are many aspects of the individual and its nature is not exhausted by any one universal;
- the particular (P) is some determination of the universal which may encompass many individuals but does not exhaust the universal. It is not imperishable, but outlives its individual participants. The particular is differentiated

from the universal due to some attribute, by inclusion in some practice, or belonging to some genus.

There is no hard and fast line separating the particular from the universal or separating the particular from the individual – it is relative. Take the following Judgments as examples: Andy (I) is an Australian (U); some people in Brunswick (P) are Australian. All three moments are valid forms of the Concept, and each moment in the example just given is a concept.

Simple propositions like this may appear to be unproblematic, but this is not the case. For example, the entire legal system is set up and operates solely to decide whether individual actions breach laws, laws which have been written down in supposedly unambiguous language and refined over centuries. In the meantime, Parliament and judges in the higher courts spend countless hours further refining and modifying these laws, trying to eliminate grey areas, aporia and contradictions. Looking at traditional logic, you would think it would be a simple matter to write a definition of murder, for example, so that a clerk could check the facts against the definition, read the sentence off a table and that would be that. Clearly the real world does not work like that. Instead of having a concept-as-such (a definition, a list of essential attributes, an archetype, ...) and trying to figure out which individuals belong to it – a problem which Wittgenstein loved to play with – Hegel takes the Particular, Individual and Universal as equally valid forms of the concept and examines the processes which arise from the contradictions between these forms, through which a concrete concept develops.

The Three Moments of the Subject

Hegel likened the first Universal, Particular and Individual Notions of the Subject to the first moments of reflection:

> Universality, particularity, and individuality are, taken in the abstract, the same as identity, difference, and ground. But the universal is the self-identical, with the express qualification, that it simultaneously contains the particular and the individual. Again, the particular is the different or the specific character, but with the qualification that it is in itself universal and is as an individual. Similarly the individual must be understood to be a subject or substratum, which involves the genus and species in itself and possesses a substantial existence.
>
> *Enc. Logic*, §164

Hegel's exposition of the three moments of the Notion and their relations is rather obscure. Let us take a look first at the Universal Notion:

> *The universal ...* is *that simplicity* which, because it is the Notion, no less possesses *within itself the richest content.* First, therefore, it is the simple relation to itself; it is only *within itself.* Secondly, however, this identity is *within itself* absolute *mediation,* but it is not something *mediated.*
> Science of Logic, §1327

The Universal has acquired its content and its necessity from its genesis in the Objective Logic (Being and Essence). The Universal is evoked by a word or symbol or tool or gesture or whatever which represents the Notion – "in free equality with itself in its specific character" (*Enc. Logic,* §163). It is simple and immediate because it is what it is independently of any relation to others. Although every word is an individual utterance, every tool an individual object, in the Universal they are united by some *norm* irrespective of their concrete nature. Any woman is the universal woman simply because she is a woman.

But the entire content of the Universal is implicit, being part of a language or other culturally constructed system of meanings or actions in which it can be used. It is *absolute mediation* as on its own it is just a dead thing, like a word from the language of a long lost civilisation, and the mediation is entirely *within itself,* potential. It is what it is independently of its use or presentation by any person, but as such it is a nothing. Take a word out of its language or an object out of the context of its use by people and it is nothing, but the meaning is still there implicitly; a key found on the road which opens an unknown lock is still a key.

The Universal Notion is *not* to be understood as an essential attribute uniting an otherwise arbitrary set of objects, as in set theory, but as a *self-subsistent genus.* In Dickens' *Hard Times,* Cissy, who had an intimate practical knowledge of horses, is humiliated by Mr. Gradgrind when she cannot give the definition of a horse, proving to her great embarrassment that she does not know that the answer is "4 legs, 40 teeth, etc., etc." Cissy, of course, knew far better what a horse was than Mr. Gradgrind.

In the quote above, Hegel points out that the universal "contains" the particular and individual, i.e., a *concrete* universal cannot have an existence separate from its instantiation in particular individuals. While the universal is always just as it is, every particular is different and it is the specific difference which makes it a particular. Like the universal, the particular is nothing other than individuals, not something side by side with individuals. Thus the individual is the *ground,* because it is the substratum in which the universal exists. The category of Ground is given in the maxim "Everything has its sufficient ground."

I find that a useful illustration to show how these moments work to take the case of the concept of 'unionism' which is instantiated in the union movement, specific trade unions and individual unionists.

The social form taken by the union movement in Australia is the ACTU – the Australian Council of Trade Unions and all trade unions are affiliated to the ACTU and all trade unionists are members of affiliated unions. Thus, the ACTU is the Universal. The ETU, AWU, NTEU, etc., are Particulars. And there are 1.8 million Individual union members. *On the face of it*, as I have presented it, the concept of trade unionism is a simple illustration of Set Theory in which the elements are individuals.

But rather than taking unionism as an object revealed in a survey form, let's take the union movement as a living organism, as a 'formation of consciousness' – the social form of an idea. And for the purpose of simplicity, let's pass over all those unionists (retired, unemployed, ...) who are not members of affiliated unions and ignore the complex internal structures of the affiliated unions, mediating between the Executives of the affiliated unions and their members (simplifications for the purpose of illustration, but which are not required for Hegel's Logic).

The Universal, the ACTU, has a range of policies, such as support for employer contributions to superannuation, which they claim flows from the concept of unionism. But it is hardly likely that every unionist supports that claim; any individual unionist you meet would have their own view. They might raise the matter with their union executive and if a sufficient number of members of, say, the NTEU, opposed compulsory super, that particular union may adopt a different policy and argue on the ACTU Executive for a change in policy. All the while, the union movement remains a coherent movement and lobbies government and employers for the ACTU policy of compulsory superannuation. The same idea goes for all the policy issues and across all the mediating structures in all the affiliated unions. The Universal is at odds with the Particular and Individual, but nonetheless remains the Universal embracing and representing *all* unionists.

If we were to ask: what is the concept of unionism in Australia? then the answer is not going to be found on a survey form or in the Macquarie Dictionary; it is found only in the real policies, structures and actions of the union movement – Universal, Particular and Individual, different in each case, but nonetheless *a* Subject. It's internal tensions are manifested from time to time in shifts in policy and activity, but the internal relations within the movement moderate these conflicts and since 1927, there has been one, ever-changing Subject of unionism in Australia.

By choosing a concept which is actually a subject with a formal structure, I have of course oversimplified the character of a concrete concept. Hegel's Logic is not tied to a formal structure of this kind. Nonetheless, the Universal, Particular and Individual concepts still make clear sense however informal the social structure of a concept may be. The Universal does not usually have a voice like the ACTU, but is rather 'represented' by a word or symbol which is interpreted in different ways by particular individuals.

How do these disparate concepts form a coherent concrete Subject?

§5   The Judgments are Logical Representations of Unmediated Actions

The first chapter of the Subject described above shows how the Subject is expressed by each of the three moments of the Subject alone – the Individual, Particular and Universal concepts.

The second chapter looks at how the subject acts in the relations between two moments and Hegel discusses these in terms of a series of JUDGMENTS.

The third chapter looks at how each of the Judgments is mediated by one of the three moments in SYLLOGISMS.

A Judgment has the form Subject | Predicate in which the Subject is one of the three moments, and the Predicate is also a moment. For example: "Ivan is a Unionist"

Continuing the metaphor of the union movement, the Judgments express the actions that each moment takes towards the other in formulating and implementing the ideals of the union movement. So, unionism is realised as a coherent concrete Subject by means of such actions as the Particular union intervening to defend an Individual member, or the ACTU taking a levy to support the struggle of a Particular union, or an Individual acting as delegate at their Particular union conference and so on. It is all these two-sided relations which draw the disparate moments of the Subject into a concrete whole.

We can grasp the meaning of Judgments even more generally and concretely by means of the maxim: "Every action is a judgment." Every time a person takes an action there is a judgment implicit in that action. As Hegel says, it is the Individual actions which are the Ground of concepts, so it is through this nexus: Action = Judgment that we can see how concepts are realised and what is more, how they *develop* as forms of human action.

The Judgments reproduce at a higher level the categories of Being and Essence. They are the Qualitative Judgment, the Judgment of Reflection, the Judgment of Necessity and the Judgment of Notion. Each of the Judgments expresses only partially what it is that brings something under the Notion, each Judgment is a successively more concrete characterisation of the Subject. This process of Judgments recapitulates the categories of Essence in the form of more and more adequate notions, but at this stage, still notions which are one-sided and deficient. The recapitulation reflects the fact that what is taking place is similar to the processes of Being and Essence (the Objective Logic) except that there is now a developing Subject which can register these moments in an increasingly concrete concept of itself.

(a) In the QUALITATIVE JUDGMENT, the subject is ascribed a single *quality*, the relevant social practice is said to be good or bad, or novel or whatever. Hegel presents a logical critique of any such judgment, hinging on the point that equating an individual with a particular is always faulty.

(b) In the JUDGMENT OF REFLECTION, the subject is given in connection with other things, so that it is not just seen as having some quality, but as *having a place in a system of social practice*, connected with other practices, of being useful for something, or whatever.

(c) In the JUDGMENT OF NECESSITY the subject is taken under its *genus*, rather than just as sharing with others a contingent property but being an organ of some living whole.

(d) In the JUDGMENT OF THE NOTION, these three judgments are brought together. Hegel gives the following example:

> This (*the immediate individuality*) house (*the genus*), being so and so constituted (*particularity*), is good or bad. This is the Apodeictic judgment. All things are a genus (i.e. have a meaning and purpose) in an *individual* actuality of a *particular* constitution. And they are finite, because the particular in them may and also may not conform to the universal.
> *Enc. Logic*, §179

This most developed Judgment has risen to a concreteness where individual, universal and particular are brought together. In the case of each of these judgments, which are after all just making *one* judgment in relation to some form of social practice, Hegel demonstrates the deficiency of the Judgment, its limitations. This demonstrates the action of sceptical critique as an existing formation of consciousness which is not yet fully conscious of itself, tries to define itself: "no it's not this or that quality, or just this or that connection with other things, and it may be this kind of thing, but that doesn't exhaust what it is, and so on." All these deficient judgments are reflected in one-sided forms of practice, that are still guided by conceptions reflecting the fact that the specific character of the relevant social practice has not been fully grasped, or in taking up a social position which obstructs the development of the notion, or taking account of just one attribute or in terms of the Subject's relation to other social practices, etc. But eventually, if the development is completed, the individual, particular and universal aspects of the Subject are brought into harmony, so to speak.

§6   Each Moment Mediates between the Other Two

In general, actions such as those represented by the Judgments are not imme-diate: actions are invariably *mediated*. For example, when an individual acts to change ACTU policy, his action is probably mediated by a resolution endorsed by the Particular union Executive. It is these mediated actions which form the Ground of the development of the Subject.

The third chapter of the Subject presents a series of *Syllogisms*, in which a Judgment connecting two moments, is mediated by one of the moments. We can grasp the meaning of these syllogisms under the maxim: "Every syllogism is a mediated action."

Each syllogism expresses the Subject more or less defectively, but gets closer and closer to the Notion. Hegel elaborates 12 Judgments and 10 Syllogisms, and I will only touch here on the most prominent points in the development to give the reader an idea of how this works. Only when all the different possible com-binations are brought together and concentrated in a single syllogism which gives weight to every aspect of the relation between Individual, Particular and Universal, may the conception "capture the Notion."

Like the Judgments, the Syllogisms also recapitulate the categories of Es-sence: the Qualitative (or Immediate) Syllogism, the Syllogism of Reflection and the Syllogism of Necessity. Each Syllogism unites an Universal, Individual or Particular Notion, with a Judgment.

The first, IMMEDIATE SYLLOGISM is the *determinate syllogism* (I-P-U), in which the Individual is brought under a Universal by virtue of coming under a Particular. This is the most straight forward and immediate of syllogisms. The deficiency arises from the fact that the individual's relation to the Universal may be fortuitous, as the individual is only participating in the Universal by virtue of one Particular which may not be sufficient, for example:

He's got such a nice way with people; he'd make a good politician.

The second Immediate Syllogism is the QUALITATIVE SYLLOGISM (P-I-U), in which a particular is subsumed under the Universal only because one of its individuals are under the Universal. This is an obviously incomplete claim as other individuals are excluded from consideration. There are altogether four such Qualitative Syllogisms.

> I'd never let an English doctor operate on me; look at that Dr. Gillingham.

Hegel says that the Qualitative Syllogisms deal with Particularity abstractly, whereas the SYLLOGISM OF REFLECTION extends this abstractness to encompass *all* Individuals. So we have the *syllogism of allness* (also I-P-U), that an individual which is under a particularity comes under the universal because *all* individuals under that particularity come under the universal. The deficit is that the major premise (that all such individuals comes under the universal) *depends on* the conclusion, namely that the individual in question comes under the particular.

> You can't tell me you're a footballer! You're only 5'6" and no footballer is that short!

The second Syllogism of Reflection is the *syllogism of induction* (U-I-P), deduces the universal from the particular, because all the particular individuals come under the universal, the deficit of which is that the particular is never complete, and does not cover *all* possible individuals, for example:

> There's more and more crime nowadays; you hear about a murder almost every day on TV.

The third Syllogism of Reflection, the *syllogism of analogy* (I-U-P), lifts an individual to the status of a universal and deduces from a particularity of one individual to another similar, but the similarity may not be such as to justify the analogy, for example:

> Vietnam has proved that a small country defending its territory can defeat the USA; it's only a matter of time in Iraq.

In each Syllogism of Reflection, an effort was made to make a generalisation based on incomplete information, leading to unsafe conclusions. The next and third category of Syllogism are the SYLLOGISMS OF NECESSITY, in which this limitation is to be overcome.

The first Syllogism of Necessity is the *categorical syllogism* (I-U-P), and here instead of an arbitrary characteristic of an individual (which may or may not unite it with another individual) being taken up, the genus which concretely unites it with other individuals is the middle term. The deficit of this syllogism is that even though particularity of an individual is deduced from its genus, without having a Notion of the genus the syllogism is still open to error.

He's a professor of neuroscience; he must know what consciousness is.

The second Syllogism of Necessity is the *hypothetical syllogism*, A implies B, A is, therefore B is. But in this B has its existence in A and the conditions which made A necessary are not necessarily the same conditions which make B follow from A. The deficit in the syllogism is therefore that the necessity of B must be known in itself, not mediately through A, for example:

The fuel gauge says we're half full; we *can't* have run out of petrol.

And so on. We can all recognise these one-sided lines of argument; in every case they fail because they have not yet grasped the relevant *notion*, but it is only in and through such deficient judgments, which prove in practice to be deficient, that the notion consolidates itself and becomes a fact, not the outcome of a line of argument, but an objective fact.

It is noteworthy that all the syllogisms dealt with are faulty logic, sometimes obviously so. But they all represent the kind of reasoning that we do come across, every day in social practice. Try discussing the impact of immigration on unemployment with a racist, or discussing with a climate-denier whether 7 of the hottest 10 years on record having occurred in the past 12 years is evidence of climate change. It seems strange to find obviously faulty logic being discussed in a book on Logic. But this is the reality.

The *Syllogism of Action* will be dealt with later as this Syllogism plays a crucial role in interpretation of the Logic.

The implication seems to be that social change happens as a result of rational debate, but this is not necessarily the case. I will deal with this more fully in Part 3, but briefly, Hegel believes that there is a kind of necessity driving the concretisation of concepts which realises the Logic of Concepts even 'behind the backs of' the actors. In any case, this is the sense in which the (logical) Subject is the active element in social change.

CHAPTER 11

Subject, Object and Idea

§1   The Subject Develops from Abstract to Concrete

The three books of the Logic are laid out in a logical sequence, and they describe a process of development, but the realized process of development does not take the form of a temporal *succession* of these categories. In a real process of development, the categories of Being come into being and pass away, and *continue* to come and go indefinitely. The succession of oppositions which overtake one another in Essence continue to generate opposing pairs of determinations. As these unfold, a new form of social practice develops self-consciousness, with a succession of new qualities, new relations, both incidental and necessary, are registered in theory, in activity and as representations. As people act on these phenomena, a more concrete form of the new social practice develops. So in terms of time, all these relations are happening at the same time. However, there is a *logical dependence of the later categories on the earlier.*

There is also a reverse process in which a new Concept reflects on Being with the result that new Qualities and Quantities are measured and manifested in new Forms and Appearances.

The development described in the Doctrine of the Notion is the development of a Concept from its first abstract form to a concrete totality, abstracted from the independent development of *other* concepts.

In the first place, the Logic represents what is *necessary* in the development, as opposed to what is contingent or accidental or as the result of caprice, so the logical process differs from the historical process in that respect.

Secondly, the subject domain of the Logic is *formations of consciousness*, or more precisely, the *units of formations of consciousness*, namely concepts. A concept is to be understood as a regular system of activity which is organized around some conception which may be taken by the participants as an entity (institution or artefact) of some kind; that is, it may be reified. Self-consciousness here implies that people involved in that system of activity bring together particular forms of activity, their individual actions and the representation of the activity into a stable relationship. The series of judgments and syllogisms represent the moves towards the formation of that mature relationship, and it is that consistent, worked-out relationship which brings about a relatively stable reification.

Abstract and Concrete

This is a good moment to recap what Hegel meant by 'abstract' and 'concrete' and we can use the contrast between the beginning and the end of Essence to illustrate this.

In a sense, Being is concrete, because it is the raw data: the tables of figures, the series of images and records of actual events, etc., all the Quantities and Qualities given to Reflection. But on the other hand, all these measurements are very *abstract* because each is a tiny 'snap shot' of reality with no rational connection with what came before or after.

On the other hand, the Notion is abstract, because it is just a thought, a theory, and is only connected to lived experience by a long and devious theoretical argument. In economics, consider a concept like 'productivity' – it takes the government three months to calculate whether productivity had gone up or down and who knows what that means for any given worker or business? And yet in that precise sense, 'productivity' is a much more concrete concept than any of the items of data that went into the calculation because it represents a quality implicit in the whole mass of data with a single figure and it is extremely hard for governments to shift it.

So the process of Essence, moving from Being to the Notion is a two-way movement: from abstract concreteness to concrete abstractions. The process of development in the Doctrine of the Notion is also such a movement. It begins with the concrete abstractions which have been produced by Essence and ends with a conceptual reconstruction of the whole, with the abstractions from which it began translated into concrete practices and institutions.

All Hegel's books follow this form: they begin from an abstraction and concretise it. Being, for example, begins with single, isolated 'readings' and concludes with averages, totals, percentages – a complete quantitative profile of the subject. This concrete is the abstract for the next phase, so each phase produces a unique kind of abstractness and a unique kind of concreteness.

In social movement terms this means that the demands thrown up by the movement – "Equal Pay! Access to Nontraditional Jobs!" – are translated into realistic, working policies. But policies have to be turned into real social practices.

Applied to the development of a science, it means taking a new concept, such as evolution, and transforming biology so that every organism is understood as a work-in-progress of natural selection.

The Method of Political Economy

There is a well-known passage in Marx's *Grundrisse* known as "The Method of Political Economy," and this passage is universally recognized as a synopsis of

Hegel's Logic which was to underlie the writing of *Capital*. I shall quote a part of this passage in full, interspersing comments to indicate the parallels.

> When we consider a given country politico-economically, we begin with its population, its distribution among classes, town, country, the coast, the different branches of production, export and import, annual production and consumption, commodity prices etc.

Marx here refers to Being: the representation of the economy in all the measures which are tabulated by businesses and government departments.

> It seems to be correct to begin with the real and the concrete, with the real precondition, thus to begin, in economics, with e.g. the population, which is the foundation and the subject of the entire social act of production. However, on closer examination this proves false.

Marx refers to these initial data as *concrete* but now he goes on to point out that the same "concrete" categories turn out to be *abstract*. Historically, political economy did in fact begin with this data, but subjected it to criticism, and the critique of this data which follows characterises Essence:

> The population is an abstraction if I leave out, for example, the classes of which it is composed. These classes in turn are an empty phrase if I am not familiar with the elements on which they rest. E.g. wage labour, capital, etc. These latter in turn presuppose exchange, division of labour, prices, etc. For example, capital is nothing without wage labour, without value, money, price etc. Thus, if I were to begin with the population, this would be a chaotic conception of the whole, and I would then, by means of further determination, move analytically towards ever more simple concepts, from the imagined concrete towards ever thinner abstractions until I had arrived at the simplest determinations.

The process of Essence concludes once it has determined the basic Concepts of modern political economy. By the time he wrote *Capital*, one category has been singled out as the key concept – *value*. This "simplest determination" is arrived at by a process which concentrates all the aspects of the whole, and is in that sense a *concrete* concept, but at the same time is the most *abstract* of all the categories. Once having possession of these abstract concepts, the concrete whole which was represented in the data in Being, is *reconstructed*:

From there the journey would have to be retraced until I had finally arrived at the population again, but this time not as the chaotic conception of a whole, but as a rich totality of many determinations and relations.

The starting point was *rich* in content, but *poor* in conceptual form. The reconstructed whole is now *conceptually* rich, at the cost of richness in empirical *content*.

Marx again summarises the whole process which Economics has followed in terms which are recognisable as corresponding to the Doctrine of Essence:

The former is the path historically followed by economics at the time of its origins. The economists of the seventeenth century, e.g., always begin with the living whole, with population, nation, state, several states, etc.; but they always conclude by discovering through analysis a small number of determinant, abstract, general relations such as division of labour, money, value, etc.

Marx then describes the development in the Doctrine of Notion, beginning from more or less adequate concepts to construct a theoretical image of the economic world.

As soon as these individual moments had been more or less firmly established and abstracted, there began the economic systems, which ascended from the simple relations, such as labour, division of labour, need, exchange value, to the level of the state, exchange between nations and the world market. The latter is obviously the scientifically correct method.

Marx then contrasts *two forms of concreteness*: the conceptual reconstruction of the real, and the representation of the real in the mass of raw data, which provides the starting point for theory:

The concrete is concrete because it is the concentration of many determinations, hence unity of the diverse. It appears in the process of thinking, therefore, as a process of concentration, as a result, not as a point of departure, even though it is the point of departure in reality and hence also the point of departure for observation and conception. Along the first path the full conception was evaporated to yield an abstract determination; along the second, the abstract determinations lead towards a reproduction of the concrete by way of thought.

Marx continues on to make some important criticisms of Hegel, but this is not the place to discuss these.

Sublation
The relation between categories and their successor relations in the Logic is that of sublation [*Aufhebung*]. Hegel uses the term 'sublation' throughout the Logic, including the relation in which one determination *passes into* another in the sphere of Being, the relation in which one opposition is *overtaken by* another in the sphere of Essence, and the way in which, successive determinations are *'taken up'* by the subject, in the Doctrine of the Notion.

Aufhebung means taking something beyond its own limits and 'negating' it, that is to say, *preserving* what was necessary in the former relation while *terminating* that which is no longer tenable. Sublation is the basic organizing principle of the Logic. It's like when something is done away with because it is outmoded, but its essential contribution is preserved and carried forward in a new form.

The form of sublation which subjectivity undergoes is the process of *objectification*. In this process, the subject enters into a relation with all the other concepts (the object) in the formation in the course of which both subject and object are changed. In the end, the Subject has become a moment of the whole formation, one its organs. For Hegel, there is ultimately only *one concept*, the Idea, which we can understand as the developing totality of the social life of a community. This Subject-Object process is the same process as what Marx refers to as a "process of concentration" and "reproduction of the concrete by way of thought."

Let us follow the subject-object relation in terms of how Hegel outlines the structure of the Object.

§2   The Three Phases of Objectification: Mechanism, Chemism and Organism

Subject-Object is a relation between entities of the same kind; subject and object are not different kinds of thing. It is simply that the subject stands in relation to other subjects as to an object. The object is both the End for the Subject, and its Means. The subject-object relation is the relation between a social practice and other social practices which are relatively foreign to it. But the normal situation is that means of mediation between subjects do exist in a community, and we are not dealing with a confrontation of the kind of the master-servant narrative, in which no means of mediation exists.

Hegel looks at three grades of the subject-object relation: Mechanism, Chemism and Teleology. I am going to refer to 'Teleology' as 'Organism' though it could also be called 'Ecology'. These ideas did not exist in Hegel's day, so he used 'Teleology' to indicate the science of living organisms.

You can visualize Mechanism, Chemism and Teleology in terms of relations between projects; between social movements and institutions; the relation of feminism to the legal system and Science; or the relations between different ethnic communities within a multicultural society, and so on, or a concept like the internet and all other relations which are transformed by the arrival of the internet. It is a relation between one project (the Subject) which is the new, active or "abstract" project and the others (Object) which are already institutionalized and constitute the components of the existing social context.

Note that if we were to use the term 'Other' here, it would be to refer to the Object, the existing institutions, in contrast to the Subject, which is the outsider, the newcomer.

Mechanism
This is how Hegel describes MECHANISM:

> As objectivity is the totality of the Notion withdrawn into its unity, ... In so far as it has the Notion immanent in it, it contains the difference of the Notion, but on account of the objective totality, the differentiated moments are *complete and self-subsistent objects* which consequently, even in their relation, stand to one another only as *self-subsistent* things and remain *external* to one another in every combination. This is what constitutes the character of *mechanism,* namely, that whatever relation obtains between the things combined, this relation is one *extraneous* to them that does not concern their nature at all, and even if it is accompanied by a semblance of unity it remains nothing more than *composition, mixture, aggregation* and the like. *Spiritual* mechanism also, like *material,* consists in this, that the things related in the spirit remain external to one another and to spirit itself. A *mechanical style of thinking, a mechanical memory, habit, a mechanical way of acting,* signify that the peculiar pervasion and presence of spirit is lacking in what spirit apprehends or does.
>
> *Science of Logic,* §1543

This brings to mind a multicultural society in which the 'ethnic mosaic' metaphor applies. In this view a collection of self-sufficient communities mutually indifferent to one another interact, but in the way of external impact on one another; neither community modifying its own nature, merely adjusting its activity to accommodate or resist the impact of another community. Or, sciences, each of which is pursuing its own research program, perhaps uncritically using the findings of another as instruments in their own work, but remaining separate branches of science. Or, a social movement that regards all other movements as irrelevant to themselves, that turn up to protest against something and happen to find other social movements there as well, and may go so far as agreeing the date and place of the protest, but no further. Or, a social movement which succeeds in having its main demand legislated, but in a way which does not integrate it into the whole, like in Indonesia, where there is a minimum wage in legislation, but no provisions to enforce it – life goes on as before.

Hegel follows the development of Mechanism through the concepts of mechanical *objects* to mechanical *processes* to systems of mechanical *relations*, particularly where one object creates a centre around which others revolve. He likens Mechanism to systems of government in which the components are united mechanically but not integrated organically; he traces the development of relations between individuals (I), organisations (P) and the state (U) using the idea of Syllogisms, an approach he uses again in *The Philosophy of Right*. This system, in which one Subject plays a central role in relation to the others, forms the transition to Chemism.

Chemism

The second chapter of Objectivity is CHEMISM, where the Subject and Object have a selective *affinity* to one another based in each's own nature. One is here reminded of the 'ethnic melting pot' metaphor used for the development of a multi-cultural society. Here subject and object are not wholly external to one another, but recognise a relation to the object within their own nature, like social movements which recognise that both are fighting a common enemy, and in making common cause strengthen that affinity and collaborate. Again Hegel follows the development from Chemical Object to Chemical process, and uses the Syllogisms developed earlier to trace the relation between Individual, Universal and Particular through which these processes develop, gradually resolving the one-sidedness of the Subjective Syllogisms.

Hegel wants to derive the notions of the Physics, Chemistry and Biology of his times logically and is preparing the basis for his Philosophy of Nature in this section, but its usefulness in this respect is questionable. There is a fine line between intelligibility and rationalisation which Hegel transgresses from time to time. But he does sketch out a plausible, escalating series of categories through which a subject objectifies itself, and ideas drawn from the natural sciences serve nicely to illustrate this development: a subject is abstract at the beginning and finds the outer world foreign and indifferent to it, and in that sense is a concept in-itself. Then through the discovery of affinities the Subject develops relations with all the other subjects in the community. A multisided network of affinities results in all round mutual dependence of Subjects, marking the transition to Organism.

Organism and Teleology

Hegel did not have at his disposal a viable natural scientific theory to explain the appearance of teleology in the natural world of plants and animals, but teleology was undeniably *real*. Kant had recognised this problem as well and concluded that it went beyond the valid limits of knowledge to deduce from the appearance of the teleological character of the organic world that there was a Designer or Final Cause behind it or any teleological explanation. Hegel would agree, but his aim was to demonstrate that the emergence of teleology in the formation of the natural world was logically *necessary*, flowing from the inherent nature of concepts. But he was opposed to any theory of evolution, whether inheritance of acquired characteristics or natural selection. (Hegel's rejection of the idea that the organic world had *evolved* will be dealt with in §8 of the next section.).

   Hegel held that in Nature there is change but no development over time, but this does not exclude relations of *logical* priority in Nature. Hegel defended the use of Teleology as a method of analysis of Nature, alongside Mechanism and Chemism. Now that everyone knows about natural selection, it is commonplace to ask the question "Why is it so?" while "How is it so?" is an impossible question. In social and cultural developments, we also find teleological relations, but we do not jump to Theistic conclusions from that, or become functionalists or presume that a conspiracy is at work.

> The more the teleological principle was linked with the concept of an *extramundane* intelligence and to that extent was favoured by piety, the more it seemed to depart from the true investigation of nature, which aims at cognising the properties of nature not as extraneous, but as *immanent determinatenesses* and accepts only such cognition as a valid *comprehension*. As end is the Notion itself in its Existence, it may seem strange that the cognition of objects from their Notion appears rather as an unjustified trespass into a *heterogeneous* element, whereas mechanism, for which the determinateness of an object is a determinateness posited in it externally and by another object, is held to be a *more immanent* point of view than teleology.
>
> *Science of Logic*, §1595

Hegel concluded that the End emerges as the truth of Mechanism and Chemism, that a Notion 'strives' to objectify itself. (More on this in Part 3).

> End ... is the *concrete universal*, which possesses in its own self the moment of particularity and externality and is therefore active and the urge to repel itself from itself. The Notion, as End, is of course an *objective judgment* in which one determination, the *subject*, namely the concrete Notion, is self-determined, while the other is not merely a predicate but external objectivity. But the end relation is not for that reason a *reflective* judging that considers external objects only according to a unity, *as though* an intelligence had given this unity *for the convenience of our cognitive faculty*; on the contrary it is the absolute truth that judges *objectively* and determines external objectivity absolutely. Thus the End relation is more than *judgment*; it is the *syllogism* of the self-subsistent free Notion that unites itself with itself through objectivity.
>
> *Science of Logic*, §1599

So here the Subject finds in the Object, in other subjects, its own End, or as it is sometimes said, the Subject finds its own essence outside of itself. Thus the development here is one in which the Subject becomes *in and for itself* through the process of mutual transformation of object and subject, which is the basis for the Idea.

The process of TELEOLOGY is the dialectic of Means and Ends. We have two maxims: on the one hand, "the end justifies the means," and on the other, "the movement is everything the end nothing." Both these maxims are limited and one-sided. The Subject strives to realize its End, at first by inadequate means, and the Realised End expresses the disharmony between the Means and the *Subjective* End – it is the truth of the subjective end. This leads to a reconception of the End and determination of a new Means more adequate to the End. Finally, *there can be no contradiction between the Means and Realised End*, ultimately the Subject realizes that the Means and End are identical. I will deal comprehensively with Hegel's critique of the maxim: "The End justifies the Means" in 17§4.

§3   The Idea is the Unity of Life and Cognition

The Idea, the final section of the *Logic*, develops through a long drawn-out process of differentiation and re-integration, objectification and internalisation, with a continual interchange between means and ends.

Hegel says that the Idea is a dialectic of Life and Cognition. That is, it is both a learning process and a life process. Subject and Object have repeatedly overcome their contradictions and transformed one another, and both subject and object are part of a single process of development. The Subject's activity develops towards its own Good, but can only do so insofar as it forms a True conception of the Object. The Idea of *the True* and the Idea of *the Good*, and the unity of the True and the Good, constitutes the Absolute Idea.

In the section on Life, Hegel discusses the relationship of Individual and Genus: the Genus can live only in and through the finite mortal individuals which realize it, and conversely the individual finds *its truth* in its Genus.

> That is to say, the process of the genus, in which the single individuals sublate in one another their indifferent immediate existence and in this negative unity expire, has further for the other side of its product the *realized genus,* which has posited itself identical with the Notion. In the genus process, the separated individualities of individual life perish; the negative identity in which the genus returns into itself, while it is on the one hand the process of *generating individuality,* is on the other hand the *sublating of it,* and is thus the genus coming together with itself, *the universality* of the Idea in process of *becoming for itself.*
>
> Science of Logic, §1676

The category of Life leads to the category of COGNITION: "Life is the immediate Idea, or the Idea as its *Notion* not yet realized in its own self. In its *judgment,* the Idea is *cognition* in general" (*Science of Logic,* §1677). In the section on the True, Hegel deals with the relation between *Analytical Cognition and Synthetic Cognition,* and Definitions and the Division of subject matter in a science.

Hegel sees Cognition as the unity of Analytical and Synthetic Cognition, but even this formulation shows itself to be defective:

> Similarly, [the unity of analytic and synthetic cognition] finds propositions and laws, and proves their *necessity,* but not as a necessity of the subject matter in and for itself, that is, not from the Notion, but as a necessity of the cognition that works on given determinations, on the differences of the phenomenal aspect of the subject matter, and cognizes *for itself* the proposition as a unity and relationship, or cognizes the ground of phenomena from the *phenomena* themselves.
>
> Science of Logic, §1721

Likewise Hegel requires that the definition of the concepts in a science and the division of the subject matter in a science be determined immanently from the Notion of the science, not arbitrarily or subjectively introduced from without.

The final concept of the *Logic* is the ABSOLUTE IDEA which appears as the unity of the Theoretical Idea and the Practical Idea (incidentally, mirroring the concluding section of the *Subjective Spirit*), that is, the identity of a practical form of life with its own self-understanding, a *concrete* identity arrived at through the long-drawn out process described. The chapter on the Absolute Idea, like the final chapter of the *Phenomenology*, reads like the "Twelve Days of Christmas," – a recapitulation of the whole structure leading up to itself, emphasizing the idea of concreteness as sublation.

And in a final unbelievable leap of Hermetic magic, the truth of the Idea is Nature:

> The Idea, namely, in positing itself as absolute unity of the pure Notion and its reality and thus contracting itself into the immediacy of being, is the totality in this form – Nature.
>
> *Science of Logic*, §1817

Despite the obvious social character of Hegel's Logic, he still makes Logic prior to human life and even prior to Nature itself!

§4   Hegel Overcomes the Individual/Society Dichotomy

What we have seen is that Hegel presented a critique of all aspects of social life by an exposition of the logic of formations of consciousness, which does not take the individual person as its unit of analysis but rather a *concept*. A concept is understood, not as some extramundane entity but a *form of activity – a practical relation among people* mediated by 'thought objects', i.e., artefacts.

If we understand that human beings live in an environment of thought-objects constructed by their own purposive activity, and that thinking, insofar as it is correct, reflects the objective relations between these thought-objects, then this is surely a viable approach to science, and the basis for a genuinely self-construing method of science.

Looked at with the benefit of 200 years of hindsight, this philosophy has its problems, this is undeniable. However, recent currents of philosophy, such as "post-humanism," which pride themselves in having "deconstructed the subject," invariably make the target of their critique a Kantian or Cartesian individual subject, passing over Hegel's solution of this problem. Hegel is often dismissed on the basis of side-issues without confronting his achievement in overcoming the aporias in Kant's notion of the subject or the Cartesian dichotomy. Hegel built a philosophy which overcame the contradictions inherent in Kantian individualism without the sacrifice of an *ethical theory*, without the sacrifice of a concept of genuine individuality, and which makes a strong concept of Freedom the central category of his theory of history and politics.

In the Logic, Hegel resolves the individual / society dichotomy as a problem in social science by means of the Individual / Universal / Particular relation. This is not the same issue as the problem of how modern individuals see their relation to the whole community. But the *Logic* does suggest a practical solution to this problem as well. We see that Subjectivity is a multiplicity of processes and relations in which individuals collaborate with one another in particular forms of social practice organized around different universals. This approach is far more fruitful than setting up two poles – the individual and 'society' – and then trying to draw some connection between them. By taking the concept, in the sense described already, as his 'unit of analysis', rather than the individual person, Hegel has produced a powerful and nuanced conception of human life.

This approach allows us to see that the individual may have a whole variety of different commitments and beliefs, participating in a variety of crisscrossing processes of social change. This is because Hegel takes not persons, not groups, but *actions* as the individual unit. By interpreting actions as judgments and mediated actions as syllogisms, he has built a Logic which enables him to explore and illuminate the widest possible range of issues within a single framework. This facilitates interdisciplinary research and makes *real life*, as opposed to the laboratory, the site for scientific practice.

§5   Spirit is Both Substance and Subject

Hegel's philosophy is certainly very strange and difficult to grasp. But we need to remember that his ideas were developed in response to specific, difficult problems in philosophy which were demanding resolution at that time. The problems at issue were chiefly those that arose from the need to transcend liberal individualism and from Kant's attempts to rescue science from the opposing forces of dogmatism and scepticism. So we should not lightly condemn Hegel, but rather give him credit for having laid the foundation for an interdisciplinary science. We should take him at his word when he says that Spirit is the nature of human beings en masse. All human communities construct their social environment, both in the sense of physically constructing the artefacts which they use in collaborating together, and in the sense that, in the social world at least, things are what they are only because they are so construed. The idea of Spirit needs to be taken seriously. It may seem odd to say, as Hegel does, that *everything is thought*, but it is no more viable to say that everything is matter.

No-one else has produced anything that can rival his Logic; and he left no room for imitators. It should be taken seriously.

At this point, the reader should be able to read the *Shorter Logic*. I recommend at this stage reading only selected passages in the *Science of Logic*, rather than attempting to read it cover to cover.

Hegel's Theory of Action, Part 1: Teleology

Mediation and the 'Cunning of Reason'

Hegel shows how it is the mediation of actions with artefacts and the objectified practices of a community (i.e., institutions in the broadest sense of the word) which ensures that whatever may be a subject's aims in some action, the outcome is the development of Spirit, the working through of contradictions intrinsic to the whole social formation. This idea of Reason manifesting itself in human actions, independently of the subjective intentions of those pursuing their own ends in the given action, Hegel calls the 'cunning of reason', and it appears in the *Logic, The Philosophy of Right,* and the *Philosophy of History.*

For example, individuals may *bring* a dispute into the legal system but the dispute is *decided* with reference to the body of legislation and case law. And where this proves indecisive, the judges are concerned with the further development of the law, not just the resolution of the immediate issue in dispute. Likewise, when people use tools acting on some material to achieve their ends, they must perforce use these tools according to their affordances and therefore in line with the constraints of both Nature and the historically determined forces of production. More and more, written procedures, tools, materials and especially algorithms embedded in machinery, play a determinant role in the labour process, and over the decades and centuries have become more and more powerful and sophisticated.

The Syllogism of Action

The SYLLOGISM OF ACTION is the last section of the Logic before the Absolute Idea.

> In the syllogism of action, one premise is the *immediate relation of the good end to actuality* which it seizes on, and in the second premise directs it as an external *means* against the external actuality.
>
> Science of Logic, §1773

So the outcome of an action realises what is implicit in Nature and the social forces of production, which may or may not be what the subject had in mind in taking up the tools to realize his or her own ends. The REALISED END therefore is a merging of the intentions motivating the subject's actions and objective tendencies inherent in Nature and culture.

The 'Subject' is any human enterprise (project) or formation of consciousness which arises within the fabric of a community. The universal requirements
of Nature and History manifest themselves in the finite actions of individuals
and social movements, thanks to the fact that no subject can achieve its ends in
the natural or social world except by using as means the universal products of
that wider world. As Hegel put it:

> Purposive action, with its Means, is still directed outwards, because the
> End is also not identical with the object, and must consequently first
> be mediated with it. The Means in its capacity of object stands, in this
> second premise, in direct relation to the other extreme of the syllogism,
> namely, the material or objectivity which is presupposed. This relation
> is the sphere of Chemism and Mechanism, which have now become the
> servants of the Final Cause, where lies their truth and free notion. Thus
> the Subjective End, which is the power ruling these processes, in which
> the objective things wear themselves out on one another, contrives to
> keep itself free from them, and to preserve itself in them. Doing so, it
> appears as the Cunning of Reason.
>
> *Shorter Logic*, §209

> Reason is as cunning as it is powerful. Cunning may be said to lie in the
> intermediative action which, while it permits the objects to follow their
> own bent and act upon one another till they waste away, and does not
> itself directly interfere in the process, is nevertheless only working out
> its own aims.
>
> *Shorter Logic*, §209n.

The subject and object are each mutually independent totalities, but
the means, *that is, the object*, is, according to Hegel, more powerful in the long
run:

> That the end relates itself immediately to an object and makes it a means,
> as also that through this means it determines another object, may be
> regarded as *violence* in so far as the end appears to be of quite another
> nature than the object, and the two objects similarly are mutually inde-
> pendent totalities.... the *means* is superior to the finite ends of *external*
> purposiveness: the plough is more honourable than are immediately the
> enjoyments procured by it and which are ends....
>
> *Science of Logic*, §1614

So whilst a person can do as he or she chooses, as natural and cultural human beings our ends are, in fact, *given* to us:

> The *tool* lasts, while the immediate enjoyments pass away and are forgotten. In his tools man possesses power over external nature, even though in respect of his ends he is, on the contrary, subject to it.
>
> Science of Logic, §1615

As Hegel says in the "Philosophy of History":

> It is not the general idea that is implicated in opposition and combat, and that is exposed to danger. It remains in the background, untouched and uninjured. This may be called the *cunning of reason*, – that it sets the passions to work for itself, while that which develops its existence through such impulsion pays the penalty and suffers loss.
>
> Philosophy of History, §36

Individual human beings and the formations of consciousness in which they act are thus, for Hegel, the forms by means of which Spirit unfolds itself.

Marx appropriated this idea in *Capital*:

> Labour is, in the first place, a process in which both man and Nature participate, and in which man of his own accord starts, regulates, and controls the material re-actions between himself and Nature. He opposes himself to Nature as one of her own forces ...
>
> An instrument of labour is a thing, or a complex of things, which the labourer interposes between himself and the subject of his labour (*Arbeitsgegenstand*), and which serves as the conductor of his activity. He makes use of the mechanical, physical, and chemical properties of some substances in order to make other substances subservient to his aims.
>
> Capital, Volume I, Chapter 6.1

The Soviet Cultural Psychologist, Lev Vygotsky, agreed. In the context of comparing mediation by tools and mediation by symbols, he says:

> With full justification, Hegel used the concept of mediation in its most general meaning, seeing in it the most characteristic property of mind. He said that mind is as resourceful as it is powerful. In general, resourcefulness consists in mediating activity that, while it lets objects act on

each other according to their nature and exhaust themselves in that activity, does not at the same time intervene in the process, but fulfils only its proper role.... man acts on behaviour through signs, that is, stimuli, letting them act according to their own psychological nature.

LSVCW v. 4. p. 61–2

I will further discuss Hegel's structural determinism in Part 3 where Parts 2 & 3 of Hegel's theory of action also appear, and will further reflect on these questions in Part 4.

CHAPTER 12

The Subject and Culture: Logic and Ontology

§1   Dichotomy is a Problem in the History of Philosophy

How does Hegel respond to the problem of *di*-chotomy? In one sense, he replaces dichotomy with *oneness* in that he begins each of his books with a single concept, be that Being or Concept or Space or Freedom, and unfolds out of that single concept all the distinctions which are implicit within it, through a process of differentiation or *diremption*. So each of Hegel's books are monist.

Each well-known dichotomy which Hegel inherited from the history of philosophy, particularly Kant, appears in his system with the opposites already rooted in a logically prior unified conception, rather than each having an independent origin and having later to be stitched together in some way.

It is often the case that the two opposites do have independent origins, but share a common history in material or historical reality before coming into a relationship with one another. For example, the monarchical state and civil society had separate origins; another example, intellect and speech which also have separate origins. However, in these cases neither the one nor the other nor the unity of the two constitute the fundamental concept. A state can be true to its concept only when it rests on a fully developed civil society, and speech is only fully developed when it is intelligent.

The two-ness of the Doctrine of Essence is another instance. Here each of the opposites (e.g. Form and Content) are the whole. But Hegel does not divide Reflection into Forms and Contents; you cannot add Form to Content or vice versa. Further, the opposites (e.g. Cause and Effect) can transform one into another. Here the opposites are the 'moments' of a whole, rather than 'elements' or 'kinds'.

It might be said that Hegel replaces *di*-chotomy with *tri*-chotomy. But 'trichotomy' is literally to cut in three, and that is not what Hegel does with his various triads. He does not sort the world into three kinds of thing. The number three comes up quite a lot in Hegel, but it is the three-ness of the three moments of the subject – Individual, Particular and Universal – which are of significance in Hegel's response to dichotomy. Does this triplet, which is the basis for all those syllogisms, which Hegel uses to elaborate the relations between various groups of concepts, really constitute a *trichotomy*? Or on the other hand, does it succeed in allowing the subject matter to develop its own distinctions whilst retaining the unity and integrity of the original subject matter?

Each of the moments of the Subject is itself a *whole*, albeit a one-sided, un-developed whole. The concrete Concept arises through interaction between and ultimately the merging of the three. But, in each instance, the Individual is the *ground* of the concept, whether that be the Universal Notion, the Particular Notion or the Individual Notion. They are not ontologically distinct.

Let's consider some object, say the 'Cussonia tree at Melbourne University'. 'Tree' is a *universal*, but the specification of the variety and genus of the plant, its location in a university and the name of the university, *particularize* the tree down to an *individual* tree. There is no ontological distinction between individual, particular and universal – all have their ground in individuals.

The 'Melbourne University Cussonia Tree' is an elementary formation of Spirit, that is, a human activity. Hegel calls it a 'thought determination' but thought in the sense we normally understand it is only something we *abstract from activity* in order to make sense of activity; it is not something that can be added to activity. It is just the same as when we talk of past historical events even though these events are utterly inaccessible to the senses – we must assume their reality in order to make sense of our world. The same is true of all the strange objects of physics and chemistry and the theories of geology and evolutionary biology: we prove the reality of all kinds of material entities because their reality is necessary to make sense of our activity. All these thought determinations are abstracted from human activity in order to make sense of the activity in which they are implicit.

§2   Hegel has Overcome the Mind-Matter Dichotomy with Logic

What about the mind-matter dichotomy? Hegel doesn't have a lot to say about 'matter' simply because there is very little to be said about it. Matter is the category of the Thing-in-itself, that is to say, it is an *empty* concept. It simply indicates the world which exists independently of human activity and nothing more.

Kant was wrong to claim that the Thing-in-itself is unknowable, because, as Hegel shows, we get to know about the material world outside of and independent of human activity *through* our activity. There is no hard and fast line separating the Thing-in-itself from Appearance.

This dichotomy, whether in the form suggested by Descartes or by Kant, has considerable support in our ordinary everyday intuitive conceptions of the world. Like all animals, we are born realists. Well, not quite *born* realists, but one of the first things infants learn is the distinction between their own action and an objective world which they do not (yet) control. This distinction has *survival value* for any organism. And in general people do suffer from the Cartesian illusion of having access to thought objects which are in some sense mirror images of real objects, belonging to a mental world which is something quite distinct from the material world it reflects. The intuitive power of this idea is undeniable, but it does not stand up to criticism.

Nowadays, among philosophically educated people, there is a widespread conviction that there is something fundamentally wrong with *any* dichotomy. We are suspicious of any conception which *sorts the world into two kinds of thing with a sharp line between them*. However implausible Hegel's ideas seem in places, we need to keep in mind that he does overcome the limitations of these intuitively very compelling systems of thought.

Hegel demonstrated in the *Phenomenology* that all the foregoing systems of Ontology and Epistemology were obsolete along with the mind/matter dichotomy. By subjecting the concept of Being to logical criticism, he subsumed Ontology under Logic.

§3   The Logic Offers a Basis for Interdisciplinary Research

After Hegel's death, there were no further attempts to develop science in an 'encyclopædic' manner. Each of the different branches of science were pursued separately and further divided and specialised as time went on, and it could not have been any other way. The insights provided by Hegel's encyclopædic approach were lost on those engaged in research in particular domains of science. Nowadays, the human sciences are extremely fragmented; not only are the human sciences divided into sociology, economics, political science, anthropology, psychology, law, history, linguistics, philosophy, criminology, etc., etc., etc., but on top of this the different currents of thinking: positivists, behaviourists, functionalists, structuralists, Marxists, poststructuralists, deconstructionists and so on, are no longer able to talk to one another. This situation poses severe problems for anyone who want to solve social problems, rather than just build an academic career.

It is widely recognised that the solution of complex social problems requires the critical appropriation of insights from a wide variety of currents and subject areas. A holistic approach is needed, one not hampered by the individual vs. social dichotomy and other ideologies based on fixed categories. Hegel's *Logic* is a framework for such a project.

The *Logic* is particularly well suited to the study of emergent social movements and projects. Whenever you are dealing with a group of people organized around an idea or a social project or enterprise of some kind, then

Hegel's *Logic* is your operational manual. No community development worker, social justice activist, voluntary group organizer, political activist or academic with an overview of their subject matter should be without it.

§4   Everything is Both Immediate and Mediated

Some writers have argued specifically *against* mediation. Hostility to all kinds of mediation is pervasive among anarchists who eschew participation in elections and intervention in other institutions in favour of 'direct action'. Dave Lamb has used the passages in Hegel's Logic cited above, about mediation and the 'cunning of reason', to argue that mediation functions against human emancipation. But the 'cunning of reason' is not conservative, but rather is a vehicle for the tendencies and contradictions immanent within the the social formation itself. If a social movement wants to change society, then it needs to do so having a mind for and *using* these inherent tendencies.

One of the arguments against mediation is that the Means very easily becomes the Object of activity. In fact, it could be said to be a law: for example, merchant capital arose as the mediator facilitating trade; but merchant capital soon became its own end, and trade merely the means of capital accumulation. Nonetheless, alongside a rapid expansion of merchant capital there was also a massive expansion in trade. Another example is the charity which transforms itself into a career in its own right, and loses sight of those it is supposed to help. These are real problems, but it is a mistake to locate the problem in mediation as such. Every action requires a means. To refuse all means is to refuse to act.

While direct action has virtues in itself, it seems to me that to deny oneself the option of going beyond direct action to challenge the institutions of capitalist rule is to desert the field of battle. Direct action and direct democracy make sense up the level of about 1,000 people; beyond that, to abstain from the use of forms of mediation is to 'drop out' of politics.

Three points about mediation. (1) *Every* action and *every* relation is mediated. It is only a question of *how* the relation is mediated. (2) The point about mediation is not to be for or against mediation, but that asking *how* the action is mediated is an heuristic device, leading to the discovery of new relations. (3) Hegel's claim is that everything is *both* mediated *and immediate*. If the mediated relation is not *also* immediate, then it is not mediated in the sense intended by Hegel. Vygotsky expresses this insight with the term 'dual stimulation' – both the Object and the Means 'stimulate' the Subject.

§5   Normativity, Attributes and the Idea

In non-Hegelian philosophy, concepts (and therefore norm) are taken to be a collection of essential attributes. It is this limited conception of norms which has given norms a 'bad name' on the 'cultural left'. Human life is impossible without norms, and as a result of cultural and historical development norms become very concrete and expansive and Hegel's Logic reflects this.

A child, a person who has not yet grasped a concept, or an artificial intelligence device, takes a collection of attributes as the means of recognizing the thing, but this is not the same as grasping the concept. Measure, the 'observer category' in which the concept is taken as a complex of quantities and qualities, is something very different from a true concept.

It is this conception of a norm which is most powerfully expressed in bureaucratic and industrial procedures – doorways are normatively 820mm wide and 2040mm high, newspapers are printed in 12pt type, and so on. These kind of norms reflect conceptions of how the products in question are to be used and consequently a normative conception of the person – who can walk through a door of this dimension and read 12pt type.

The myriad of attributes of a person are indeed connected with the concept of a person, but they are *not* definitive. Each of the attributes which can be said of a person – vocality, dexterity, sightedness, attentiveness, etc., etc. – are themselves universals like "person," and in most cases don't have a cut-and-dried meaning.

Whether in the case of a concept of 'person' or concepts like 'vocality' and 'dexterity' – the simplest abstract form of the concept is typically taken to be the norm, but for Hegel this is false.

In the section of the Logic on the Object, Hegel describes how concepts interact with one another, and he takes these interactions in three grades – Mechanism, Chemism and Organism. In each interaction both subject and object changes. So the concept of person (the norm) changes as it interacts with the concepts of 'dexterity' and 'vocality', and so on and these concepts in turn change whenever they interact with the concept of 'person'.

Now it so happens that what counts as 'dexterity' and what counts as 'vocality' varies and of course the characteristics of each person are different, and the interactions between all these concepts happen in evolving cultural contexts. The *truth* of the concept, that is, the *Idea* of dexterity (as it comes to be understood after undergoing extensive criticism in social life), the idea of vocality and the idea of a person is the totality of all the meanings determined under each concept. The concrete idea of person, vocality, dexterity, etc., can only be realized through infinitely many such real interactions in the course of the historical development of a culture. The concrete universal concept of each encompasses all these particulars as they are manifested in all the individual interactions.

It is not possible to form a concrete concept, whether of 'dexterity', 'vocality' or 'person', by considering that concept on its own, in isolation from all the other concepts it interacts with, that is, its cultural and historical context.

In *The Philosophy of Right*, Hegel attaches a very definite meaning to 'person': a person is someone of our species who has 'taken possession of their own body'. Other than this, no attribute of a person counts as to whether they are a person or not, consequently there are persons of every imaginable measure. The imperative of life in any state is: "Be a person and respect others as persons."

§6   Hegel and Deconstruction

Deconstruction, originally a technique of literary criticism initiated by Jacques Derrida in his *Of Grammatology* in 1967, has proved to be an effective tool in the hands of social movements. Its power has been demonstrated above all in the success of the LGBTI... movement in the past 30 years in breaking down gender stereotypes and opening the way for the removal of practices discriminating against people identifying outside the traditional male/female norms.

Deconstruction is fundamentally an application of Hegel's dialectical approach to reality, but Derrida was at great pains to distinguish Deconstruction from Hegel's dialectic.

The technique is to call into question a relevant binary distinction in discourse, social customs or institutionalised practices. Initially, the attack takes the form of a Hegelian type of criticism of the relevant distinction, with the aim of making it unsustainable in discourse. The verbal criticism then opens the way to changing not only forms of words ('political correctness') but practices and laws (unisex toilets, right to adopt for same sex parents, etc.) The resulting changes in social practice then change everyday experience and consolidate the new norms, and the next round begins.

The underlying ontology is the same as that outlined in the Preface to Hegel's *Phenomenology*, namely, that independently of human practices the world is irreducibly unorganised, complex and unstable, and human practice introduces order into this world, captured in our concepts. Our concepts are not 'copies' of distinctions existing in Nature.

Derrida's concern (and Bakhtin voiced the same concern) is with the idea that when 'contradictions' such as a binary opposition like male/female, are subject to criticism by Marxists informed by Hegel's dialectic, the aim would be to *resolve* the contradiction by reducing the difference to subordinate types of the same whole (thus a kind of 'humanism'), such as when seeking to eliminate gender discrimination in discourses and social practices. Deconstruction, on the other hand, discovers so many varieties of gender that no-one can even remember all the letters of the alphabet by which they are referred to and no term such as 'gay' or 'other sexualities' can be used to lump together what is taken to be in reality irreducibly multiple and unstable differences.

There is no doubt that there is a difference in strategy here, and it seems that the Women's Movement benefited from the use of the strategy of dissolving differences, while LGBTI... people have benefited from the opposite strategy of validating difference. It also seems that the success of the Deconstruction strategy depends upon the prior success of the non-discrimination strategy. In fact, Deconstruction could have had perverse outcomes if the principle of non-discrimination on grounds of gender had not already been secured. What is overlooked is that Deconstruction does in fact *resolve* the contradictions entailed in binary gender differences – we are all persons, and all entitled to be respected as persons.

The problem of women's disadvantage in economic life is a wicked problem in a way which is not shared by the stigmatised categories: gender equality in the workplace is only possible when women and men share the burden of domestic labour equally, and yet that can only be achieved if women have the same earning capacity at work. In other words, the disadvantage women face is due to the contradiction between stereotyping in the public sphere on one hand and in the private sphere on the other. Neither strategy on its own is going to resolve this one so long as distinct private and public spheres exist. A false dichotomy between Deconstruction and Dialectic is no help.

§7   Is Hegel's Logic a Monologue?

Mikhail Bakhtin (1986) claimed that Hegel's dialectic was "monological" and counterposed his 'dialogic' approach to Hegel's 'dialectic' on the basis that the dialogic approach allowed for a multiplicity of voices, while Hegel's dialectic was a monologue.

In brief, my response is to point the reader to the section of the Logic on The Object. This section explicitly deals with the development of a subject through a many-sided interaction with other, independent subjects within the same community, in which both subject and object are transformed. What marks out Hegel's view from other approaches to dialogue is that Hegel is interested in whatever shared social and cultural conditions the participants to a dialogue bring with them. No two voices are completely foreign to one another. Do they share a common language? Do they have something to offer each other? Do they have preconceptions of each other? Is collaboration possible? It is this attention to the wider context of interaction which marks Hegel out from some proponents of discourse analysis.

This is not to suggest for a moment that Bakhtin's theory is superseded in some way by Hegel's Logic. Bakhtin built a discourse theory on the basis of the 'utterance' as the unit of analysis, and as such, it offers certain insights not given by a theory based on the concept as the unit of analysis. Hegel's Logic is not a discourse theory; it is a Logic. Whether Bakhtin's discourse analysis offers a methodology for the human sciences as a whole is another question altogether.

§8   Brief Outline of *Philosophy of Nature*

The *Encyclopædia of the Philosophical Sciences* has three Parts: Logic, Nature and Spirit. Of all Hegel's works, his *Philosophy of Nature* is the one which has had the least positive impact in the years after his death. It is often derided, even by people who otherwise admire Hegel. I think it is important for the reader to know how Hegel moves from the *Logic* to *The Philosophy of Right* (the second book of the Philosophy of Spirit), but there is not a lot to be gained from a detailed study of the Philosophy of Nature. However, it is not as misguided as it is often claimed to be. Hegel drew on all the scientific literature available in his day such that it could be said that the *Philosophy of Nature* was a critical appropriation of natural science as it was in the 1810s and 1820s.

Like all of the *Encyclopædia*, the *Philosophy of Nature* was revised throughout Hegel's lifetime. The definitive edition of the *Philosophy of Nature* was published in 1842, based on editions of 1817, 1827 and 1830, and I will be using an English translation of this edition as my reference.

The *Philosophy of Nature* has three books: Mechanics, Physics and Organics. MECHANICS begins with the abstract notions of Space, Time and Matter as far as Gravity, covering the topics taught in my school days as 'Applied Mathematics'. This domain was revolutionised by Einstein between 1905 and 1916. PHYSICS deals with all the Inorganic phenomena, covering both Physics and Chemistry. ORGANICS covers the "Terrestrial Organism" (the history of the Earth), Plants and Animal Physiology, but does not include the nervous system or the various processes which underlie and constitute the psyche at even the most primitive level. These come under the *Philosophy of Spirit*.

The first part, Mechanics – 18 paragraphs covering material which in its modern form is almost entirely mathematical – is where Hegel's most prescient insights are to be found. Of course Hegel knew nothing of the world of atoms and subatomic particles, the weird physics of speeds approaching the speed of light or Maxwell's equations of electromagnetism. Nor did he know anything of the cell life underlying the organic world, invisible without the aid of microscopes.

It is clear that Hegel seriously underestimated the extent of what the expanding scope of technology and industry would reveal about Nature. The Nature Hegel knew was the same range of phenomena which had been observed since antiquity. Consequently, it was not hard to fall into the illusion that all these phenomena – given to the senses and incorporated in everyday practical activity – could be organised into a single, coherent rational system of natural science based on the logic of the concept. In hindsight it is now obvious that this project was doomed from the start.

However, in the domain of Mechanics, it would not seem out of reach. After all, in 1910–1913, Bertrand Russell and Alfred North Whitehead published *Principia Mathematica*, aiming to derive the whole of mathematics from a few axioms like a geometric theorem. They failed, however, and contradictions were disclosed and in 1931 Gödel proved that their task was in principle impossible. In the case of Mathematics, then, it took 100 years after Hegel's death to show that Formal Logic could not do what Hegel had wanted to do with Dialectical Logic, so Hegel's work here cannot be said to have been entirely misconceived.

But it is Einstein's revolution in the domain of Space, Time and Gravity where Hegel has proved to have been so prescient.

§9 Einstein Confirmed Hegel's Approach to Mechanics

Hegel never accepted Newton's concept of forces acting at a distance as an explanation for gravitational or electromagnetic phenomena. He held that gravitational attraction had to be conceptualised as a *form of motion* inherent in matter. He never brought this idea to fruition, and nor could he have without the developments in mathematics and the experimental observations of the late 19th century. It is remarkable however, that Einstein's General Theory of Relativity resolves the problem of gravity without recourse to the concept of force, but by the critical revision of the notions of space, time and matter.

Maxwell's theory of electromagnetism likewise reduced the so-called electromagnetic *forces* to appearances to be explained in terms of *fields*.

It is in Einstein's Special Theory of Relativity that we see the Hegelian approach in its most fruitful application. The Special Theory hinges on a critique of the concepts of space and time. Space-time exists independently of human activity, but to then presume that *measures* of space and time are therefore objective properties of these natural entities, is exactly the kind of reification which Hegel opposed. Our measures of space and time are *reifications* of the practices of measuring space and time. Einstein carefully reconstructed the measurement of intervals of time and space as forms of human practice, and on the assumption that the laws of Physics were invariant with respect to inertial movement, discovered the relativity of these measures.

This critical examination of practice is, we have learnt, the essential meaning of Hegel's Logic. But neither Hegel nor anyone before 1905 could suspect that Euclid's Geometry, which reified spatial relations, and which had stood unchallenged for more than 2,000 years, would fail in the context of cosmological masses and speeds.

Hegel famously said: "In Nature there happens 'nothing new under the sun'," by which he meant that there is no *development* in Nature. He was aware that the Earth and its continents had a history – indeed he makes the history of the Earth the starting point for the *Philosophy of Nature*. But he worked on the assumption that plant and animal life arose from the ground according to *invariant* Natural laws.

In the light of the Big Bang Theory it seems unbelievable to deny development in Nature. However, the Big Bang Theory was devised on the *assumption that the most basic laws of Physics have remained invariant* at least for the 14 billion years since the Big Bang. Were it not so it would be impossible to draw any conclusions about events in the distant past. So Hegel was quite correct on this question.

The domain of Spirit is another matter altogether however.

PART 3

The Philosophy of Right

∵

CHAPTER 13

Subjective Spirit

§1   Subjective Spirit, Objective Spirit and Absolute Spirit

Whenever you are reading Hegel, you need to know just where you are in the 'circle of circles' which constitutes the *Encyclopædia* and in particular, the immediately foregoing and succeeding sections (Fig. 3). Although Hegel's social theory is contained in a separate publication called "The Philosophy of Right," this book is an extended version of the Objective Spirit, which is the second book of the Philosophy of Spirit. The Subjective Spirit is the first book of the Philosophy of Spirit.

Although an English translation of the Subjective Spirit was published in 1894 as part of the whole Philosophy of Spirit, this edition did not include the *Zusätze* – the notes clarifying the main text, drawing upon notes of Hegel's lectures by taken by his students. The *Zusätze* are crucial to understanding the bare and abstract text, and had been included in the 1873 translation of the *Shorter Logic* and the 1896 translation of *The Philosophy of Right*, ensuring

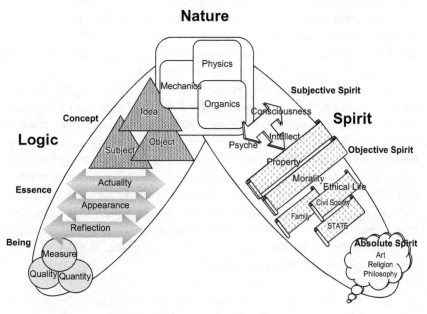

FIGURE 3   The Encyclopaedia of the Philosophical Sciences

the wide distribution and relative popularity of these works in the English speaking world. However, it was only in 1971 that the Wallace translation of the *Philosophy of Spirit* was republished, now including Ludwig Bouman's *Zusätze*, thus making Hegel's Psychology accessible to an English speaking readership for the first time.

In the absence of an accessible edition of the Subjective Spirit, Hegel's views on psychology were widely taken to be what is to be found in the 1807 *Phenomenology*. Such was the influence of the *Phenomenology*, that even with the publication of the *Philosophy of Mind* in 1971, only two book-length English language treatments of Hegel's Psychology have been published in the almost 50 years since.

We can only hope that people will tire of the master-servant narrative at some point, and the profound and complex structure of the *Subjective Spirit* will capture the attention it deserves. It may surprise readers to see that Hegel presents a view of the mind which provides a plausible material basis for thought, while also making it possible for us to reconcile the *experience* of conscious awareness with this material substratum. Hegel was writing at a time when the microstructure of the body was hardly even suspected let alone understood, so his psychology is based on speculative reasoning, his experience as a tutor, teacher and lecturer, and the very limited scientific knowledge of time. Nonetheless, the complex structure he suggests for the mind is plausible and challenging, and gives modern science cause to take it seriously.

The structure of the SUBJECTIVE SPIRIT changed over the years since it was first published in 1817, and different translators have used different words to translate Hegel's terminology. I have selected English words which I think best convey Hegel's concepts for a contemporary readership.

When we say 'Spirit', this is an English translation of the German word *Geist* which is also sometimes translated as 'Mind' and for Hegel carries the implication of being *rational* process. I have said that 'Spirit' can be understood as human activity, but this does not fully convey Hegel's meaning. According to Hegel, Spirit is both Substance and Subject. That is, Spirit does not just happen, it *does* things. We cannot view the unfolding of history in the same way we view a natural process like the weather or continental drift (which are viewed just as 'Substance'). The fact is that everything in history happens through the combined action of many wills, even if, like the movement of the pointer around a Ouija board, the resultant escapes the intentions of most of the players.

Marx was aiming at Hegel when he said:

> History does nothing, it 'possesses no immense wealth', it 'wages no battles'. It is man, real, living man who does all that, who possesses and

> fights; 'history' is not, as it were, a person apart, using man as a means to achieve its own aims; history is nothing but the activity of man pursuing his aims.
>
> *The Holy Family*, IV.2

and this would be more in accordance with modern consciousness which prefers to see the great social processes like the economy as quasi-natural forces. But there is no need to counterpose what is done by humanity to what is done by Spirit. The point is that Spirit is the "activity of human beings en masse" – it is what people *do* on a mass scale.

In the Subjective Spirit, it is this 'en masse' aspect which is missing. It is only when human beings build social formations which extend beyond the cultural horizon of any individual that individuals find themselves shaped not only by a natural environment, but by a civil society – law, culture, custom, social division of labour, etc., etc. – a *human* product, OBJECTIVE SPIRIT. Subjective Spirit describes animal life, up to and including human life, absent Objective Spirit, and provides the precondition and stimulus for the formation of Objective Spirit.

Mind is a *form of motion* or activity, rather than an attribute of an organism, let alone a state or substance inside the skull. The grades of Spirit, then, do not single out the individual, but on the contrary, take individual *actions* as moments of a whole formation.

ABSOLUTE SPIRIT includes Art, Religion and Philosophy (and one would nowadays include Science, which Hegel included under the heading of 'Philosophy') – all those products of human activity which are 'above politics', and which in modern society are kept separate from politics and government. The state does not legislate the approved art movement, a state religion or to resolve scientific disputes.

Hegel gives to each of the phases of Spirit – Subjective, Objective and Absolute – a definite directionality, not predetermination, but directionality. I will discuss this in more depth later on in connection with *The Philosophy of Right*. The *Philosophy of Spirit* expounds on its subject matter *logically* not historically. His *Philosophy of History* and his histories of the various components of Spirit are contained elsewhere. The relation between all the books and chapters of the *Philosophy of Spirit* is a logical one, not an historical relation. His views on ontogenetic development are to be found in remarks in the Subjective Spirit, so all those interested in child development and education should read the Subjective Spirit.

The *Philosophy of Nature* took us from space, time and matter up to the various systems of plant and animal organisms, including the autonomic nervous system, irritability, etc., but stops short of anything which could be construed as embryonic consciousness or a psyche, anything *mediating* between physiology and behaviour. So Nature gives us animal organisms which have all the biological prerequisites for a sentient being capable of having feelings, sensations and thoughts. Hegel cannot explain how such organisms come to be endowed with feelings, but he makes his start in the Subjective Spirit from the most primitive forms of psyche imaginable. But structure of the Hegel's subjective mind no more corresponds to neurological map of the brain than did Freud's Id, Ego and Super-ego.

§2   Psyche, Consciousness and Intellect

One of the features of Hegel's approach is that he does not take the individual mind to be a homogeneous process, but a *three-layered process*. Each category is a moment of a whole, viable and self-contained organism, not a functional sub-system.

The Psyche

First there is what Hegel calls *die Seele* or 'Soul', but which I will call 'the Psyche'. The PSYCHE is a moment of the nervous activity of an autonomous organism. It encompasses the entire organism, registering the neurophysiological totality of the organism as its own given being. Its determinations are *feelings*, but the Psyche does not register these feelings as intuitions *of* an object nor therefore does it take itself as a subject. Its mental life lacks both subject and object – it just *feels* afraid, content, anxious, angry, sleepy or whatever. The Psyche encompasses both the outward behaviour and the inward feelings of the organism, mediating between the two, and is an integral function of the whole organism.

The Psyche develops by means of *habits* and *habituation* so that the organism comes to distance itself from the immediacy of its own body. The distinction between itself and objects which belong to an external world thus begin to stand out in relief against this background. The most primitive organisms are not capable of habit-forming and habituation, but those which can open the way to Consciousness.

Consciousness

Mind which is habituated to its own feelings and orients itself to stimuli evidently coming from outside, is called CONSCIOUSNESS [*das Bewuβtsein*]. What distinguishes Consciousness is that it takes an object with which it interacts to be something with an independent unity of its own – something *else*. The out-of-the-ordinary feelings, feelings to which it is *not* habituated, are imputed to an objective world, and are called *sensations*. While Consciousness directs the body in its activity in relation to given objects, the Psyche all the while continues its work of regulating the movement and functioning of the body, now responding in addition to the stimuli of its own Consciousness. Indeed, Consciousness can only sense objects thanks to the feelings of the Psyche.

But Consciousness is not at first *self*-consciousness. In the earliest stages of Consciousness, even though Consciousness takes the object to have an independent unity, it is not self-aware. It comes to know its own subjectivity only mediately through interactions with other, objectively existing self-consciousnesses. Once it comes to see its own subjectivity reflected as something objective and objectivity as something which can be subjective, then it has reached the threshold of Spirit as such – Reason.

The Intellect

This third grade of Mind, based on Reason, Hegel calls Psychology but I will call the INTELLECT, because for us 'Psychology' is taken as inclusive of feelings. The crucial stage in the development of the Intellect is *language*. However, there is pre-linguistic Intelligence, which knows its object to be a meaningful thought determination, but has not yet acquired *universal* self-consciousness made possible by acquisition of language. Intelligence is universal self-consciousness, an entire world of pure meanings.

Whereas the Psyche knows nothing of subject and object, and Consciousness takes its object to be objective, the Intellect understands its objects to be both subjective and objective, to be both a thought determination and an object which exists in the world independently of its own activity. With Intelligence we have not only self-conscious activity, but *thinking* activity. Intelligence becomes *actual* when its will becomes objective, in private property and laws.

Each individual mind is a concrete whole, but differentiated according to the categorically different relations to the world characterising Psyche, Consciousness and Intelligence.

§3   The Forms of Movement in Subjective Spirit

On its own, the Psyche would be the mental life of a primitive, autonomous form of life. Consciousness presupposes the Psyche and together with it, also constitutes a viable and self-contained organism, as it does at each stage of its development. But whereas the Psyche does not ascribe its intuitions to anything, but merely feels, these same intuitions may be taken by Consciousness to refer to an object outside of and independent of the subject. Likewise, whereas Consciousness is 'realist' and takes the objects of its perception to be objective, the Intelligence ascribes to the objects of perception subjective significance, requiring interpretation. Thus, while the Psyche communes with itself, Consciousness rests on the Psyche, and the Intelligence rests on Consciousness. The reverse applies as well, objects recognised by the Intelligence are sensed as objective by Consciousness, and objects of Consciousness are felt by the Psyche.

Secondly, these three processes are not 'modular' in the sense of acting externally to one another, executing distinct functions, and interacting causally. Rather they *include* one another, while each remains a distinct whole, or *Gestalt*. The Psyche is entirely self-contained and in communion with itself. Consciousness takes every one of its determinations, whether feelings or perceptions of objects in the external world, to be equally objective determinations of consciousness, and in that sense also, Consciousness always refers to itself, absorbed in an objective world. (Even hunger and fear, etc., have an object). The Intellect moves within the world of universal consciousness, in which language comes to play the central role.

> Given the name lion, we need neither the actual vision of the animal, nor its image even: the name alone, if we *understand* it, is the unimaged simple representation. We *think* in names.
>
> *Enc.,* §462

Thirdly, each sphere of mental life begins from something which arises in the lower sphere, but which *stands out* from the norm in the lower sphere. It is this 'standing out' which it takes as the basic unit of its sphere. This is actually how the internet works – all messages are just 1s and 0s, but certain sequences 'stand out' and cause succeeding sequences to be interpreted differently, until another 'stand out' sequence terminates that 'message'. AM and FM radio signals use the same structure. This structure is replicated layer upon layer up to the point of marks on our screens which are meaningful to us humans (Fig. 4).

In the Psyche, responses to stimuli are merely feelings, but thanks to the development of habituation and habit, certain feelings stand out in relief, as it were, as that to which the organism is *not* habituated and these intuitions are taken to be *sensations* of something *else*, and these sensations become the basic units of consciousness.

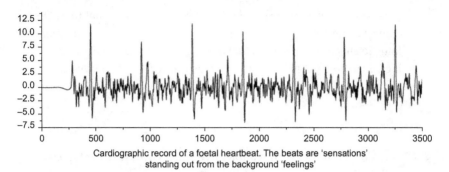

Cardiographic record of a foetal heartbeat. The beats are 'sensations'
standing out from the background 'feelings'

FIGURE 4   Form of movement in Subjective Spirit

Intelligence is aware that every sensation indicates some objective process, but certain forms 'stand out' from the natural background and are taken by consciousness as signs having meaning. It is the sign-meanings rather than sensations which are the basic units of the intellect.

This is a distinct form of movement, different from the forms of movement found in the Logic in Being, Essence and the Notion.

Each of the forms of life described in the Subjective Spirit is a form of movement of *an individual taken together with its environment*, engaged in a symbiotic, metabolic relationship. In the beginning, we are dealing with only the simplest kind of organism. All that is implied is that the environment provides suitable, natural conditions for the individual organism to thrive. But once we reach the stage of intellectual life where the organism regards its determinations as both subjective and objective, then the human being finds its environment to be a product of its *own activity* and that of like minds. The tools, signs and other artefacts which the Intellect uses are meaningful products of the Intellect, but at the same time, material things, objective in relation to the individual subject.

It is only possible to attain the level of development of Mind constituted by Intelligence in a situation in which words, tools and other products of human labour are an integral part of the life of the community. These artefacts are bearers of norms, that is to say objective thought-determinations. So, *Subjective Spirit* describes the necessary structure of natural forms of life which are capable of living a genuinely human life, with its laws, culture, customs, technology, language, politics and so on.

Objective Spirit, which is the domain of social life and world history, bears this name because its content is forms of Mind which are actualized and made objective. Without *Objective Spirit*, the organism can only develop within limits imposed by the nature of the organism itself. As Hegel put it:

This world confronting the soul is not something external to it. On the
contrary, the totality of relations in which the individual human soul
finds itself, constitutes its actual livingness and subjectivity and accordingly has grown together with it just as firmly as ... the leaves grow with
the tree.

> *Enc.*, §402n.

§4   A Contradiction within Subjective Spirit Gives Rise to Objective Spirit

Hegel says that Nature is the presupposition for Spirit, but it is not a *product* of
Nature. Spirit has *produced itself* – Spirit begins with the strivings of elementary forms of life to determine themselves. Spirit there has the form merely of
the feelings of a simple, unconscious organism, but nonetheless, it is a form of
life. Hegel saw Spirit in this process of struggling to *free itself* from the external
determinacy of Nature, where Spirit lies in itself.

I have claimed that Spirit is the nature of human beings en masse. How
can I say that the feelings of a microbe is Spirit? Because in the feelings of the
microbe we have the first and simplest existing form of Spirit; but Spirit is true
to its concept only at the *end* of its journey, in Absolute Spirit, when human beings attains a form of life true to the concept of Spirit, that is, Freedom. At the
beginning of Subjective Spirit it is still Spirit in its natural determinacy.

Within the domain of Subjective Spirit certain forms of heteronomy can be
overcome, or putting it another way, certain forms of freedom can be realised.
People can gain a certain mastery over external Nature, a certain level of mastery of their own desires and an ability to control their own thought processes.
However, none of these forms of freedom can be taken beyond a limit extend
which could be called a *subjective* freedom. Human beings have only ever
achieved significant mastery of Nature by the cultural development of tools
and knowledge and their social application. Control over our own internal processes depends on the development of art, culture, science, religion and philosophy, activities which cannot be developed other than in a social and political
community. Further, perhaps the greatest threat to freedom comes from pas-
sions and oppressive practices of other human beings with whom we interact.

Thus, in itself – that is, without any form of recognised law and custom – Subjective Spirit does not have the resources to attain real, that is to say, *objective*
freedom. For that it shall be necessary to shape Objective Spirit – law, politics,
the economy, etc. – so as to make genuine freedom a reality. The preconditions

for the free development of spirit must be given a social form. In §474 of the Subjective Spirit, Hegel concludes:

> What are the good and rational propensities, and how they are to be co-ordinated with each other? resolves itself into an exposition of the laws and forms of common life produced by the mind when developing itself as *objective* mind – a development in which the *content* of autonomous action loses its contingency and optionality. The discussion of the true intrinsic worth of the impulses, inclinations, and passions is thus essentially the theory of legal, moral, and social *duties.*
>
> *Enc.* §474

This is a problem which confronts all individual human beings, and it is one which can only be solved through the formation of a *state*. But a state cannot be conjured up by even a mass of individuals from the sheer need of it.

The solution of this contradiction is the basis for Objective Spirit, also known as *The Philosophy of Right*.

CHAPTER 14

Social Science as Hegel Saw It

§1   Hegel Unfolds Social Theory from the Concept of 'Right'

It is Hegel's contention that Spirit arose out of Nature in the form of living organisms struggling to free themselves from natural determinacy, and Spirit is this relentless struggle to overcome all kinds of dependency, heteronomy and limitation on its free activity and development. In the phase of subjective spirit this went so far as the development of self-conscious and intelligent human activity. But within the domain of subjective spirit, that is to say, in the forms of activity characteristic of and constituting human individuals, there remain severe limitations on the quality and extent of the freedom which Spirit could attain. Only by creating social and political institutions could Spirit extend beyond the limited forms of life characterised by subjective spirit. This next phase of Spirit is called 'objective spirit'.

On the foundation of objective spirit, the subjective spirit is able to objectify itself as free intellect in the pursuit of art, religion, philosophy and science without alien social or political constraints, and this is 'absolute spirit'. But it is objective spirit as Hegel outlined it in *The Philosophy of Right* which is the topic here.

The *social*[1] form of Freedom is Right. The German, *Recht*, has much the same range of meanings as the English, 'right', but Hegel broadens the meaning of the word considerably. A whole range of juridical, sociological, moral and ethical concepts arise, as he sees it, out of the abstract concept of Right, and Hegel treats them all as *forms of* Right. Consequently, *The Philosophy of Right*, turns out to be not just a treatise on law, but also morality, civil society, the state and 'world history' – all those forms of 'objective mind' which Spirit produces and requires for its free development.

Thus, as the title implies, the subject matter of *The Philosophy of Right* is Right. But Right is an extremely concrete concept for which the entire treatise is required to elaborate. As with Hegel's other books, the *abstract* concept of Right is not deduced within *The Philosophy of Right*, but is rather given to it by Subjective Spirit, which arrived at the contradiction that Freedom could only

---

1   Strictly speaking, I should say "societal." "Social relations" fall under Subjective Spirit, while "societal relations" fall under Objective Spirit. But "societal" is not a word which is widely used, so I will generally use "social" in its broader sense, inclusive of "societal," and rely on the context.

be attained by means of social and political rights (some say 'recognition'), something which lay beyond the horizons of subjective spirit.

The *first* social form of Freedom is (private) property.

I have put 'private' in brackets because according to Hegel, property is inherently private and what could loosely be called 'public property' is not property at all. So in all that follows, 'property' is synonymous with 'private property'.

Further, even the abstract concept of Right exhibits a development from a phase which still falls short of the juridical relation of ownership up to more socially elaborate forms of property. Property as such is the key concept in the phase of the development of Right which Hegel calls 'Abstract Right'. So the first category of *The Philosophy of Right* is Abstract Right.

According to Hegel, "In this treatise we take for granted the scientific procedure of philosophy, which has been set forth in the philosophic Logic." (*PR* §2. ad.)

This procedure is to begin with one concept, here 'Abstract Right', and subject the concept to internal critique. 'Internal critique' means to test by logical enquiry whether the concept is Absolute, that is to say, whether the given concept of Right is able to secure a person's freedom absolutely, or whether it comes up against a limitation or internal contradiction which demands a new concept. In the absence of the spirit of human beings to overcome all limitations on their free activity, such a logical procedure would be an empty exercise, and indeed Right could not exist at all. But insofar as Spirit is, as Hegel believes, something real, and human activity is not simply a natural process driven by neurological processes and conditioned reflexes, then *The Philosophy of Right* is a valid approach to social science.

That the *Logic* sets out the procedure to be applied in *The Philosophy of Right* requires some caveats. (1) This does *not* imply that the *Science of Logic* is some kind of *model* for *The Philosophy of Right* or that we should expect a one-to-one equivalence between sections of the two books; (2) The forms of movement exhibited in *The Philosophy of Right* are distinct from those exhibited in the *Logic* or Hegel's other books; (3) Whereas the *Logic* is the 'pure essentialities' exhibited in the development of *all* formations of consciousness, *The Philosophy of Right* bears specifically upon those formations which foster the development of social forms Freedom treated in the book.

These issues will be treated in more detail later on.

§2   Right may not be True to its Concept

The concept of Right is Freedom in the societal domain. Right is a concrete concept, and for Right to be true to its concept requires millennia of many-sided cultural development. Indeed, in advance of such development, no philosopher can hope to formulate such a conception. In any given realisation of the concept of Right there will be circumstances where Right manifestly falls short of social freedom.

So, for example, the typical liberal concept of Freedom, sometimes referred to, following Isaiah Berlin, as 'negative liberty', is a concept of Right which falls demonstrably short of being an adequate, concrete concept of Right; it approximates that 'state of Nature' where an individual is free to do anything but can achieve nothing. 'Negative liberty' self-evidently runs up against the contradiction that if everyone else enjoys freedom from constraints, then ipso facto they will impinge on your liberty – one person's 'negative liberty' can only be realised by denying the 'negative liberty' of others.

In beginning *The Philosophy of Right* from Abstract Right, a.k.a. private property, Hegel must not be seen as an advocate for this liberal conception of Freedom. On the contrary. And nor is *The Philosophy of Right* a discourse on abstractions of this kind. Although it begins with an abstract (i.e., undeveloped) conception of Freedom, it progresses by a rational procedure through to exceedingly concrete (i.e., developed) conceptions of the social and political conditions for Freedom. Unlike John Rawls, Hegel does not begin with an abstract (lacking a basis in reality) counterintuitive 'thought experiment' like the 'veil of ignorance', but on the contrary he begins from the very concrete (i.e., immediate) human need to be relieved of the need to be forever on guard against attacks by one's neighbours – to be *recognised* as a person and be treated as a person by others.

It is not enough that Right should be a mere conception to which the world ought to conform. The concept of Right must exist in the external world, at least implicitly in existing social relations, as an ideal. It must have a basis in external reality. For Hegel, Freedom is 'a state of mind', but it is not *just* a state of mind. To be Free, a human being must know themselves to be free, and that freedom must have a real basis in their existing situation. Indeed, it makes nonsense to consider a person free according to the maxim attributed to Gandhi: "You can chain me, you can torture me, you can even destroy this body, but you will never imprison my mind." A freedom which is merely implicit but not capable of taking an objective form is illusory. What the British could not imprison was not Gandhi's mind, but the millions of Indians who would indeed ultimately free him. So to say that human beings are 'inherently free' means that they must be free *in reality*, not implicitly or in fantasy. Their reality must correspond to their concept as a human being.

To enslave a person, or to submit to enslavement (even in the face of death) is a failure to treat a person (including yourself) according to their concept, and is therefore wrong. Slavery cannot be justified by the submission of the slave. In antiquity, when a person could be enslaved as if they were a natural entity, "it occurs in a world where a wrong is still right" (*PR* §57). That is, wrong had *validity* and slavery was *real*, but once genuinely ethical conditions come into existence, slavery is an absolute wrong.

§3   Concepts have an Inherent Tendency Towards 'Perfecting Themselves'

If a concept represents some phase of Right, and therefore a necessary stage in the actualisation of Freedom, then we have seen that Hegel believes that there is an inherent tendency in historical development for that concept to be actualised. This idea can be generalised. Any concept which represents the object of some practice has normative force for that practice. The Logic depicts how this works in logical form, but in turning to Hegel's social theory it would be timely to illustrate how this logic translates into historical tendencies. The idea that because an idea of Right exists in a community then that concept will necessarily be realised in more and more adequate forms of practice over historical times seems idealist in the extreme. But this idea is no stranger to common sense even when common sense is at home. Let's look at how the idea works for the concept of 'chair'.

What makes something a 'chair'? Chiefly it is that a person can sit comfortably in it, i.e., its sittability, but also that when you sit in it, it raises you a respectable distance off the floor, suitable for sitting at a table, and should rest stably and safely on the floor. A chair which bears all these attributes would be called a 'good chair' and one that did not would be regarded as a 'poor chair' or not a chair at all. It is solely these functional attributes which makes a chair a chair, so these would be called the 'essential attributes' of a chair. So we have a clear idea of the 'norm' for a chair, and there is no physical feature of a chair, its colour, the material it is made of or any such sensuous attributes which, as such, belongs to the concept of being a chair. As it happens the concept of 'chair' is not only functional, but also intentional: if a chest happened to meet all the functional attributes of a chair, it is still not a chair.

The precise way in which the physical features of a chair contribute to its being a good chair are open to debate and cultural context, but someone who manufactures chairs will be skilled in determining and realising these features and will do so or they will not remain in the business of chair-making. It is an essential feature of the concept of 'chair maker' that you make chairs which well conform to the concept (sittability with stability, strength and table-height). The same applies to the people who buy chairs and those who place them around the home or office – they do their job well or badly insofar as they practice the selection and placement of chairs on the basis of sittability, etc. So everyone involved in designing, making, buying, situating and using chairs acts according to the maxim: 'a good chair is one which accords with its concept', i.e., the concept of chair acts as a norm for everyone involved, and there is a clear tendency towards chairs instantiating the concept of 'a good chair' which is *immanent* in all the relevant practices.

Therefore it makes sense to talk of the 'self-actualisation' of the concept of 'chair'. Other things being equal, abstracting from the capitalist economy, there is clearly a tendency for the concepts of all such useful artefacts to actualise themselves in *good* realisations of the concept, adapting to changing social and cultural demands. Given the understanding that a concept is a form of practice, this is just *common sense*, and to the extent that chairs are used in much the same way across entire communities, this is a strong tendency.

The modern concept of a chair as an item of household furniture has only been around since the 16th century however. Before that there were thrones and they conferred status rather than comfort and everyone else sat where they could. Growing industrial strength and an egalitarian sentiment made it possible for *everyone* to have a throne, and the concept of chair underwent a radical change. A new concept of chair as a piece of household furniture then arose and widely actualised itself.

Can this idea be validly extended to concepts representing social practices such as those analysed in *The Philosophy of Right*? Sceptics will be quick to show that production and use of useful artefacts such as chairs does not work as a model for all human practices, practices such as asbestos production, nuclear weapons, cigarettes and fast food or concepts like constitutional monarchy and the patriarchal family which are rationalised by Hegel as forms of Right.

The functionalist idea that *every* social practice is *eo ipso* satisfying a corresponding social need would be to imagine a world somewhat like the USSR, in which the Politburo set targets for all industries in a rational administration of the nation, or the fictional world of market fundamentalists 'planned' by the invisible hand of the market. In each case, the concept is not immanent to the practice, but imposed on it from outside.

There are always other concepts at work in a society so that contradictions can arise which will radically shift the concept in question. For example, in the late 1990s a collaboration between a section of medical science and a section of the union movement in Australia set out to expose the dangers of asbestos and by 2003 asbestos use was banned, with the concept of a 'miracle fibre' transformed into the concept of a 'deadly thread'.

The Logic tells us that the self-actualisation of an abstract concept can include its transformation from a good to be realised into an evil to be eradicated. There is nothing inconsistent with Hegel's procedure in this. However, there is no guarantee that the philosopher will correctly discern the destiny of a practice, and Hegel knows this.

Hegel believes that Right is a concept which exhibits a strong tendency towards its realisation because he sees freedom as essential to human beings. Of course, at any given historical moment, people are *not* free, political institutions are *not* conducive to freedom, etc., but in a long view of history his thesis stands up very well. Nevertheless, there are times when, in hindsight, it can be seen that he has seriously misread the status of certain practices. We will discuss these issues as they arise.

§4   What is Rational is Real and What is Real is Rational

There are some very famous passages in the Preface to *The Philosophy of Right* which can help shed light on some important issues about the nature of this work. The first is:

> What is rational is real;
>   And what is real is rational.
>   ... Against the doctrine that the Idea is a mere idea, figment or opinion, philosophy preserves the more profound view that nothing is real except the Idea. Hence arises the effort to recognise in the temporal and transient the substance, which is immanent, and the eternal, which is present. The rational is synonymous with the Idea, because in realising itself it passes into external existence. It thus appears in an endless wealth of forms, figures and phenomena. It wraps its kernel round with a robe of many colours, in which consciousness finds itself at home.

What does Hegel mean by "the Idea"?

The Idea is the intelligible narrative which lies within the "many coloured robe" of chance events and incidental characters; it is how we make sense of historical events. The Idea should not be seen as some kind of pre-determined law as if things could not have been otherwise, but it exists in the events themselves and not "in the eye of the beholder." It is the task of the philosopher to *discern* the Idea within the turbulence of immediate events. The Idea is to be understood in terms of the working out (or resolution) of problems and contradictions within existing social situations. The 'Idea' here is the same as concept which we met in the Logic, as the final grade of the Logic of the Concept, the unity of a concept with its reality.

What does Hegel mean by "real"?

It would be timely to cite Engels on this question:

> But according to Hegel certainly not everything that exists is also real, without further qualification, [and citing Goethe] In accordance with all the rules of the Hegelian method of thought, the proposition of the rationality of everything which is real resolves itself into the other proposition: All that exists deserves to perish.
>
> *Ludwig Feuerbach*, 1886

In terms of the categories of the Logic, one should expect to find a consensus of all sane, cooperative and honest people about "what exists," which more or less means the simple facts. 'Existence' appears very early in the phase of Reflection. 'Actuality' however, is the highest grade of Reflection, immediately preceding the Concept. The German word being translated as "real" is *wirklich*, and *Wirklichkeit* is the German word for "Actuality." What is real (or actual, i.e., having effect) is the whole range of facts which are connected by definite lines of causality to 'what is going on', the essential meaning (or content) of the current conjuncture.

What does Hegel mean by "rational"? "Rational" is a translation of the German *vernünftig*, an adjective from the noun, *Vernunft*, meaning Reason. For Hegel, what is necessary and intelligible in the unfolding of historical events is virtually synonymous with 'Reason'. In explaining the procedure exhibited in the Logic I said it was based on testing the limits of claims that a certain concept is absolute. That is what happens in history, except that the logic of history is clothed in accidental and contingent events.

Understanding the current social and political conjuncture is therefore a matter of *judgment*, and requires discernment and an understanding of the essential problems and contradictions at work in the existing social situation. So far as possible the philosopher wants to understand *why* a given event occurred. Why was Trump elected in the US (because he got more delegates to the Electoral College is not a valid answer)? Which aspects of the event are accidental? (the Russian meddling? his TV persona? his wealth? his abusive manners?) and what is the *reality* of the event? (The degeneration of the GOP? The class resentment of Trump voters? The rejection of politics-as-usual?)

But whatever you decide, you must see the essential features of events (the election of a man-child as US President) as manifesting real features of the conjuncture, real changes and historical tendencies. More pertinently to reading *The Philosophy of Right*, currently the UK, Spain, Belgium, Holland, Denmark, Norway and Sweden are all constitutional monarchies and yet these seven countries are all exemplary liberal democracies. Crazy as it seems, this is a reality because it has shown itself to be a consistent and stable aspect of modern Europe. We have to ask ourselves: what is rational in this reality? Conversely, sometimes there are 'crazy' features of the existing state of affairs which we can say are not *real*. I think it is possible to say that the existing level of inequality which now has six men holding as much wealth as the poorest half of the world is *not rational*, and consequently cannot be *real*. Such an extreme of inequality is something which has developed since about 1980, and expresses a contradiction in the existing world system which *cannot* last.

§5   Philosophy cannot Teach the State What it should Be

Hegel is dead set against 'building castles in the sky':

> This treatise, in so far as it contains a political science, is nothing more than an attempt to conceive of and present the state as in itself rational. As a philosophic writing, it must be on its guard against constructing a state as it *ought to be*. Philosophy cannot teach the state what it *should* be, but only how it, the ethical universe, is to be *known*.

This is a good moment to reflect on the claim that *The Philosophy of Right* is simply a *rationalisation* of the existing Prussian state and what exactly is the relationship between the the existing state which Hegel knew and the state he outlined in *The Philosophy of Right*.

'To rationalise' means 'to explain on a rational basis, make conformable to reason, intelligible,' but usually carries the connotation 'to explain *away*' or 'justify with plausible but specious reasons'. Were it the case that the ideal state depicted in *The Philosophy of Right* was a representation of the Prussian state in which Hegel lived then the case would be proved. But this is not the case. At the time Hegel wrote the first draft of the *Encyclopædia* in 1817, the "Objective Spirit" would have been taken as a reform agenda for the relatively benign but *absolute* monarchy of Friedrich Wilhelm III, but the *Zeitgeist* took a turn to the right, plans for reform were dropped and Hegel was subjected to censorship. So *The Philosophy of Right* stands in relation to the existing state as a *philosophical reform manifesto*. As I remarked above, after his death, Hegel's name was synonymous with radical political reform; the criticisms implicit in *The Philosophy of Right* had considerable purchase in those times.

On the other hand, all of the elements of this ideal state either existed in Germany, in other European countries, or were extensions of what existed or had existed in the past in Germany or other European countries in some form. Hegel invented nothing.

When I refer to the state described in *The Philosophy of Right* as an 'ideal state', 'ideal' refers to what is implicit in the existing state of affairs, *not* a model or a concoction of the mind of a philosopher. It represents what is rational in the real, the Idea.

§6   Here is the Rose in the Cross, Now Jump!

I will quote this passage from the Preface at length:

> Ιδου Ποδοσ, ιδου και το πιδιμα
> Hic Rhodus, hic saltus.
>   To apprehend what *is* is the task of philosophy, because what *is* is Reason. As for the individual, every one is a son of his time; so philosophy also is its time apprehended in thoughts. It is just as foolish to fancy that any philosophy can transcend its present world, as that an individual could leap out of his time or jump over Rhodes. If a theory transgresses its time, and builds up a world as it ought to be, it has an existence merely in the unstable element of opinion, which gives room to every wandering fancy.
>   With little change the above, saying would read:
>   *Here* is the rose, *here* dance.
>   The barrier which stands between Reason, as self-conscious Spirit, and reason as present reality, and does not permit Spirit to find satisfaction in reality, is some abstraction, which is not free to be conceived. To recognise reason as the rose in the cross of the present, and to find delight in it, is a rational insight which implies reconciliation with reality. This reconciliation philosophy grants to those who have felt the inward demand to conceive clearly, to preserve subjective freedom while present in substantive reality, and yet thought possessing this freedom to stand not upon the particular and contingent, but upon what is and self-completed.

"Hic Rhodus, hic saltus" is the Latin translation of the punch line from Aesop's fable, *The Boastful Athlete*, usually translated from the Greek as: "Rhodes is here, here is where you jump!" The story is that an athlete boasts that when in Rhodes, he performed a stupendous jump, and that there were witnesses who could back up his story. A bystander then remarked, 'Alright! Let's say this is Rhodes, demonstrate the jump here and now.' The fable shows that people must be known by their deeds, not by their own claims for themselves. In the context in which Hegel uses it, this could be taken to mean that a political philosophy must have a basis in the *actuality* of modern society ("What is rational is real; what is real is rational"), not the theories and ideals that societies create for themselves, or some dream counterposed to existing conditions: "To apprehend what *is* is the task of philosophy," as Hegel goes on to say, rather than to "teach the world what it ought to be."

The epigram is given by Hegel first in Greek, then in Latin, and he then says: "With little change, the above saying would read (in German): "*Hier* ist die Rose, *hier* tanze": "Here is the rose, dance here."

This is taken to be an allusion to the Rosicrucians, a sect dating from the early 17th century who claimed to possess esoteric knowledge with which they could perform great feats. The 'rose in the cross' symbolised the consolation for suffering to be found in esoteric knowledge. But "Here is the rose, dance here" means that the material for consolation for the philosopher and relief of suffering is given in the social situation itself, not in some other-worldly theory, punning first on the Greek (*Rhodos* = Rhodes, *rhodon* = rose), then on the Latin (*saltus* = jump [noun], *salta* = dance [imperative]).

In *18th Brumaire of Louis Bonaparte*, Marx quotes the maxim, first giving the Latin, in the form: "Hic Rhodus, hic salta!", – a garbled mixture of Hegel's two versions (*salta* = dance! instead of *saltus* = jump!), and then immediately adds: "*Hier ist die Rose, hier tanze!*", as if it were a translation, which it cannot be, since Greek *Rhodos*, let alone Latin *Rhodus*, does not mean "rose". But Marx does seem to have retained a form of Hegel's meaning, as it is used in the observation that, overawed by the enormity of their task, people do not act until:

> a situation is created which makes all turning back impossible, and the conditions themselves call out: Here is the rose, here dance!

and one is reminded of Marx's maxim in the *Preface to the Critique of Political Economy*:

> Mankind thus inevitably sets itself only such tasks as it is able to solve, since closer examination will always show that the problem itself arises only when the material conditions for its solution are already present or at least in the course of formation!

So Marx evidently supports Hegel's advice that we should not "teach the world what it ought to be", but he is giving a more active spin than Hegel would when he closes the Preface with the owl of Minerva.

§7   The Owl of Minerva Takes Flight at Dusk

> Only one word more concerning the desire to teach the world what it ought to be. For such a purpose philosophy at least always comes too late. Philosophy, as the thought of the world, does not appear until reality has completed its formative process, and made itself ready. History thus corroborates the teaching of the conception that only in the maturity of reality does the ideal appear as counterpart to the real, apprehends the real world in its substance, and shapes it into an intellectual kingdom. When philosophy paints its grey in grey, one form of life has become old, and by means of grey it cannot be rejuvenated, but only known. The owl of Minerva, takes its flight only when the shades of night are gathering.

Minerva was the Roman goddess of wisdom (and the title of a reformist journal to which Hegel subscribed), so the simple meaning of this aphorism is that science (or philosophy) is only able to discern the ideal implicit in reality at the moment when it has already made its appearance. This is not to say that the relevant social transformation has been achieved, but just that the new social movement has come on the scene, so to speak. In its grey, i.e., colourless as compared to the rich fabric of actuality itself, philosophy discerns the rational in the new tendency, and therefore understands its significance – but cannot "teach the world what it ought to be."

I think that in the writing of *The Philosophy of Right*, Hegel is generally true to this dictum up until the final paragraphs, when even Marx abandoned his 1843 annotations on *The Philosophy of Right*, and Hegel descends into silliness. Further, I think Marx took this advice much more seriously than did Hegel himself. Hegel at times oversteps what can be elucidated by philosophical speculation alone, whereas Marx showed more restraint in predicting the future or rationalising the distant past, or speculating on natural scientific problems the solutions to which were not yet evident.

At this point, the reader should read the Preface to *Philosophy of Right*.

Hegel's Theory of Action, Part 2: The Free Will

Most of the Introduction to *The Philosophy of Right* is taken up with a discourse on the development of the Will. The question to be answered is this: how can human action be genuinely free, rather than being determined by basic psychological drives, structural imperatives, ideology, human needs and so on?

> The territory of right is in general the spiritual, and its more definite place and origin is the will, which is free ... the system of right is the kingdom of actualised freedom.
>
> *PR*, §4

Hegel has said that the 'second nature' constructed by human activity can be unfolded from the abstract concept of Right, the simplest societal form of Freedom. An alternative formulation is that *The Philosophy of Right* is the science of the Will. The Will is the origin of Spirit, and the successive phases of Right can be seen as phases in the development of the Will.

The focus on the development of Free Will shows how Objective Spirit is a formation of "the activity of human beings en masse," rather than just showing what is necessary for human freedom. These passages of the Introduction to *The Philosophy of Right* form a connecting link between Hegel's Psychology and his social theory. Although they are explicitly written with the individual subject in mind, they provide good material on which to meditate in connection with the development of the Will of any social agency, including a social movement.

> That which is free is the Will. Will without freedom is an empty word, and freedom becomes actual only as will, as subject.
>
> *PR*, §4ad.

As Hegel sees it, it is part of the very idea of Will that it is free. So to speak of Will which is *not* free is a contradiction in terms. And yet the natural will – such as that exhibited by an animal which is merely acting out instinctive drives – is not free. Hegel's approach to this contradiction is to say that the natural Will is *implicitly free*, and in the development of human life this freedom which is implicit in the Will makes itself explicit through successive phases, and these phases correspond to the phases of development of Right.

The first phase of the Will is the natural or direct will. The direct will is all the "impulses, appetites, inclinations, by which the will finds itself determined by Nature" (*PR* §11). Nonetheless, this content comes from the rationality of will, because as natural beings what we strive for is given by our vital needs, not caprice or fancy, so the Will is also implicitly rational, but "in its immediate directness it has not yet the form of rationality."

Human beings however are not so determined. As natural beings, we are subject to impulses, but it depends on my will whether I embrace an impulse or not.

The contradiction inherent in the direct will is that it "exists only as a *multiplicity* of impulses, ... but at the same time universal and undetermined, having many objects and many ways of satisfaction" (*PR* §12). The will only actualises itself by resolving this conflict. Thus every action is a Judgment. Given the multiplicity of mediations entailed, one could argue that every action is a *Syllogism*.

Social movement activists will be familiar with this as an issue for collective action, but it is ubiquitous even in the life of an individual. Every moment I act, I make a judgment between a multiplicity of possible objects each with a multiplicity of possible means. But there is no criterion at hand in order to arrange them all into some kind of system, and yet the truth of the Will is that these impulses must be arranged in a rational system.

This conflict between different impulses and means is resolved by reflection. In thinking, for Hegel, we are active, and the intellect and the Will are inextricably tied up together in this activity. The only distinction is that between the theoretical relation and the practical relation – they are not two distinct faculties, and both are present in every action. Hegel is often criticised for having an intellectual attitude towards action, but it is more accurate to say he has a practical attitude towards thinking.

Hegel says that Will, at this stage, is necessarily untrue and finite because the subjective side is still different from the objective side, so the Will still does not have itself for content and cannot form a 'closed circle' The Will is therefore other-determined. Hegel explains this in terms of the great artist who, when completing their work, knows that it *had* to be just so. Any action, if it is rational, is found to be necessary, and not a matter of 'free choice'. Consequently, "when I will the rational, I do not act as a particular individual but according to the conception of ethical life in general" (*PR* §15).

The human Will is undetermined and therefore universal – human beings can turn their Will to any task. But in order to be free, the Will must make *itself* its own object. That is, rather than willing this or that, the subject must rationally determine what it is that they should be trying to do. Only by closing upon itself in this way, making a circle, can it become infinite, rather than being determined by some other.

The activity of the Will is to transcend the contradiction between subjectivity and objectivity, transferring its end from subjectivity to objectivity, while objectivity as means is transferred from objectivity to subjectivity. This activity is the essential development of the Idea (*PR* §28). Therefore the actualisation of the Free Will is what is meant by Right – in general, Freedom as Idea.

In order not to remain abstract, Free Will must, in the first instance give itself reality in external things, and this leads to the first category of *The Philosophy of Right*, Property.

CHAPTER 15

The Three Parts of *The Philosophy of Right*: Right, Morality and Ethical Life

§1   Right, Morality and Ethics

To make sense of the early chapters of *The Philosophy of Right* we first need to clarify the variety of concepts indicated by the word SUBJECT (*Subjekt*). In the Logic, the subject could be an idea, a social movement, a person – it is a purely logical concept, and this logical meaning is retained in the Philosophy of Nature and the Philosophy of Spirit. However, in the philosophy of spirit, 'subject' has two different meanings over and above its logical meaning.

In the Subjective Spirit, any living thing is a subject, up to and including a human being. A subject, in this sense, becomes a *person* only when they acquire the right to own property, including the right to exclusive control of their own body. The imperative of participation in a human community is: "Be a person and respect others as persons."

> It is only through the development of one's own body and mind, essentially through one's self-conscious apprehension of oneself as free, that one takes possession of oneself and becomes one's own property and no one else's.
>
> *PR*, §57

To be a person entails "taking possession of one's own body" and having the Right to own property – not any specific kind or quantity of property, but just the bare right to own property. A subject must be treated as a person, their body must not be violated contrary to their will, and their right to property must be respected. The category of 'person' abstracts from all attributes, indicating just the bare 'I'. This is the essential meaning of the ABSTRACT RIGHT, the first part of *The Philosophy of Right*.

The recognition of the person arising from their engagement in *contracts* (a form of Property) opens the way to the person becoming a *moral subject* – a distinct concept of 'subject'. The concept of 'moral subject' introduced here is closer to the Kantian sense of a 'subject'. The activity of the moral subject is the content of Morality, the second part of *The Philosophy of Right*.

MORALITY is a distinct phase of Right over and above abstract right. Morality does involve 'rights' such as the right not to be made responsible for unforeseeable consequences of lawful actions, the right to pursue one's own welfare, etc., but in Hegel's way of speaking, 'Morality' is a 'phase of Right' in the broader and more concrete sense. The demanding requirements for the subjects of a state to enjoy Freedom cannot be achieved by everyone simply respecting each other's rights, but is dependent on raising the moral and cultural level of the entire community.

The German concept of *Bildung* – meaning to acquire the culture of one's community and contribute to that culture – is relevant here. The point is that a moral subject must know that they can achieve their own welfare only in a community which has established an ethical order in which cooperation towards the common good is supported. The moral subject therefore acts to support that ethical order, and indeed Freedom can only be realised through the activity of moral subjects who act as citizens of the state.

The third part of *The Philosophy of Right* is 'ETHICAL LIFE' (*Sittlichkeit*), which covers the entire sphere of social life built on the relations of abstract right through the collaboration of individuals. The divisions of Ethical Life are: the FAMILY (where we get Hegel's ideas about the paternalistic family, gender, education and the rights of the child), CIVIL SOCIETY (which covers the economy, class relations, regulation, the justice system and voluntary association) and the STATE (the Constitution, international relations and 'World History'). In Ethical Life, individuals are taken to be fulfilling particular roles, to be shaped by their social position and to pursue their own welfare, whilst remaining moral subjects with rights. A key concept of Ethical Life is *mediation*.

In this part, Hegel gives us a logical reconstruction of an entire social and constitutional system followed by a sketch of his ideas about history of civilisation.

Note that the conception of the actor is different in each part, reflecting the *principle* of each part. In Abstract Right, the actor is a bare *person* lacking all particular attributes, demanding 'negative liberty' for their own person and granting it to other persons; in Morality, the actor is a *moral subject* who seeks their welfare in a well-ordered community of which they are an agent; in Ethical Life, the actor is an *individual* with all their distinctive personal characteristics, social interests and duties.

§2   Hegel Rejected the Individualism of Kant's Moral Philosophy

'Morality' (*Moralität*) and 'ethics' (*Sittlichkeit*) derive respectively from Latin (*more*) and Greek (*ethos*), both meaning 'mores' (*Sitte*) and there used to be no systematic difference in the meaning of the two words in philosophy. It was Hegel who introduced a distinction which did not previously exist.

'Morality' stresses the 'inner' will and intention of a moral subject, as opposed to 'ethics' or *Sittlichkeit*, which is the institutions and norms of a social formation. Morality is associated with duty, the good, responsibility, virtue and conscience, and like Kant, Hegel held that Morality was *rational*, rather than being determined by revealed religion. However, what Hegel meant by 'rational' is something quite different from what Kant meant.

According to Kant, every subject has an innate faculty of Reason, and through their own reflection could agree upon moral rules grounded on Reason. Based on this idea, Kant produced a system of Moral Philosophy with the well-known principles of universalisability of moral maxims, the categorical imperative and so on. For Hegel, what is rational is not discovered through the logical reasoning of individuals, but is to be found in the customs and institutions of the historically evolved community to which the individual belongs. So it is the principles and customs of the existing ethical order which direct the subject to what is rational. However, this does not mean that the subject must simply obey the law and go along with whatever is customary, because what is "rational is real," but what exists is not necessarily real (or rational). Morality entails a *critical deference* to the existing ethical order. The individual who is led by their own reflection to go outside the mores of their own historical community runs the risk of doing evil.

The central tenet of Hegel's morality is the realisation that one's own welfare is only secured through the welfare of the community as a whole. Consequently, to act rationally means to act according to the rational ethical order of which one is a part. The good order of the state presupposes that individuals will pursue their own ends, just as much as it requires that citizens pursue their welfare having regard to morality and respect the rights of persons.

The respect given to the ethical order is far from resolving every moral question which a subject must face however, and in Part 3 on Hegel's theory of action, below, we find that Hegel's Morality has much to say to the social movement activist whose aim is to *change* the ethical order. Of interest also is Hegel's conception of the 'world historic hero' (such as Napoleon). Hegel held that it was inevitable that such a person who overthrows one social order in order to establish another will inevitably violate not only the morality of the social formation they overthrow, but also of the new society they usher in. And yet, there is no suprahistorical criterion on which to judge such heroes.

§3   Hegel Rationalised the Paternalistic Family

When you read *The Philosophy of Right*, I think, insofar as you can follow Hegel's arcane manner of writing, and tolerate his occasional rants against his contemporary protagonists, everything makes abundant sense ... until you get to the section on the Family. Suddenly one finds oneself confronted by such an atrocious, paternalistic misogynist prig that one could be forgiven for tossing the book away and having nothing more to do with Hegel.

Earlier, I refuted the claim that Hegel 'rationalised' the Prussian monarchy of his own day, but 'rationalise' is the perfect word to describe Hegel's 'deduction' of the 19th century paternalistic family. Father is the head of the household and has legal coverture over his wife and children. Women are there to produce and raise children and are unsuited for participation in the economy, the state or philosophy. And it is all 'proved' on the basis of the natural division of labour built around the woman's biologically determined role.

To a certain extent Hegel is simply making intelligible the existing and very longstanding paternalistic family of his own times. However, he was surrounded by women who were in the front ranks of the liberal feminism of the day, including his mother and sister and two wives of friends, Dorothea and Caroline Schlegel. He had plenty of opportunity to acquaint himself with the feminist critique of patriarchy. Mary Wollstonecraft's *Vindication of the Rights of Woman* had been published in 1792 and would have been well-known in the circles in which Hegel moved. But it would seem that he took these criticisms to be a version of the 'castles in the sky' of which he was so dismissive in connection with political utopianism.

I think that this failing of Hegel's needs to be seen in the same frame with his acceptance of the Biblical story of Genesis for want of any scientific explanation of the origin of species. Nothing that Hegel would have learnt from the new science of Anthropology or from his acquaintance with the mores of different European countries, or of quite unknown prehistoric times would have given Hegel any hint that things had ever been otherwise. Even what was known of the animal kingdom would have only reinforced conventional wisdom about the gender division of labour among human beings. He was, after all, a creature of his times.

Mary Wollstonecraft's central thesis was that the apparent weakness of the female sex and their unsuitability for work outside the domestic sphere was a *product* and not a *cause* of the gender division of labour, and that the few women who had managed to escape the straightjacket fitted for them had proved that once given the education and opportunities of men, women were equally able. Hegel could not see this. The structure of his system blinded him to the interplay of Nature and Culture in the formation of the human phenotype, including its intellectual and spiritual capacities. It never seems to have occurred to Hegel that gender and ethnic differences are *products* of human culture.

This is a serious fault. But in my opinion it is easily surpassed. Unlike Hegel, we have the benefit of 200 years of human development during which time the

Women's Liberation Movement has not only educated us about gender matters, but changed the social structures themselves and changed the nature of men and women.

Is there something intrinsic to Hegel's philosophy which is either patriarchal or open to 'essentialism' in the sense in which this term is used in feminist discourse? I say no. But it was not going to be a conservative gentleman like Hegel who would be the one to see that it was the age-old theory of female inferiority and not contemporary Feminism which was in error. Hegel placed limits around the dialectic which only need to be moved aside for Hegel's philosophy to prove itself a powerful weapon in the hands of feminist critique, as it is today. Indeed, feminist critique owes more to the critique of categories elaborated in Hegel's Logic than any other source.

§4   The Family, Civil Society and the State

There are three divisions in Ethical Life: the Family is "the immediate substantiality of Spirit", characterised by love; Civil Society is the stage of difference which develops in the space between the Family and the State, characterised by reciprocity; and the State, which is the 'actuality of the Ethical Idea' in which duty and right are united.

The FAMILY is seen as a process: Marriage, formation of the family capital (the family is the basic unit of Civil Society in all economic and social affairs), raising of children and the dissolution of the Family with the children moving on to different families and the family capital distributed among family members (in accordance with the law rather whim). Hegel saw the family as a patriarchal nuclear family, and downplayed the role of larger 'clan' groups.

'CIVIL SOCIETY', in a literal translation from the German (*Bürgerliche Gesellschaft*) is 'bourgeois society', and this would be a better term, because 'civil society' does not have the same meaning in contemporary discourse. But we have to stick to the conventional Hegel translation. Civil Society encompasses the economy ("the system of needs") as well as the various entities which regulate life outside of both the family and the state. These extend from PUBLIC AUTHORITIES such as the police and regulators of various kinds to the justice system and the CORPORATIONS, all charged with protecting life and property and governing day-to-day life.

Nowadays we would regard the public authorities and justice system as part of the state, but Hegel saw the responsibility for governing and regulating Civil Society to be a function of Civil Society itself. 'Corporations' refer to the guilds, town councils, universities, professional associations, friendly societies, religious groups, and so on. These voluntary associations flourished in mediae-val times but were under pressure from the bourgeoisie as Germany began to industrialise after 1815. Hegel wanted to *revitalise* them to play a central role in mediating between the State and life in Civil Society.

Hegel saw the Classes as anchored in Civil Society, but Hegel's idea of class dates from a time before modern class conflict had developed in bourgeois society. The classes were each rooted in one of the three sectors of the society: *agriculture* in the countryside, *business* activity in the towns, and the *civil service*. Hegel did not foresee class conflict of the poor peasants against wealthy landowners, wage workers against capitalists or public employees against the senior civil servants. Indeed, he would have regarded such conflict as destructive. He took it for granted that the 'leading' figures in each sector would represent the interests of the whole class: the landowner speaking for the peasant, the capitalist speaking for the wage workers and so on. Indeed, this had been the accepted practice in medieval times.

The STATE has three components: The Crown, the Executive and the Legislature.

The CROWN is hereditary with succession determined by primogeniture in a constitutional monarchy somewhat like the UK where the Queen merely signs Bills into law. However in Hegel's state the monarch appoints the members of his/her cabinet who function as the heads of the civil service, and the monarch is Commander-in-Chief of the armed forces and plays an active role in international affairs. Although the monarch is playing a purely symbolic role in signing the Bills recommended by the Executive, this non-decision is the product of a long history of the organic development of the State during which the monarch is able to rule with a lighter and lighter hand until his role becomes purely symbolic. Self-evidently, in an immature state this arrangement would be unworkable.

The EXECUTIVE is the heads of the civil service, effectively the Cabinet, and is appointed by the Crown, as had been the practice in Britain until not long before Hegel was writing. The civil servants are selected on merit from all social classes without regard to their wealth, etc., but according to their expertise in all the roles required by the State and are expected to selflessly serve the universal interest without regard to their own background or even their interests as employees of the state.

The LEGISLATURE is reminiscent of the Estates General of pre-Revolutionary France, its members being nominated through the mediating structures of the three Estates.

It is very easy to get confused between the Estates and the Classes, the more so because they are both translations of the same German word, *Stände*.

The Estates are *political* entities, the nearest equivalent to political parties in Hegel's scheme; they represent the Nobility, the Church and the Bourgeoisie respectively. The Classes on the other hand organic components of Civil Society; they are the Agricultural Class, the Business Class and the Civil Service, which Hegel calls respectively the Immediate, Particular and Universal Classes. He does not use such designations for the Estates.

The most startling aspect of Hegel's conception of the Legislature is that he is dead set against elections from the general population by universal suffrage. He had no illusions about elections being able to represent the interests of the masses. In my opinion, he argues his case here very effectively but his alternative of relying on election or nomination via the internal structures of the Estates has just as many faults and Hegel seems to be blissfully unaware of these faults. It is the same with his unwarranted confidence that the civil service can be relied upon to be true to its concept and serve the universal interest.

The section on the State is divided into two sections. All the above is part of the INTERNAL CONSTITUTION of the State. After that Hegel turns to INTERNATIONAL RELATIONS, where the Monarch plays an active role. Interestingly Hegel regarded international relations as more or less the law of the jungle. Treaties between nations should be respected, but he had little confidence in the Law of nations and even less confidence in ideas like a United Nations (which Kant had proposed) and in fact, regarded war as a positive to the extent that he took the notion of a 'perpetual peace' as tantamount to putting the world into a coma.

The final section on 'World History' is the kind of 'grand narrative' which opponents of Hegel find most open to derision.

§5   Hegel's Critique of Rousseau on the State

Hegel positioned his theory of the State against that of Rousseau, most particularly because the French Revolution had self-consciously set out to implement Rousseau's idea of the State. Hegel credited Rousseau for making the Will the principle of the State, as opposed to a gregarious instinct, force, the need for protection or for mutual benefit and so on. As we noted above, Hegel accepted this thesis in his own terms. His criticism was that Rousseau:

> takes the Will only in a determinate form as the individual will, and he
> regards the universal will not as the absolutely rational element in the

will, but only as a 'general' will which proceeds out of this individual will as out of a conscious will. The result is that he reduces the union of individuals in the state to a *contract* and therefore to something based on their arbitrary wills, their opinion, and their capriciously given express consent;

> PR, §258n.

In fact, the social contract, rests on a *fiction*. Here is how Rousseau formulated it:

> What, then, strictly speaking, is an act of Sovereignty? It is not a convention between a superior and an inferior, but a convention between the body and each of its members. It is legitimate, because based on the social contract... So long as the subjects have to submit only to conventions of this sort, they obey no-one but their own will; and to ask how far the respective rights of the Sovereign and the citizens extend, is to ask up to what point the latter can enter into undertakings with themselves, each with all, and all with each.
>
> ROUSSEAU, 1762, §2.4

Not only is the social contract a fiction in that no such contract was ever made, but conceptually it subsumes the State under Civil Society as if it were a contract made between citizens to secure their life and property; but the State is a *political* tie, which raises itself above the affairs of Civil Society. Further, since an individual does not have option of separating themself from the State, it cannot be the subject of a contract.

For Hegel, the state is the essence of the self-consciousness of all its citizens. In other words, the State is a concept which embraces them all as individual elements. The State is then a paradigm of Hegel's *concept* as elaborated in the Logic.

The state is a product not just of the behaviour of its citizens, but of their *actions*. That is to say, it essentially involves the subjects' intentions. But it is not the subjective will, with all its illusions and capriciousness, which is decisive, but the *objective will*, which is not just a manifestation of the subjective will, but through its mediation with the external world and the actions of others, is what is *rational* in the Will:

> ... the objective will is rationality implicit or in conception, whether it be recognised or not by individuals, whether their whims be deliberately for it or not.... its opposite, i.e. knowing and willing, or subjective freedom

(the only thing contained in the principle of the individual will) comprises only one moment, and therefore a one-sided moment, of the Idea of the rational will, i.e. of the will which is rational solely because what it is implicitly, that it also is explicitly.

> *PR*, §258n.

People set out with all sorts of intentions and conceptions of what it is that they are doing, but (and this is the fact which forced Rousseau to resort to a fiction) the result is not a multiplicity but a single, universal product – the State. Of course not every State provides ideal conditions for what is rational in the Will of its citizens to manifest itself, but:

> The state is no ideal work of art; it stands on earth and so in the sphere of caprice, chance, and error, and bad behaviour may disfigure it in many respects. But the ugliest of men ... is still always a living man.
>
> *PR*, §258ad.

Readers may have difficulty with the way Hegel talks about the State: "The State is the march of God in the world," and "has supreme right against the individual, whose supreme duty is to be a member of the state," and so on. My advice to the reader is that instead of "the State" read "the Revolution" or "the struggle." For Hegel, the State was more like what it is to a fighter in a national liberation movement than what it means to individuals living in a modern imperialist country.

§6   Logic and History

Hegel makes it very clear that *The Philosophy of Right* is a *logical* derivation of the various phases of Right, but the question inevitably poses itself as to to the relation between the sequence in which the categories as presented in *The Philosophy of Right* and the sequence in which they appear in history.

Evidently the two sequences are not the same, as a couple of examples suffice to prove. The Family appears in *The Philosophy of Right* only after the section on Property, and yet the family pre-existed property rights. Also, the State pre-existed the emergence of Civil Society but follows it in the logical exposition.

If one could confine oneself to the development of a single concept, then one would be entitled to expect that historical development would, albeit loosely, replicate logical development through the actual resolution of the real contradictions analysed in the logical exposition. But none of the very concrete concepts dealt with in *The Philosophy of Right* experience such an isolated historical development. On the contrary, they are all part of an organic whole.

Each of the categories first arose in very ancient conditions, conditions unsuited to its free development. Property arose, for example, under conditions where there was no State to regulate property law and its enforcement; the State arose when there was no Civil Society to regulate civil life and educate the citizens; the Family arose before its possessions could be secured and inherited via developed property relations, and so on. But each category requires concrete, developed forms of the other categories for the full development of their own concept.

Each category therefore undergoes its own historical development, but in close interaction with the development of all the other categories in a complex kind of interlocked spiral of historical development. Only as a result of the entire process do they appear as elements of an organic whole. It should be noted that this process of interconnected development has continued since *The Philosophy of Right* was written, giving us the benefit of experiencing much more developed forms of the categories.

On the other hand, Hegel must elaborate the logical development of *each* category according to the method exhibited in the Logic. That is, he begins with the abstract concept, and then through the discovery and resolution of contradictions implicit in the abstract concept moves towards the analysis of the concrete whole as a result, rather than as a presupposition.

The order in which the main categories of Right are taken then is determined only by their place in the organic whole which is the result of the whole development. For the purposes of logical exposition, Hegel puts the abstract or immediate categories first and the most concrete and developed forms later, irrespective of their historical relations.

The form in which a State or any other institution first *appears* and the complex path it traces towards its modern form is material for the historian, but according to Hegel, is a matter of indifference so far as its *conception* is concerned. Thus Hegel remarks:

> But if we ask what is or has been the historical origin of the state … all these questions are no concern of the Idea of the State.
>
> *PR*, §258n.

and

The historical origin of the judge and his court may have had the form of a patriarch's gift to his people or of force or free choice; but this makes no difference to the concept of the thing.

PR, §219n.

Whether the theoretician can treat historical development of an institution as a matter of indifference to its conception is something to which we will return.

§7   The State in Germany and Europe in Hegel's Times

Before beginning a step by step run through of *The Philosophy of Right* it is worthwhile to refresh our minds as to the condition of Germany at the time Hegel was writing.

As outlined in the Introduction to this book, Germany in Hegel's day was made up of a dozens of small princedoms, with populations averaging 600,000, each with their own distinct history dating back to early medieval times, each with their own nobility and customs, either Protestant or Catholic. Surrounding them were great nation states - Austria, Britain, France and Russia as well as other peoples like the Swiss and the Italians in similar conditions to their own, and the smaller nation-states such as Holland and Denmark which were moving in the direction of constitutional monarchies.

A number of nation-states, such as Britain, had a constitutional monarchy, which was in Hegel's day widely recognised as the most successful state form. France's efforts to establish a republic had been followed by a Restoration as had England's earlier attempt under Oliver Cromwell. America was not regarded by Hegel as having achieved Statehood at all. During Hegel's lifetime, Britain was ruled by George III and George IV who played a very marginal role in affairs of state. Prussia, like the majority of the German states, was an absolute monarchy. As an advocate for constitutional monarchy, Hegel was regarded as a radical reformer.

At the time Hegel was in Jena, the population of Jena was a few thousand, and that mostly because of the prestige of the university, whereas Erfurt had a population of a few tens of thousands and Berlin had a population of 200,000. The majority of the population lived in the countryside and was employed in agriculture, but the towns were home to artisans, merchants, teachers and professionals of all kinds as well as Universities with quite large student populations. Servants were employed in the homes of the local nobility and bourgeoisie. Following the end of the Napoleonic Wars in 1815, the bourgeoisie had high hopes for German unification and industrialisation began, but was still embryonic in 1821 when *The Philosophy of Right* was written. The artisan and merchant guilds opposed industrialisation and the introduction of factory labour, and in Hegel's day were still able to protect the conditions of the townspeople and hold back the advance of industrialisation. The Carlsbad Decrees of 1819 had marked a sharp turn to the right in German politics, opposing modernisation. It was not until after the defeat of the 1848 Revolution that industrialisation and German unification began to advance.

The leading lights of European philosophy, music and literature were in Germany and Germany would soon blossom into the leading nation in natural science as well as the arts. The education system in Germany, based on the classics, was renowned throughout the world – all the founders of American academia were educated in Germany.

This contradiction between the backwardness of Germany's economic, social and political development on one hand, and its supremacy in the arts on the other, was the central problem for the modernisation of Germany. Meanwhile, the universities were turning out far more young intellectuals than the economy could provide jobs for.

CHAPTER 16

Abstract Right

§1   The Right to Property is Necessary to Being a Person

The German for 'to possess' is *besitzen*, literally, 'to sit on', and this conveys very well the meaning of 'possession' and why it is a category which is within the capacity of Subjective Spirit but presents problems which can only be solved by Objective Spirit. You can sit on something, and fight off all comers, but this is not a human life. You need *recognition* as the owner of that possession so you can get on with your life. POSSESSION is the first category Hegel deals with under Abstract Right, but it is not in fact a category of Objective Spirit, which begins with Property.

But Hegel eschews pragmatic answers to explain why subjects need to possess or own things. Granted, the Will can only have effect (i.e., be actual) if it is mediated through an external object (including but not limited to parts of the body). But possession and property are something more than just *using* an external object.

At first, the Free Will is self-conscious, but only inward. I know myself to be completely limited (subject to my desires and the hard necessity of the external world) but I also know myself as universal and free. But this knowledge is entirely internal and remains so despite the use of external objects as mediating artefacts. I don't really exist. Existence means to exist *for others*. Subjects need to be recognised as *persons*, that is to say, to *exist* in an external world. Thus they must make their Will into something existent in the world, that is, own property. If a thing is my property, I do not need to 'sit on it' in order for my Will to exist in the thing; it has its own existence, and remains so even in my absence.

Hegel sees this drive as something more than the pragmatic need of a subject to have their possession of something guaranteed. For example, I think a lot about Hegel, but until these thoughts are written down and are out there in the world independently of me, they don't really exist. But it's not just about *my* individual needs. Hegel scholarship can exist and develop only if people publish. In order for the fully developed Will to exist as Idea, it must first exist as the immediate, individual Will, and beginning with Property, this process unfolds independently of any one person's Will.

This right for one's possessions to be recognised as their property is secured by the universal imperative: 'Be a person and respect others as persons', independent of any particularity. Consequently, the commands of Abstract

Right are limited in the final analysis to *prohibitions* – not to infringe the rights of other persons, specifically a person's rights in their own body and their property.

In order to exist as Idea, and to be part of an evolving human culture rather than just the day-to-day struggle for existence, a person's will must be given an external, ideal form, which is Property.

Hegel then proceeds to examine the means by which something becomes Property. The first principle is that a thing is the property of the first person in time to take it into their possession. This is the principle of *res nullius*. Hegel's categorisation of Property is an *active* one, hinging on the transformation of external objects by human action.

The three phases of Property are (A) Taking possession, (B) Use, and (C) Alienation.

TAKING POSSESSION can be by directly *grasping*, by *changing* the form of something (such as clearing land) or by *marking* it. In effect, grasping and using are forms of marking, so marking is the most complete form of taking possession.

It is in the category of USE that Hegel introduces the concept of *value*. Because the use of an object determines it qualitatively and quantitatively in relation to a specific utility, and the thing becomes *comparable* to other things of like utility. This is the thing's *universality*, abstracted from the thing's quality – its *value*. Thus Hegel takes value to be both qualitative and quantitative, and accepts the naïve view that the exchange value of a thing is determined by its usefulness, with money as a symbol of this value. Marx, by contrast, proved that the value of a thing is determined in exchange and, mediated via the market, is determined the labour time socially necessary to replace it. Marx thereby disclosed an internal contradiction in the concept of value, between use-value and exchange-value. Hegel's only qualification is that if the owner is unable to sell the thing, then the thing is not really Property, but he did not pursue this contradiction.

It may seem odd to include ALIENATION as, not only a moment of Property, but the moment which expresses the *truth* of Property. Use of the thing negates specific properties, but Alienation negates the thing as a whole. And while it is possible to take possession of something or use something without owning it, it is in fact impossible to alienate something which is not one's property in the first place. Alienation means to take possession of the thing by at the same time alienating it. Alienation is the unity of the taking possession and the use of a thing. It is Alienation which definitively makes a thing into Property.

For example, an indigenous people which takes possession of a land and uses it, does not thereby make it Property, but as soon as they alienate it, it becomes property. This is a real problem for traditional owners of the land in Northern Australia, who remain impoverished so long as they retain traditional ownership. Once they take up the right to alienate their land, they become owners of valuable real estate and enjoy benefits such as credit. It also means, of course, that they lose the protection that traditional ownership gave them and risk falling even deeper into poverty. Another example: the Marxists Internet Archive publishes material which is in the public domain, that is we take possession of it and use it; people sometimes ask us for permission to reproduce material, but we can't do that, because we don't *own* the material.

Since Alienation is the truth of Property, those characteristics of my own personality which are by their nature inalienable, are my personality as such – my Free Will, beliefs, intelligence, morality, etc. – are not Property, even though a person *takes possession* of their body when they put there Will into it. Consequently, a person is responsible for their own actions and may break a contract which requires them to do anything unethical.

A person can give the *use* of their abilities to another person for a finite period of time, as is the case in wage labour (See §67). Hegel says that the time restriction is necessary, for it is only by this restriction that the distinction between the substance of a power (labour power) and the use of that power (labour) is maintained. Were a person to give the use of their capacities for an indefinite period of time that would be tantamount to alienating their personality, effectively making themselves a slave.

Intellectual Property

In the course of dealing with Property, with external things like land as the archetype, Hegel covers the whole range of forms of property and related problems, including intellectual property, copyright, leasehold, freehold, mortmain, trusts, labour-power, public monuments, graves and plagiarism.

Hegel defends copyright on the basis that although on alienating the work to others, the author does not reserve the right to use the work or to make copies of the work, she or he does reserve the right to use it as a *capital asset*. He contends that insofar as any product is divisible: one part can be alienated while another is retained, and the use to which a work is put makes such a division. Property is complete not by taking possession or by use, but only by alienation, and the use of the work as a capital asset entails the alienation of the entire asset, so the author is entitled to sell the work without abandoning its use as a capital asset (See §69).

Note that Hegel does not appeal to any intangible 'mental objects' such as 'knowledge' or 'ideas', but grounds his analysis solely in external things and human actions. It is only insofar as the Will and its products are in external things (including human bodies) that the rational historical process which is at the centre of Hegel's concern can unfold.

Hegel was Opposed to Common Property

> Since my will, as the will of a person, and so as a single will, becomes objective to me in property, property acquires the character of private property; and common property of such a nature that it may be owned by separate persons acquires the character of an inherently dissoluble partnership in which the retention of my share is explicitly a matter of my arbitrary preference.
>
> *PR*, §46

This paragraph rules out privatising the air and the water, etc., as the elements are indivisible, but it does not rule out ownership of property by corporations (churches, unions, body corporates, companies, and so on, or the State and its component parts), and common ownership was meaningless within the paternalistic family. So this paragraph anticipates current practice. What it rules out is independent persons being joint owners of their common property. Hegel gives a number of reasons for this, but it is clear that he believes that so far as is feasible all property should be private. He accepts that the state must own assets which are essential to its function, but he expresses himself in favour of privatisation where this is possible.

It seems to me that Hegel's insight that the individual Will must be expressed in external objects for the person to exist, needs to be extended to what he has to say about the State. The state is not "an inherently dissoluble partnership," because "it does not lie with an individual's arbitrary will to separate himself from the state," and according to Hegel it is only as a member of the State that an individual has objectivity. So State property functions to make *real* the State as the essential being of every individual citizen. A State which privatises everything negates its own existence.

Equality Belongs to Civil Society not Abstract Right

Abstract right, which covers 'rights' in the narrow sense of the word, only goes to the *right to own property*, and has no bearing on *how much* property a person has. The right to own property, that is, to be a person, presupposes the right to the integrity of one's own body, which would cover some of what counts as 'rights' nowadays, but to the modern eye, this seems to be a very impoverished conception of 'rights'. Abstract Right is the *sine qua non* of civilised human life, but it is not a developed system of social rights.

We must recall that Hegel is not a Kantian who claims to establish Right by recourse to our individual faculty of Reason, whether by reflection or argument. It is well-known that what counts as a right and many other aspects of justice and morality varies considerably from one culture to another. Since cultural relativism is part of the modern spirit, the attempt to 'derive' rights by rational argument within a modern context inevitably leads to "empty formalism" (*PR* §135n.).

For Hegel, all of those principles which we know as 'rights' are products of Ethical Life, the third part of *The Philosophy of Right*. The first principle, outlined in Abstract Right, is simply recognition of each other as persons, which implies the 'negative freedom' of not having one's personality interfered with. On this foundation, people become responsible moral subjects and build ethical lives together. They do not do so in the common rooms of Philosophy Departments but in the course of their cooperation and conflict in social life. Facing all kinds of conflicts and tragedies, we figure out principles to regulate ethical life, and these include making provision to ensure that all have access to health services, education, means of subsistence, justice in the resolution of disputes, generally aimed at securing parity of participation in Ethical Life for all.

It could be argued, however, that the right not to be treated prejudicially on the grounds of race, gender, sexual orientation, ethnicity, and so on, constitutes a concretisation of Abstract Right rather than belonging to Ethical Life, inasmuch as these rights are demands to be treated as *persons without regard* to any particularity. On the other hand, in Civil Society, we are to be treated as *individuals taking account* of particularity. Justice cannot be secured in all cases by 'blindness' to particular differences but often requires appropriate modification to norms.

§2   Contract and Exchange

Being an external thing and an embodiment of my Will, in my property my Will exists for other persons, and thus other Wills. But this relation of Will to Will mediated through my property is a implicitly CONTRACT, which thereby gives reality to our common will, and is an objective realisation of my recognition as a person. Thus, Contract is implicit in Property.

The common Will expressed in Contract is not however a *universal* Will, and as mentioned above, Hegel rejects the idea that the State can be seen as a 'social contract'. The Wills involved in Contract are the Wills of finite persons.

Hegel also rejects the idea that Marriage can be subsumed under Contract. Marriage is in essence an *ethical* tie, and cannot be reduced either to one of mere reciprocal usefulness nor one of the subjective and transient aspects of love.

The phases of Contract are (A) Gift, (B) Exchange, and (C) the Pledge.

A GIFT is a *formal* contract because it requires only the Will of one to alienate and the Will of the other to appropriate. A Contract is *real* when both Wills have the moments of alienating and appropriating, and remain so as in Exchange. The Pledge, such as a mortgage or surety, is made where there is a cleavage between possession and ownership, and the *value* of the property is offered immediately, until possession is brought into line with ownership. The Pledge completes the contract,

The making of a contract differs from its performance and the idea must be given external, determinant existence in some form of symbol, be that a gesture or a signed document. By this means, the identity of different Wills is made existent.

A Gift properly so called, or a loan or favour, is formal. But nonetheless, since I can only realise my Will by alienating the thing, this relation makes explicit what was only implicit in Property.

An EXCHANGE can be (1) Exchange pure and simple or a purchase and sale, in which one side counts as value only and the other side as utility only, (2) the lease of all or part of a thing in which the lessor remains the owner, and (3) "Contract for wages – alienation of my productive capacity or my services so far as these are alienable, the alienation being restricted in time or in some other way."

Hegel does not go anywhere with exchange for money or wage labour. His concern is that these relations are immediate and dependent on chance as to whether their particular will actually correspond to the implicit Will, even though the implicit Will (i.e., the Idea) can only be realised through such immediate Wills. That exchange relations are in fact constrained by laws of political economy seems to be no compensation and nor is Hegel interested in pursuing them at this point, although it is known that he read and admired the British political economists. The economic angle is not pursued at this point.

The PLEDGE is intended as a guarantee against the possibility of wrong, by one party failing to complete the contract after the transfer of property. Thus the Pledge explicitly posits the possibility of wrongdoing.

The problem is this: just how can contracts between *particular* persons realise the Idea? Just as Alienation turned out to be the only way that the transformation from Possession to Property could be completed, the only way Contract can make the transition to the universal is by Wrong!

Because Contracts are made according to particular Wills, they are at the mercy of Wrong, and the truth of the show of rightness which is cancelled by Wrong is the negation of Wrong and the restoration of Right. Right thus reasserts itself by negation of the negation, and Right thereby makes itself into something real and actual, whereas in Contract it was only transitory, immediate and implicit.

Since Abstract Right contains only prohibitions, it makes sense that its truth turns out to be the negation of Wrong, with punishment proving to be essential to the realisation of Abstract Right.

The phases of WRONG are (A) Non-malicious wrong, (B) Fraud, and (C) Crime.

NON-MALICIOUS WRONG can happen because what is Right is determined in each instance by particular persons from their specific point of view and in such a case there can be disagreement as to what is Right, but both parties recognise the same principles of rightness, and the wrong can be put right without punishment. In the case of FRAUD, both parties agree as to what is demanded by Right, but one party takes Right as inessential and sets it aside. CRIME is Wrong in the full sense, showing no respect for Right, infringing both the particular and the universal, but nonetheless manifesting a Free Will, which could have *chosen* to do what was lawful.

Much of what Hegel has to say about Crime is concerned with establishing that coercion is Right when applied to cancel a Wrong. Wrong licences the use of force, and the punishment must be seen as the criminal's own act if the criminal is to be treated as a rational being. Hegel finds however that the measure of punishment administered by sentencing is entirely a matter of precedent and cannot be determined by "mere thinking." Hegel allows that compensation is appropriate where only external things have been injured, but regards revenge, the first form in which punishment appears, as a primitive conception of punishment reliant on a subjective Will and liable to lead to an infinite regression, and insists that considerations like deterrence and rehabilitation are secondary to the imperative of justice in the determination of sentencing.

All Hegel's lengthy discussion of crime and punishment lead to the conclusion that justice needs so far as possible to be freed from subjective interest and from reliance on might, and in short, that reliance on punishment for the establishment of Right is fraught with difficulties. This leads to the "demand for a will which, though particular and subjective, yet wills the universal as such. But this concept of Morality is not simply something demanded; it has emerged in the course of this movement itself" (*PR* §103).

The truth of Abstract Right is that the implicit Will shall be embodied in something external (the judge who punishes Wrong according to a universal code), "but the next requirement is that the will should be existent in something inward, in itself. It must in its own eyes be subjectivity, and have itself as its own object" (*PR* §104ad.) – being one's own judge, i.e., Morality.

§3   The Form of Movement in Abstract Right

The transitions through all the phases and grades of Abstract Right takes a similar form. The relevant concept of Abstract Right proves to be defective, failing to completely determine Right, and at the same time is shown to have implicit within itself, a new concept which is more complete in its determination of Right.

Taking Possession by Grasping does not indicate how much of the thing is grasped (for example, how can it be justified that planting a flag in Port Jackson annexes the whole of Australia to the British Crown?), but by imposing a Form on a portion of land I do determine the extent of the thing claimed, but only with respect to the relevant use (for example, farming it does not exclude travelling across it or mining it). But both these forms of taking possession Mark the object, and a symbolic mark, though indeterminate, can by convention mark Property entirely. The Use of a thing more securely marks it as Property, for if something is not being used it can be taken to have been abandoned, but by Alienating something I definitively mark it as Property, which neither the taking of possession nor use of the thing can do since these can be consistent with not being the owner of the thing. Alienation is a form of Contract, and all Property is in fact an implicitly a Contract with others who respect your Property. But a Contract of Gift is one-sided and therefore incomplete, while Exchange has both parties alienate or appropriate either utility or value, but in the event that possession of the thing cannot be immediate, a Pledge is required to secure the Contract. But even pledges are open to misunderstandings and therefore Non-malicious Wrong, but even if there is common understanding of what is demanded by Right, one party may be acting as a Fraud, or discount Right altogether and commit a Crime. Right can be restored by punishment for an act of crime, but only partially and imperfectly, therefore each person must will the Universal – thus Morality.

At each point what appeared to be Right turns out to be Wrong (or vice versa) and the relevant concept of Right has to be revised and made more concrete. Hegel carries out this development by the method already expounded in the *Logic*. In reality, the development happens by means of collective re-flection on conflicts which have generated crises in the community, and the objectification of decisions in the form of new customs and laws.

  Please excuse the unavoidable imprecision in summarising all these tran-sitions in a single paragraph. Note that occasionally the incompleteness is a problem for the property-owner, but only sometimes, and on occasion it is the reverse. The necessity which is driving the progression is the demand that Right find an objective and universal form, that is, a *rational* form. This entails that the immediate Will find an external and increasingly impersonal and *ideal* form. The transition to a law-governed Will takes place while retaining and enhancing the Free Will which is inherent to personality.

  The last category in a grade (respectively Alienation, Pledge, Wrong) each have the contradictory character of *negating* the category (Property, Contract, Abstract Right) in relation to the particular, while at the same time completing the category from the standpoint of the universal.

  This form of movement makes sense: in so far as Right is particular it will always be subject to challenge by others. But provided the immediate Will is given an external form, its Right will be subject to rational development, like a natural process.

Hegel's Theory of Action, Part 3: Purpose, Intention and the Good

The most developed component of Hegel's theory of action is situated within the middle section of *The Philosophy of Right*, entitled 'Morality'. Here Hegel tackles the difficult questions of what a subject has moral responsible for. To the activist who wants to bring about social change rather than waiting for 'structural forces' to bring about change of its own accord, this has more than a moral significance. Are you responsible for unforeseen or chance side-effects of your action, or the negative impact of counter-measures by your opponents? Or, for that matter, can you claim responsibility for the positive outcomes of your actions?

Hegel's theory of action is for social theory what causation is for natural science, and provides the best foundation for a morality of social movements, though it needs to be critically appropriated for our times. Further, whether in terms of their motivation, means or consequences, all actions are irreducibly collective, and only derivatively individual.

I will include in what follows observations taken from the Logic which help to complete the picture.

Action

Our action is what w*e* did and what *we* are responsible for. An action is a *unit* of social practice,[1] a primitive concept and the relevant purpose, knowledge, intention, responsibility, goal, motivation, etc., arise from an analysis of and/ or from the development of the action itself, which at the beginning may lack all of these characteristics. So it would be wrong to say, for instance, that an action is a 'unity of' behaviour and consciousness. Rather, consciousness and behaviour are *abstracted from* actions.

'ACTION' (*Handlung*) here refers only to *human* action, and *purposive* human action at that, rather than the preconscious behaviour characteristic of

---

1   The German word translated for Hegel as 'action' is *Handlung*, in contrast to *Tat* (deed) from which we have *Tätigkeit* (activity). This contrasts with Marx's usage in which *Tätigkeit* means activity in the sense of 'social practice', and *Tat* means a deed or purposive act. But for Hegel *Tat* is the change the actor brings about in the world irrespective of the consciousness (if any) with which it is done, while *Handlung* is 'action' (or 'activity') from which the actor's consciousness and their deed can both be abstracted.

non-human forms of life or the autonomous functions of the human organism, such as hiccups, goose bumps or withdrawing the hand from fire. It seems that 'action' includes, however, those actions which are first done with conscious awareness and control, but with mastery, come to be carried out unconsciously, such as tying shoelaces or stepping over the kerb. Although not done with conscious awareness, these operations are consciously acquired and if something unexpected happens, they are called back into conscious control. So for example, using a sexist expression which violates social norms Hegel would take as an action for which the speaker is morally responsible, even though it was unconscious.

Hegel does not explicitly discuss the question of what is a unit of action, but it is possible to reconstruct his answer to this problem. One of the meanings of *Handlung* is 'plot' or 'story line', and this parallels the way the action for which an agent is responsible hangs together as a unit extended over time and space. Hegel takes a subject's action as one continuous story line, uniting both inner and outer aspects of activity in a way which makes the 'story line' intelligible.

Purpose, Intention and Welfare

Purpose, Goal and Means

Every action, even actions carried out without conscious awareness, has a Purpose – what the subject set out to do (irrespective of the benefit the agent saw in doing it, and of the particular goal by which this purpose was fulfilled). The action must use some Means, which is to be distinguished from the Object which it is the agent's purpose to transform. These are the immediate elements of an action.[2]

The PURPOSE is the universal concept of the action (e.g. 'break a window'), the particular content (e.g., here and now that window) and the judgment to do it. The MEANS is the external object (a cobble stone), my activity to make it my means (ripping it up for a projectile) and my activity in using the properties of the Means against the object (throwing it at the window). The OBJECT (a shop) is transformed into the Realised Purpose (its window is broken), the changed object is meaningful (a symbol of my anger) and my purpose is preserved in the realised purpose. The cobbled street which was my Means has been partially 'worn out', even though it persists and was not my object.

---

2   The German word translated as "purpose" is *Vorsatz*. Purpose is linked with *Zweck*: what is aimed at (*Zweck* originally meant the bull's eye in a target), for which I will use "goal" or "aim." The *Mittel* (means) is the external thing used by the subject to act upon the object (*Gegenstand*), transforming it into the realised purpose.

But "action *presupposes* an external object with a complex environment" (*PR* §115) and so has consequences which are deemed to be *part of* the action as the purpose unfolds and is realised. So the action is not complete when the subject stops acting. If I throw a stone, the action is not complete until the stone hits the window and the last shard of glass has landed. My intention – my reason for doing it – is so far immaterial.

The purpose goes through a development in the course of the action as my subjective will interacts with the complex and infinitely interconnected external world. Initially the purpose is a *subjective purpose* – a universal concept of a goal embedded in the external world. The discrepancy the subject perceives between the subjective purpose and its object (*Gegenstand*) produces an action to resolve the discrepancy. The subjective purpose is transformed by the action into the *realised* purpose. The realised purpose inevitably differs from the goal, but the purpose is nonetheless preserved in the realised purpose because as a result of the action, the object bears the impression of my subjective purpose. Even if the window fails to break, the scratch on the glass and the stone lying nearby remain evidence of my purpose. The realised purpose unites the subjective purpose with the objectivity of the external world, and becomes part of the changing conditions for further action. "The End achieved consequently is only an object, which again becomes a Means or material for other Ends, and so on for ever" (*Enc. Logic* §211).

The means, the "middle term" between subjective purpose and realised purpose "is broken up into two elements external to each other, (a) the subject's action and (b) the object which serves as Means" (*Enc. Logic* §208). This object is an external object brought under the power of the subject as a means for the subject's purpose, and directed against other objects, and using its mechanical and chemical properties to shape the object to the subject's own purpose. The distinction between the activity of the subject in using the means, and the means itself is important and the two should not be conflated. Whereas the subject's own activity is subjective and manifests the subject's own will, the means is external and exists, interacting with the object as a part of a whole, interconnected, external world – the complex objective environment beyond the subject's control. For example, if I am in the habit of burning off my garden waste, but do this same action on a hot, dry day, my action may prove to be dramatically different, even though my subjective purpose is the same as usual. This external world is a material culture which is objective, that is, independent of the subject's will, the product of the activity of past generations, as are the norms which I acquire and which shape my intentions. It is from this material culture, in which all human action is embedded, that the 'implicit teleology' which Hegel calls 'Spirit' arises, apparently acting 'behind the backs' of the actors themselves.

In the meaning of 'action' and 'purpose' in connection with the actions of an individual person, the external object is not something general like the weather or knowledge of English or a situation – it is a *material object*, even if that material object is a part of the subject's own body. The subject's will cannot be made objective without the use of a material object as means. If I want to go to Sydney, I can use a car, a plane or my feet, but I cannot fulfil my purpose without using *some* external object.

The same logic applies when the subject of action is not an individual person but a corporate actor, institution or social movement of some kind. Here, 'external' means 'Object' in the sense of the Logic, activity whose centre is not the subject itself but another. In this wider sense, we should add to the "mechanical and chemical properties," *social* properties, that is, the social significance or meaning of the objects concerned in the relevant cultural environment. A party or social movement cannot achieve an external aim solely by means of its own internal resources; it has to use the people and institutions beyond its own ranks as a Means.

The object is *transformed*, but the means is *preserved* in the action, although it is 'worn out' by is use and in repeated use is ultimately used up:

> the Subjective End, which is the power ruling these processes, in which the objective things wear themselves out on one another, contrives to keep itself free from them, and to preserve itself in them. Doing so, it appears as the Cunning of Reason.
>
> *Enc. Logic*, §209

That is, by acting in the external world, the subject subordinates itself to processes immanent in the wider world, including both the object and the means, and "I must be aware of the universal character of any isolated deed" (*PR*, §118 ad.). So the NGO worker who intervenes in a community with the purpose of helping stigmatised individuals cannot ignore the likely reaction of other members of the community which could lead to everyone being worse off. For example, a worker who has enjoyed fair wages at a foreign social enterprise may never be given work again in their own town. The supporter who acts violently on a picket line may cause the union members to be isolated after the strike is over.

Further, by taking a particular action and thereby changing the object, alternative actions that may have been available may be subsequently *excluded*. So giving food to the starving also has the effect of undermining the viability of local farms.

Responsibility

Most of the discussion about Hegel's theory of action is concerned with the interconnection of the subject's purpose with the whole external environment to determine the agent's RESPONSIBILITY for the changes that take place as a consequence of the deed – where does *my* action and *my* responsibility begin and end?

Commentators on Hegel's theory of agency usually follow Hegel in using the lighting of a fire to illustrate his idea, and I will use this example as well as it very graphically exhibits the main features of Hegel's idea. However, a natural process cannot adequately stand in for the process of world history about which Hegel's theory of action is intended to enlighten us. Nonetheless, interventions into social problems sometimes trigger 'runaway' responses not unlike a bushfire. Hegel takes this problem under the heading of Morality, concerned with assigning *responsibility* for some change in the world. But it can equally well be read as a practical *social theory* for the activist who takes on responsibility to make changes in the world.

So, consider the position of someone, say Guy, who sets fire to the dry grass in his back yard. The first thing is that Guy is responsible for that immediate deed, irrespective of his intention. If it was a day of total fire ban, it is no good Guy telling the police "But Mrs. Fawkes told me to do it" or "I hadn't checked if it was a fire ban day" – he is responsible.

Further, for Hegel, the action does not end with Guy throwing the burning match into the grass, the immediate deed. If the fire spreads to the neighbouring property and burns down the neighbour's house, on the face of it, that is part of Guy's action, for which he is responsible, too.

Guy's subjective purpose in lighting the fire – whether just to burn off his own land or to create a firebreak – are immaterial. But:

> The will's right, however, is to recognize as its action, and to accept responsibility for, only those presuppositions of the deed of which it was conscious in its aim and those aspects of the deed which were contained in its purpose ... – this is the right to know.
>
> *PR*, §117

The 'right to (not) know' is a *formal* right which turns out to have a limited scope, because when Guy decides to set fire to the grass he has the responsibility to know that the fire could get out of control and could spread to his neighbour's property. If he meant that the fire should spread *or* if he did not take the trouble to see if it might or take action to prevent its spread, he is responsible, because the spreading of the fire was implicit in his purpose.

But what if Mrs. Fawkes had secretly hidden her savings in a box in the grass and the money was destroyed by the fire? If Guy had no reason to believe that something of value could be hidden there, he is not responsible for the destruction of what his wife hid in the grass – it was not part of his purpose. Hegel contrasts this with the ancients for whom the agent's knowledge was not to be taken into account in assigning responsibility – Oedipus was condemned for killing his father, even though he could not have known at the time that King Laius was his father.

Formally, the agent is not responsible for unintended consequences of their action which were not implicit in his purpose:

> the moral will has the right to refuse to recognize in the resulting state of affairs what was not present inwardly as purpose.
>
> PR, §115ad.

The agent's purpose is realised in the action and the consequences of the action belong to the action, so the subject is responsible for all the consequences of their immediate action. What frees Guy from responsibility for the destruction of the money his wife hid in the grass is that the actions of another subject with another purpose intervened and their action combined with Guy's action so as to bring about the unfortunate consequence.

> The action, as the aim posited in the external world, has become the prey of external forces which attach to it something totally different from what it is explicitly and drive it on into alien and distant consequences. Thus [in this case] the will has the right to repudiate the imputation of all consequences except the first, since it alone was purposed.
>
> PR, §118

So the subject is free of blame for "something interposed from without and introduced by chance, ... quite unrelated to the nature of the action itself" (PR §118 n.), and conversely cannot take credit for it. But what of "moral luck," that is, when a wrong action may or may not lead to serious consequences? Hegel takes a 'hard line' on this:

> It happens of course that circumstances may make an action miscarry to a greater or lesser degree. In a case of arson, for instance, the fire may not catch or alternatively it may take hold further than the incendiary intended. In spite of this, however, we must not make this a distinction

between good and bad luck, since in acting a man must lay his account with externality. The old Proverb is correct: 'A flung stone is the devil's.' To act is to expose oneself to bad luck. Thus bad luck has a right over me and is an embodiment of my own willing.

PR, §119ad.

Hegel's idea here is that the state has made laws which are designed to avoid harm caused by unintended as well as intended consequences, and the subject who steps outside of the law, if they are a rational agent, must take responsibility for consequences which they, lacking the historical wisdom of the state, did not foresee. On the other hand, if a subject acts in a way which is consistent with law and custom, then they cannot be blamed for *unintended* and *unforeseeable* consequences of their action. If serious unintended consequences transpire, this may be an occasion to make a new law.

What if Guy didn't light the fire, but a youngster he hired to tidy up the garden did? In this case, Guy is responsible even though the lighting of the fire cannot be imputed to him – his action was in failure to supervise the youngster's work.

Since an action unites both purpose and deed, the action extends temporally and spatially beyond the immediate deed, as consequences unfold and the agent continues the action in response to the unfolding consequences. It also extends back in time, such as when I plan my day at work while commuting in the morning. The quality of my planning is manifested in the deed which it has prepared. Indeed, all the imaginary voices, dreams of glory and other fantasies I have exist only in the actions which express them in the external world. People are unreliable reporters of their own thoughts, which are to be judged only by the series of their actions. As Hegel puts it in the Remark to the very first paragraph of *The Philosophy of Right*: "Philosophy has to do with ideas or *realised thoughts*, and hence not with what we have been accustomed to call mere conceptions."

Intention

If the subject's purpose is exhausted in the realised goal then the action is not a rational action at all. All forms of life manifest purposes of this kind, in which the Intention is identical to the Purpose and the subject's desire is satisfied immediately in consumption of the object, and not mediated through a conscious intention. Rational action implies a purpose which differs from the intention.

As a rational being, the subject is aware of the complexity, interconnectedness and contingency of the world they act in. Among the consequences which flow from the completion of my purpose is my INTENTION:

> The consequences ... represent the universal implicit within that state of
> affairs. Of course I cannot foresee the consequences – they might be pre-
> ventable – but I must be aware of the universal character of any isolated
> deed. The important point here is not the isolated thing but the whole,
> and that depends not on the differentia of the particular action, but on
> its universal nature. Now the transition from purpose to intention lies in
> the fact that I ought to be aware not simply of my single action but also
> of the universal which is conjoined with it. The universal which comes on
> the scene here in this way is what I have willed, my intention.
>   *PR*, §118ad.

A rational action (and it is only such actions which are the substance of Hegel's
social philosophy) is done *for a reason*, a reason different to the purpose, which
may be worthless in itself. The intention is realised only by a *series* of such
actions, each of which is a means to some more remote end, and each of the
series of actions is generally done by a different subject. That is, when a subject
takes a rational action, they are relying on the actions of others to complete
their intention which is universal in nature. All actions are irreducibly social
in nature.

The opening up of a difference between purpose and intention marks the
beginning of action proper, doing something for a reason. When Hegel talks of
a "series of actions," actions united by a common intention, it is the contradiction between purpose and intention which marks off each unit in this series,
continued in the consequences of and reactions to the deed.

But where the intention is identical to the purpose, that is, the action is a
simple reflex, the subject is probably not a rational agent (a child perhaps) who
cannot be blamed for their action.

As a rational human being, I am free, being capable of forming intentions
which are contrary to my immediate desire and inclination or the will of others. The WORTH (*Wert*) of the action and the reason I think it good to do it is
my INTENTION. If my intentions are rational, this worth must be a universal.
For example, my intention in handing out food may be to alleviate a famine,
to raise my country's humanitarian credentials, or increase business at my res-
taurant; in each case, the purpose is a step towards the Intention which is the
ultimate motivation, but is not fulfilled by the deed alone. Analysis of rational action means taking into account the Intention with which the action was
taken, related to the benefit (WELFARE) sought and the concept the subject
had of their action – their intention in doing it, not just the immediate purpose
of the action.

A person always has responsibility (*Schuld*) for their deed, without qualification, and for the immediate purpose they pursue. If the deed was in

contradiction to the purpose (the brakes failed), then I may disown that action, but good intentions cannot justify a wrong act. Hegel takes a very 'hard line' on this question. A slave or servant who is obliged to carry out a wrong action under duress is still responsible for their action, and in fact, according to Hegel, a slave is responsible for being a slave even if rebellion is punished by death. A person's will cannot be forced, even if the consequence of a person's refusal of an action is their own death.

> Yet if a man is a slave, his own will is responsible for his slavery, just as it is its will which is responsible if a people is subjugated. Hence the wrong of slavery lies at the door, not simply of enslavers or conquerors, but of the slaves and the conquered themselves.
>
> *PR*, §58ad.

On the other hand, Hegel supports the 'right of distress', under which a person in imminent danger may steal or trespass or whatever blamelessly, and a debtor should never forfeit the tools of their trade which would render them unable to earn a living.

The Truth of Intentions

The purpose undergoes a transformation through the action which transforms subjective purpose into the realised purpose; what was implicit becomes explicit. The intention is the reason for the agent's action, so while the purpose is exhausted in the realised purpose, the universal content of the action (its meaning for others), the intention, remains, and will be manifested in further actions.

> The universal quality of the action is the manifold content of the action as such, reduced to the simple form of universality. But the subject, an entity reflected into himself and so particular in correlation with the particularity of his object (*Zweck*), has in his end his own particular content, and this content is the soul of the action and determines its character.
>
> *PR*, §121

Thus, a series of actions is bound together by a shared content, the intention, whatever else may happen in consequence of the original deed, and each individual deed expresses a particular purpose subsumed under a universal concept of the intention. the intention is not merely implicit, but is known to the agent and is what provides the motivation for the action.

Two things follow from this. Firstly, the subsequent actions are generally done by other agents, each continuing or contributing to the intention with their own particular purpose, each a means to each others' ends. Secondly, the intention is not limited to the immediate context of the goal, but is realised in the development of the concrete whole. The logic of this process is the subject-object process described in Hegel's *Logic* – the subject (an intention) interacts with other projects and is manifested concretely in the development of the whole community. Things do not generally work out just as anyone originally intended, but the outcome is not that of the subject alone, since other agents will contribute to the unfolding of the intention. Nonetheless, as the intention unfolds and concretizes itself the subject sees the truth of their intention. Throughout, the subject is guided by pursuit of their own welfare as they see it, which is *implicitly* the Good of the whole community.

Welfare

The content of the intention is the WELFARE of the subject as the subject conceives it. Welfare is a unity of Happiness and Right. Although Welfare is the reflection of the Will on itself (i.e., what it should will, rather than simply what it immediately desires) and is implicitly elevated to the universal, it remains the thought of finite subjects who cannot be expected to apprehend Freedom as such.

When Hegel says that: "A person is the series of their actions" (*PR* §124), he means that the personal motives someone may have had in participating in some project – the pleasure gained from collective action, the honour and praise awarded for their achievement or even less laudable pleasures such as the exhilaration of command – are irrelevant estimating the worth of a person's work. A subject's intention may be to further the welfare of all, but it equally well may not conform to what serves the welfare of all.

Whether my intention is my own welfare, the welfare of others like myself, or the welfare of all cannot justify an action which is Wrong, that is, an action which violates abstract Right. However, an action is not to be judged wrong and therefore inadmissible according to whether it furthers the general good. The idea of the 'general good' does not, for Hegel, belong to the sphere of Morality, but rather to Ethical Life and the State. The moral subject is not responsible for determining what serves the 'general good'. The moral subject *is* responsible for interpreting and understanding the *law*, but is not in a position to make absolute judgments about the 'general good', and discount in their actions what the law requires.

The Good and Conscience

The Good is the Idea as the unity of the concept of the will with the particular Will. In this unity, abstract right, welfare, the subjectivity of

> knowing and the contingency of external fact have their independent
> self-subsistence superseded. ...
>
> *PR*, §129

Subjects come to know enough, and confront a sufficiently rational situation, that in seeking their own welfare and respecting abstract right, they progressively realise Freedom. It turns out that the welfare and right of the particular is essentially universal welfare. The Good can only be realised by means of the subjective will, so the subjective will has to be 'caught up in' the Idea of the Good, which can only be the outcome of a long drawn out process of development of rational laws and the education of the people.

A subject's *own* apprehension of the Good and their acceptance of this as obligatory for themselves is Conscience. The subject no longer looks to religion or the law to be told what is Good, but rather their own insight is what is decisive. However, their "insight is capable equally of being true and of being mere opinion and error" (*PR* §143n.) and potentially Evil. EVIL, the Will to realise what is opposed to universal right and welfare, in the name of a subject's own conscience, can only be overcome by Ethical Life and the State.

The process by which the conflicting intentions of many diverse subjects combine to produce this process, called the Idea, where subjects are more and more able to align their particular welfare with the universal welfare, is that described in the Logic. Thus in Hegel's theory of action we have come *full circle*, back to the *Logic as the truth of human action*.

*

Most of the above is written as if the subject were an individual person. But in general the subject can be a corporate actor such as a political party or an institution, or a social movement united by some universal concept in the absence of actual organizational ties. The subject identifies itself by means of a concept of itself and its welfare and shared intentions.

What this suggests is an approach to a social theory in which agency is given its rightful place through units, each of which is an *intention* – some universal concept which is the shared content, the soul, of each aggregate of actions. The term I prefer for this unit is 'project'.

The theory outlined above, which forms the basic content of the middle section of *The Philosophy of Right* on Morality, has raised some problems for social movement activists. I will examine these in a reflection on Hegel's Morality.

CHAPTER 17

Morality

Morality is about acting rationally, according to one's Conscience, rather than simply in response to immediate desires or in conformity with social norms, so it is just as it should be that Hegel's theory of action occupies the central place in his chapter on Morality. However, it turns out that the very concept of Morality contains an inescapable contradiction.

§1   Conscience and Duty, Good and Evil

The subjective totality of the moral subject's intentions is CONSCIENCE, through which the subject determines their actions in pursuit of their own welfare and that of others, mindful of the constraints imposed by abstract right and the facts of the external world. Freedom can be realised only thanks to the action of moral subjects guided by their own conscience. However, as has already been remarked, limited by the finite extent of their own knowledge, no moral subject is in a position to determine the 'general good' which is an irreducibly social process (in Hegel's jargon: "the concept of Right"). A subject's conscience may equally well be the expression of particular interests, destructive of universal welfare, as in accord with universal welfare.

This is something of the greatest importance for all those who choose to be social change activists and guided by their own Conscience rather than by the laws and customs of the society to which they belong. Other subjects have determined the general Good to be quite other than you have, otherwise there would be no point in activism. By what right do you believe that you know best? There is an inherent "moral risk" in being an activist. The maxim that 'the road to hell is paved in good intentions' has a basis in social experience. The subject guided solely by their own Conscience may equally well do Evil in the world as do Good. Provided abstract right is respected, there is no criterion within Morality which distinguishes between Good and Evil.

Morality can take you as far as the conviction that you must do your DUTY, the point that Kant had reached by relying on an innate faculty of Reason available to every moral subject. But Kant could not get beyond the emptiest generalities like "Do your duty" or "Act according to a maxim which could be laid down as a universal principle." He could not determine the *content* of

Duty. A wicked person can as well be a good Kantian as someone who does good.

Hegel points out that:

> since action is an alteration which is to take place in an actual world and so will have recognition in it, it must in general accord with what has validity there.
>
> *PR*, §132n.

So the only way that a subject may ensure that, guided by their own conscience, they do good and not evil, is to ensure that they conform to the customs and laws of their community, including the very rules they seek to overthrow.

For anyone working for social change within established institutions such as parliamentary political parties or the legal system, this is a given. The newly-appointed General Secretary of the Australian Council of Trade Unions, Sally McManus was asked on ABC TV: "We live in a country where there are laws that are established by a parliament that all citizens are expected to abide by ..., regardless of whether you agree or disagree with those laws." Personally, I was delighted when McManus responded: "I believe in the rule of law where the law is fair, when the law is right. But when it's unjust, I don't think there's a problem with breaking it" (*7:30 Report*, 15 March 2018).

Hegel would have agreed with the interviewer's position. According to Hegel, moral choice is limited by the law of the land, as rightly interpreted, and whoever steps outside those limits bears responsibility for any wrong which may result.

These laws are of course not something static, but on the contrary are determined by social processes which, under Hegel's concept, belong to Ethical Life, a social process which constitutes the resultant of many conflicting wills. Sally McManus is right because the question put to her was not one of moral choice but of her responsibilities as leader of the Australian union movement (and not as a future Labor MP), that is, of a problem of Ethical Life. Clearly, there are complex issues in play here which will be dealt with below. But the social change activist needs to see that Hegel is right in this: – the individual Conscience of a moral subject is *not* a valid basis for setting oneself in opposition to what has validity in this world.

Still, the unity of the subjective will and the universal Good cannot be achieved within the sphere of Morality, whether the moral subject is guided by Pure Reason or by Revealed Religion. It can only be achieved in Ethical Life, in the evolving institutions underlying and constituting the State, through

which the individual participates with others in determining the duties of
each individual.

§2   Hegel's Morality and Present-day Issues in Moral Philosophy

In the treatment I have given of Morality in Hegel's *Philosophy of Right* and
of Hegel's theory of action which forms the core of his theory of Morality, I have only skimmed the surface, with the aim of bringing out the main
lines of Hegel's argument. But this part of the work is extremely rich, touching on numerous problems of human action. The reader should study the
text for themselves remembering that the equivalent in social theory of causation in natural science is not 'social psychology' but *moral responsibility*: to
say that you are morally responsible for something is equivalent to saying you
caused it.

All respected Law Schools today include a study of Hegel's *Philosophy of
Right* in their legal theory course, because Hegel deals systematically with all
those problems which arise in the application of law, and his results by and
large have stood the test of time for the past 200 years.

Activism is generally about problems of unresolved injustice, and social
issues centred on 'wicked problems', that is problems which are resistant to
resolution because of their being deeply embedded in the entire social system.
It is precisely Hegel's approach – taking all moral problems as rooted in the
whole, with every action taken to be infinitely interconnected with every other
action – which is suited to tackle such 'wicked problems'. Further, activists are
often involved in publicly advocating for the injustice of situations which may
be denied or regarded as unproblematic, and will frequently have to engage
in moral and ethical argument going to fundamental principles. A familiarity
with Hegel's arguments in connection with the numerous contradictions dealt
with in the section on Morality are an important resource.

I must postpone till after I have dealt with the third Part of *The Philosophy of
Right* a comprehensive critique of Hegel's seeming insistence that it is the duty
of every citizen of a modern state to conform to the law of the land, something
which social change activists will have trouble with, since this would rule out
entire classes of social activism. These issues go to the heart of Hegel's philosophy and how it can be appropriated for social change activism, and must
not be dealt with in an off-hand way. His arguments have considerable force.
Below, I will deal with several aspects of Hegel's Morality with the aim of clarifying and defending Hegel's position.

Consequentialism, Deontology and Virtue Ethics

Hegel's critique of Morality has demonstrated the limited domain of problems which the exercise of individual Conscience is called upon to resolve. Most of the problems which have important social and political significance Hegel has pushed out to what he has defined as Ethical Life, rather than individual Morality. Nonetheless, there is significant scope for the exercise of individual Conscience within the limits set by the imperative to conform to custom and the law of the land – after all, for most people most of the time, this is the field on which they are called upon to act as moral subjects.

In this context, it would be useful to reflect on what Hegel has to say about the main contending principles of moral philosophy in present day discourse: Consequentialism, Deontology and Virtue Ethics.

Consequentialism

Consequentialism is the principle that the rightness of an act must be judged according to its consequences. Hegel finds two defects in Consequentialism. (1) In this complex world, the subject cannot know what will be the ultimate consequences of their action, and (2) the summation of the various good and bad consequences of an action can only be an arbitrary and subjective opinion. In any case, particular or even universal welfare can never make a wrong into something moral (See *PR* §126). In particular, Consequentialism pays no heed to the requirements of Justice.

At the same time, Hegel holds that the subject is responsible for all the consequences of their action which were predictable or foreseeable at the time they acted, up until the intervention of other actors (such as repressive countermeasures by one's protagonists) which necessarily make further consequences unpredictable, and no longer your *own* action. However, everything carries the proviso that the action is in accord with the subject's duty as a citizen of their state. The subject is responsible for *all* the consequences of their action insofar as they go beyond social norms, irrespective of whether the consequences are predictable. So Hegel incorporates the Consequentialist principle in his Morality *within* the bounds set by socially determined rules.

However, key to Hegel's Morality is his theory of action in which the difference between Purpose and Intention is a marker of rational action. An absolute rejection of Consequentialism, as in the case of Anarchist moral philosophy (See Frank 2010), is an absurdity. The demand that a practice, such as direct action, should be adopted for its own sake, and not for its consequences – that is, not *in order to* achieve some positive outcome such as winning a dispute or making an effective protest – is to demand that the subject acts like a child.

Adult humans, social movements and all rational actors do things *for a reason*. In fact, anarchist opposition to 'consequentialism' is not in reality a position in moral philosophy at all, but a social theory, namely the theory of contamination, according to which socialism can be achieved by force of example, creating miniature socialist societies and in the hope that the relevant practices will spread by 'contamination' (Maeckelbergh 2009).

The most widespread formulation of Consequentialism is Utilitarianism as applied in present day Economics. Objection (1) is resolved by the doctrinaire assertion of market fundamentalism, according to which the operation of the free market will ensure that the best of all possible outcomes will result by each actor pursuing their own welfare alone (the Pareto Optimum). Objection (2) is resolved by the assertion that every good has a price and the operation of the market will always act to maximise the sum of values in an economy. Thus governments measure their performance by the GNP. The doctrine of the 'triple bottom line' is an attempt to rescue Utilitarianism from the exclusively economic interpretation, but it cannot overcome the two objections applying to all Consequentialist dogmas or any attempt to turn a principle of Morality into a principle of Ethical Life.

Deontology

According to Deontology, the rightness of an act must be judged by its conformity to a set of rules. Foremost amongst such rules is the Golden Rule: "Do unto others as you would have done unto you." The Golden Rule had its origin in religion – all the great religions include a version of it. Hegel's main protagonist in 1821 was Kant's rational deontology which is the source of most present day moral philosophy on the Left. Kant endeavoured to formulate a deontological moral philosophy based on Reason, including a secular version of the Golden Rule, the Categorical Imperative. Hegel demonstrated that this approach could yield nothing beyond empty truisms.

In formulating his Communicative Ethics, Habermas (1984, 1987) attempted to overcome this problem by proceduralism. Proceduralism shares with Hegel the recognition that the content of moral action cannot be determined by the subject alone, but has to be determined by participation in Ethical Life. According to Communicative Ethics, decisions about how to act must be made according to rules governing how *collective* decisions are made: consulting all those affected, benefiting the most disadvantaged, eschewing domineering or exclusionary speech, etc. Others have further developed this Proceduralism, but Proceduralism can only partially compensate for the limitations inherent in Morality. Being limited to the individual's own Conscience, Morality cannot provide a basis for social or political theory.

Hegel does not attempt to colonise social theory with his theory of Morality, but on the contrary, develops his theory of Ethical Life from the outcome of his critique of Morality which showed that the moral subject is unable to determine their Duty by consulting their own Conscience. However, the section on Morality plays a crucial part in the overall structure of *The Philosophy of Right*. A community based solely on 'negative freedom', that is, respect for property rights and the rights of the person, can never produce the conditions for Freedom without the cultivation of the subjective will, without the formation of moral subjects who will the welfare of all. Hegel's view of how this is achieved is summed up in this remark:

> When a father inquired about the best method of educating his son in
> ethical conduct, a Pythagorean replied: 'Make him a citizen of a state
> with good laws'.
> *PR*, §153n.

A good state is impossible without the moral education of its citizens and the moral education of the citizens depends upon the state having good laws.

Virtue Ethics

Virtue ethics accepts that moral decisions rely on calculation of the consequences of one's actions and the application of relevant rules of conduct, but it also accepts the defects of all varieties of Consequentialism and the fact that no set of rules can ever determine without remainder the right course of action in every circumstance without ambiguity. Right conduct requires the cultivation of what Aristotle called *phronesis* – the capacity to judge which rule is appropriate to determining right in any given concrete situation and how to interpret that rule. Every subject's knowledge of the social context and the relevant laws has to be supplemented by a mature faculty of moral judgment, cultivated by participation in the ethical life of a good state.

The structure of *The Philosophy of Right*, suggests that Hegel can be read as promoting a Virtue Ethics, but as such, Virtue belongs to the third part on Ethical Life, not the second part, on Morality. According to Hegel (See §§150–155.), "Virtue is the ethical order reflected in the individual character," but is to be distinguished from simple conformity with the individual's duties which Hegel called 'rectitude'. Virtue is a feature of an individual's character (not necessarily exceptional) which is generally manifested however only in exceptional circumstances or when one obligation clashes with another. In ancient nations lacking a developed civil society, virtues were manifested only by exceptional individuals, but with cultural development, virtues become the acquired characteristics of all or at least most individuals.

§3   Civil Disobedience

It is not possible to give a satisfactory response to Hegel's insistence on the imperative to do your duty as determined by the law and customs of the community to which you belong until we have made a critique of Hegel's conception of the State. However, it is worth noting at this point that Hegel's demand of obedience to law is not absolute.

As I showed in §16.3 above, the categories in Abstract Right are subject to a characteristic form of movement. As the entire form of life develops, each formation of Abstract Right – that is to say, the underlying customs and laws defining and defending the rights of the person and property – proves to be inadequate. The contradiction arises because an apparent Right turns out to be Wrong (or vice versa), a social crisis results, and the customs and laws have to be changed.

But how does this happen in reality? If moral subjects meekly deferred to law and custom no crisis would ever arise; the community would stagnate and become hidebound by antiquated laws and customs. In fact, when a custom or law comes into conflict with the social practices which have grown up within them, people *do* object, and knowingly violate customs and laws and insist on their being Right and the relevant law being Wrong. In other words, law develops by means of either civil disobedience, or post facto defence of their actions by people who unwittingly committed a wrong. Surely, rational civil disobedience is higher than unwitting wrong?

The only qualification which I can see in Hegel is his observation (See *Enc. Logic* §158n.) that the punishment a subject receives is a part of their own action, and they must therefore take responsibility for that. I think this has to be qualified by the same limits (*Enc. Logic* §127n.) referred to below which require that an action in law can in no circumstances be right if it extinguishes absolutely the subject's existence. My reading of Hegel on the right of civil disobedience then is that the subject who defies a law with the intention of stimulating a change in the law must *accept responsibility for all the consequences of their act*, including their own punishment under law so long as this punishment does not threaten their existence. Given that Hegel denies that any benefit can justify a wrong, this places strict limits on what he would regard as legitimate civil disobedience.

However, Hegel allows for further situations in which it is right to break the law.

Firstly, the 'right of distress':

> In extreme danger and in conflict with the rightful property of someone
> else, this life may claim (as a right, not a mercy) a right of distress, because
> in such a situation there is on the one hand an infinite injury to a man's
> existence and the consequent loss of rights altogether, and on the other
> hand only an injury to a single restricted embodiment of freedom, ...
>   *PR*, §127

So for example, under Scottish law a starving person had a right to steal a sheep
to forestall their own death or that of their family. Likewise, according to Hegel
(*PR* §127n.), a debtor has the right to retain their tools, etc., needed to earn a
living and cannot be denied these by a creditor.

Secondly, Hegel held that a slave has no duty at all and:

> It is in the nature of the case that a slave has an absolute right to free him-
> self and that if anyone has prostituted his ethical life by hiring himself to
> thieve and murder, this is an absolute nullity and everyone has a warrant
> to repudiate this contract.
>   *PR*, §66ad.

So in a situation in which an absolute wrong is mandated by law, that law has
no force over the moral subject, who has not only the right but the obligation
to repudiate the supposed obligation. (Note however that Hegel supports the
'higher right' of the State to override abstract right such as in compulsory purchase of property or in compulsory military service, and in the latter instance,
to even demand that a subject give up their life.)

Finally, there is the 'right of heroes'. I will deal with that separately, below.

§4   Ends Justify the Means?

Hegel dismisses the maxim "The end justifies the means." (See the footnote
1(c) and (d) to *PR* §140). Provided the end is truly just and the means is truly a
means, it is a tautology, he says, because a means is nothing but the end which
is its purpose. But Hegel is being obtuse here; the 'means' here refers, not to
the means used in an action, but to the *Purpose*, and the 'end' refers, not to the
Purpose, but to the *Intention*, the reason for doing it. So, Hegel continues, what
is usually meant, is "to commit a crime as a means to a good end." Rather than
responding with a qualified variation of the maxim, Hegel demolishes it logically. He has already dealt comprehensively with the morality of the Purposes

and Intentions of actions in the section on Morality, and no version of the ends-means maxim can substitute for that analysis.

Hegel begins with a critique of what he calls the "abstract good" by which he means the will simply to do good, in abstract, without regard to the duties and ethical obligations of the individual in their actual social situation. He points out that every action will have both good and bad in it, and the question is: which aspect of the action, the good or the bad, is to be deemed essential? In the case of an action in which the intention is abstract good, it is only the subjective opinion of the actor that it is the good which is essential. "In the strict sense there are no wicked men, since no-one wills evil for the sake of evil ... simply to will the good and to have a good intention in acting is more like evil than good, because the good willed is only this abstract form of good and therefore to make it concrete devolves on the arbitrary will of the subject." Pursuit of your own abstract opinion about what is good, irrespective of objective ethical and moral constraints imposed by Ethical Life, is just what Evil is.

How did Hegel see Means and Ends though? The first thing for Hegel is that Means and Ends have to be understood holistically. The End is a condition of the whole community (the object), in which one aspect is singled out by the subject as desired, the subject's Intention. Likewise, the Means is divided into the object and the activity of the subject. The realized end is the whole of the object, transformed by the activity of the subject with the means. In what was reviewed above, Hegel has outlined the moral parameters of action, and the justice of the action does indeed depend on the ultimate consequences. However, the subject must also have in mind that he or she is not in a position to know or judge of what is good nor in control of the ultimate consequences of their action. Every person who wants to step outside the normal bounds of custom and practice has to realize that they risk doing evil and take a corresponding responsibility on their shoulders for that.

In general, for Hegel, Morality requires that a person seek to further the welfare of the community, having a mind for the unforeseeable consequences of their action and participate in the life of the community, having regard to rights and duties which are not of their own personal creation, but are products of Ethical Life. The law, as Hegel saw it, has developed historically, and on the whole is a repository of objective wisdom that is beyond what is available to the individual, subjective judgment.

It is worth mentioning at this point that in his consideration of punishment, Hegel was absolutely against the use of sentencing to 'send a message' or deterrence or even rehabilitation other than within the bounds of what is *just* in the given instance. A cruel punishment cannot be justified in order to deter others.

The argument sometimes brought against "end justifies the means," that a cruel or deceptive purpose must fail to realise a good intention is not of course a moral or ethical argument, but a social theoretical claim which needs to be answered concretely, not in an abstract maxim.

The considerations mentioned above – the evolution of custom and law through legal crises, the right of distress, the practice of civil disobedience and the obligation to repudiate unjust obligations – qualify Hegel's rejection of the maxim of "the End justifies the Means." Further qualifications may be necessary in the light of an historical consideration of the State, which I will deal with in Chapter 20.

In the meantime you should read Part Two of *The Philosophy of Right* on Morality.

§5   The Right of Heroes

Hegel was an ardent admirer of Napoleon and he introduced the category of 'hero' into his social theory having Napoleon in mind. He recognized that sweeping changes like the abolition of feudal relics in Germany and the introduction of the *Code napoleon* could only be made by heroes – individuals who act as instruments of the Idea, History if you like – with a 'higher right', to sweep away old institutions and create new ones, and these heroes would necessarily, by lights of their own community, do wrong, even evil and what is more would generally not be thanked by posterity either.

Hegel talks about the role of heroes in founding new states out of a state of nature, but "Once the state has been founded, there can no longer be any heroes. They come on the scene only in uncivilised conditions" (*PR* §93ad.).

However, he also says (*PR* §351) that the same 'right of heroes' extends to, for example, 'civilized' nations which trample on the rights of 'barbarians', and pastoral people who treat hunters and gatherers in the same way. In other words, in the case of *an historic leap in state form*, such as that posed between hunter-gathers and pastoral peoples or between pastoral peoples and 'civilized' states, and so presumably between capitalism and socialism. Such leaps cannot be achieved by the gradual evolution of the existing laws and customs, but can only be achieved by 'rightful' coercion and the sweeping aside of the old laws.

CHAPTER 18

Ethical Life

§1 Ethical Life is the Idea of Freedom in the Existing World

Hegel describes ETHICAL LIFE (*Sittlichkeit*) as "a subjective disposition, but one imbued with what is inherently right" (*PR* §141n.). Ethical Life is an entire way of life; not just any way of life, but one characterised by the unity of a system of objectified rights with the subjectivity of moral subjects. Ethical Life is composed of ethical units (households) – independent of one another, with private rights and free from despotic state intrusion – which are 'caught up' in the shared pursuit of the Good according to custom (*Sitt*).

Abstract Right and Morality cannot exist independently: "[abstract] right lacks the moment of subjectivity, while morality in turn possesses that moment alone" (*PR* §141ad.). Only the evolving system of rights-and-duties realised in Ethical Life can provide the support for both the objective and subjective sides of Right. Ethical Life is the actuality of the Idea of Freedom.

Duty sounds like a restriction on Freedom, but to know your duty is a liberation from determination by mere natural impulse, and from the indeterminacy – the indeterminacy of subjective Conscience which does not touch reality and the objective indeterminacy of the ultimate consequences of one's action. It is the achievement of *positive* freedom, for it is through Ethical Life that individuals can realise their freedom.

People learn to be ethical by their participation in Ethical Life. However, when individuals simply *identify* with the actual order, Ethical Life appears as just custom, as a *second nature* – just as Nature has its laws which are fulfilled by the animals, plants, stars, etc., this second, mindful nature is habitual. However:

> At this point the clash between the natural and the subjective will disappears, the subject's internal struggle dies away. To this extent, habit is part of ethical life as it is of philosophic thought also, since such thought demands that mind be trained against capricious fancies, and that these be destroyed and overcome to leave the way clear for rational thinking. It is true that a man is killed by habit, i.e. if he has once come to feel completely at home in life, if he has become mentally and physically dull, and if the clash between subjective consciousness and mental activity

has disappeared; for man is active only in so far as he has not attained his end and wills to develop his potentialities and vindicate himself in struggling to attain it. When this has been fully achieved, activity and vitality are at an end, and the result – loss of interest in life – is mental or physical death.

PR, §151ad.

Thus, for Hegel, Ethical Life is only truly *life* when its individual participants do not simply do their duty out of habit, but challenge and re-affirm (sublate) the customs and laws of their community and actively negate what is given, and appropriate it as their own. By this means, Ethical Life is subject to continual change and reinvention.

Ethical Life is actual, real. Its customs and duties, its social positions, classes and its various institutions are what is real, not abstractions from the real. Individuals, however, are the 'accidents' of this actuality. "Whether the individual exists or not is all one to the objective ethical order." Just as there are laws of nature which are given and intelligible, while the individual plants, mountains, rivers and whatever, have no such firmness, and are taken to be accidents, items of reality which could just as well have not been as been. The institutions and forms of Ethical Life are, according to Hegel even "more firmly established than the being of nature," but the individuals which make it up, like the various items we find in Nature, are mere accidents. The evolving institutions of Ethical Life, on the other hand, are *rational*, and the serial exposition of these relationships manifesting the Idea of Freedom, is the immanent 'science of duties'.

§2   The Family is the Unit of Ethical Life

In Chapter 15, I dealt with the appalling sexism and misogyny which saturates Hegel's treatment of the FAMILY. Rather than labouring this any further, I will outline Hegel's idea of the Family *minus* the distraction of his laughable ideas about women, so that what is meaningful in this section of the work can be registered as part of his whole concept of Ethical Life.

The Family is the *immediate* substantiality of the Ethical Idea, whereas Civil Society is the *appearance* and the State the *actuality* of the Ethical Idea.

The Family is characterised by *love* – I am in the family not as an independent person but as a *member*; I do not *wish* to be a self-subsistent and independent person but find myself in another person (my partner) and made objective to us in our children.

Although the family may originate in sexual love, in time this changes to self-conscious love, an ethical union on the level of Spirit. Although the family is formed by a (marriage) contract, it transcends the contractual relationship, in which the persons would be regarded in their individuality as self-subsistent units. Rather, the family becomes *one person* (i.e., a corporate personality), and the individuals its members, just as in Ethical Life as a whole, individuals are inessential to the whole but must play their part. The Family is thus the immediate ethical relationship, not a contractual relationship of reciprocity.

Hegel is insistent that "in accordance with the subjective principle of the modern world," however marriages may be arranged in different cultural traditions, the free consent of the couple must exist. The family bond relies on feeling, and this is a weakness of the institution. According to Hegel, this feeling needs to be supported by surrounding marriage with symbolism and ceremony validated by some public authority – it makes no difference whether this be the Church or a court – so as to make the bond as secure as possible. Marriage is 'in principle' indissoluble, which means that legislators should make it relatively difficult to terminate a marriage so that divorce is not done capriciously; but once the feeling is lost and the couple are alien to one another, then the family must dissolve and form new families.

The function of the Family in Ethical Life is the raising of children and the formation and distribution of the family capital.

The care and education of the children is the duty of all members of the family, so that the children may each become independent and self-sufficient individuals in their own right, fit to participate in civil society and the state. Restriction of the children ensures that children *urgently wish* to grow up and leave the family for their own place in civil society. But parents do not have absolute rights over their children, and every activity in the family must be directed towards their care and education. And parents do not have exclusive control over the children's education, as education of its members is one of the functions of civil society. The courts and other authorities of civil society have a right to intervene in the family should the right of the child to maintenance and education not be upheld in a family. Hegel also supported universal public education and opposed home schooling (though he earned a living as a youth as a home tutor!).

The family capital is not merely property, but something permanent which is a common possession of the family and maintained by the family to support productive labour and participation in civil society. Upon the dissolution of the family, with the children making their own way and the death of the parents, the family capital is distributed amongst the children. Hegel recognises a diversity of cultural traditions of inheritance, but he is most concerned that inheritance should be governed by some definite *rule* and not subject to the whims and favouritism of a deceased parent.

For Hegel, the Family means the nuclear family, a couple bound together by love for the maintenance and raising of children – a cyclical process which forms from diverse elements and then dissolves again into diverse new families. He regards clans and 'houses' as detrimental to modern ethical life and discounts their role in the family as a unit of civil society. He seems to take a different view, however, when it comes to the nobility, when he is insistent on primogeniture and 'family' in the clannish sense, necessary for the formation of a constitutional monarchy.

Hegel is acutely aware of the contradiction entailed in the institution of common property in a family taken as a single person. He allowed that 'prenuptial' contracts may facilitate the restoration of property to the individuals after the family dissolves. Clearly, in our times, when both parties are equal and independent participants in civil society and the state, this contradiction cannot be held off until the couple parts. This is not a problem which Hegel could resolve however, but it seems reasonable to say that the family is an institution in which independent persons participate as members (not as parties to a contract), without their personality being exhausted by their membership of the family. The members of a family are both members of a unity in the family *and* independent persons in civil society and the state. But this is a unity based on ethical feeling, not a *contract* between mutually independent individuals with reciprocal rights and duties – such relations belong to civil society. Were the family to be legitimised as a transactional relationship, then responsibility for the raising of children would fall to the State, which contradicts both the Idea of the Family and of Civil Society.

§3   Civil Society is the Self-governing World of Particular Interests

'Civil Society' – '*bürgerliche Gesellschaft*', literally 'bourgeois society' – covers a far wider field than the same term does today: basically, every aspect of life in the gap between the family and the state. If one reflects on the idea that modern society arose through the gradual separation of kinship relations and political relations during the mediaeval period – under the pressure of the growing dominance of trade, and the modern classes which grew up in the towns – then the importance of Civil Society in this sense becomes clear. Not only does Civil Society include the economy – agricultural, industrial and commercial, but the entire justice system and the various regulatory authorities, as well as the voluntary sector, and most importantly the 'Corporations' – which include the precursors of modern trade unions and professional associations, town councils, universities and companies, whose bonds derive from neither kinship nor the state, but are *voluntary*.

Hegel's vision of Civil Society retains elements of mediaeval life, in which civil society largely *governed itself* with only minimal interference from the state or even the nobility, whose interest in civil society was largely limited to creaming off a share of the surplus to support their own life style and foreign wars. Hegel lived at a time when the characteristic institutions of mediaeval civil society had already atrophied, so his assertion of their rationality and his railing against features of modernity such as the factory system, universal suffrage and deep penetration of the state into daily life, reflects neither 'castles in the sky' nor a rationalisation of the status quo. Rather, the rationality of these features of Ethical Life need to be assessed in view of their historical longevity, providing a critical counterpoint to burgeoning bourgeois modernity with all the social ills it brought with it. Hegel neither justified what existed nor welcomed what was coming. Elements of Germany's past provided concepts which he saw as rational responses to the growing inhumanity of modern capitalism.

Civil Society is a self-governing social formation. As Marx noted, however, there is a kind of dualism of functions in Hegel's vision of Civil Society and of the State, and this can be confusing for the reader. Civil Society does not *simply* govern itself, but rather the peak bodies which would constitute the self-government of civil society are met with an opposite number in the State. This dualism has historical precedent and remains a ubiquitous feature of reality to this day. For example, the universities have formed various bodies to manage the life of their sector, and these bodies confront a government department which regulates the university sector with laws, regulations and budgetary allocations. Hegel sees rationality in this dualism, which is in turn verified by its continued ubiquity. I will note the confusing duplicates when we come to them in the section on the State.

Civil Society is the domain of *particularity* as against the immediacy of the Family and the universality of the State, both of which it presupposes. It is characterised by reciprocity, difference, plurality, mutual interdependence and mediation. Every person pursues their own ends, but can gain satisfaction only by means of others, thus fostering a sense of universality, which restricts the play of particularity. Civil Society is the domain of the Understanding, in contrast to the State which is the domain of Reason.

For the Idea of Right to realise itself in a concrete universal, it must pass from immediacy in which division is suppressed, through the stage of division, and overcoming the contradictions so as to form a unity whose necessity is immanent and concrete. Civil Society is this phase of division, whose existence is essential to a mature and stable state formation.

In Civil Society, according to Hegel, needs and desires expand indefinitely, but conversely, so does want and destitution, along with the resultant inequality and discord. Only the state can bring harmony to this situation. Civil society cannot exist without the care and maintenance of individuals provided by the Family and the taming of conflict and extremes by the State. Education (*Bildung*) is therefore an important function of Civil Society, with the aim of bringing individuals to consciousness of the universal and thus liberation from the narrowness and particularity with which Civil Society is infected.

The moments of Civil Society are: (1) the SYSTEM OF NEEDS, i.e., the economy, up to and including the classes of Civil Society; (2) the ADMINISTRATION OF JUSTICE, including the legal system and the courts; and the (3) PUBLIC AUTHORITIES and CORPORATIONS, i.e., the public regulatory and self-regulatory bodies in civil society. The heart and life-blood of Civil Society is the economy, in Hegel's terms: the System of Needs.

§4   The System of Needs and Labour is the Essence of Ethical Life

Marx had begun with a critique of Hegel on the State, even going so far as to write a plan for a book on the state in November 1844, but the plan was never fulfilled. Instead, Marx devoted his life to a critique of Political Economy. Since it is widely agreed that Marx relied on Hegel's Logic in this critique, it is interesting to see what Hegel did with his own critique of Political Economy.

Hegel is full of praise for Political Economy which, he says, "finds laws for a mass of accidents" (*PR* §189ad.) and early on in his philosophical career, Hegel had seen Adam Smith's notion of an invisible hand as prefiguring his own concept of Spirit. Hegel's treatment of the economy shows many insights into tendencies immanent in capitalist development, but his analysis is markedly inferior to Marx's, and Hegel was not able to offer solutions to the serious problems he anticipated in economic development.

Hegel saw that the division of needs into separate parts, through the infinite elaboration of the division of labour, led to 'abstract needs', remote from any naturally-felt human need, and as a result, relations between individuals become more and more abstract. The system of needs and labour can be described as a process of real abstraction. But it is through the purchase of products of their labour that individuals receive recognition, and at the same time, individuals become more and more dependent on others, both materially and spiritually. Everything private becomes something social.

The demand for equality arises here out of incessant exchange and comparison, as does the need for a person to assert themselves as distinctive in some way. Hegel says that the market provides a form of liberation, but it is an *abstract* liberation. Meanwhile, "social conditions tend to multiply and subdivide needs, means, and enjoyments indefinitely ... – this is luxury. In this same process, however, dependence and want increase *ad infinitum*, and the material to meet these is permanently barred to the needy man because it consists of external objects with the special character of being property" (*PR* §195). Growing inequality, generated by the same process which generates the demand for economic equality, produces *Cynicism*. Although bourgeois society accentuates and generalises inequality, Hegel holds that the demand for equality is a "folly."

> Men are made unequal by nature, where inequality is in its element, and in civil society the right of particularity is so far from annulling this natural inequality that it produces it out of mind and raises it to an inequality of skill and resources, and even to one of moral and intellectual attainment. To oppose to this right a demand for equality is a folly of the Understanding which takes as real and rational its abstract equality and its 'ought-to-be'.
>
> *PR*, §200n.

Hegel was fully cognisant of the growing contradictions generated by the market, but whereas Marx was able to reveal the roots of these contradictions in the commodity form of value, Hegel stopped short of analysing the contradiction which his own analysis exposed.

Hegel had already derived the concept of 'value' under Property (see §16.1 above), and specifically under Use, so that value was taken naively as a measure of the usefulness of a commodity. Although the value of a product is conditional upon the capacity to exchange it, value is not determined in Exchange. Similarly in this section, Hegel says (*PR* §196) that it is Labour which confers value on products of Nature and that "it is products of human effort which man consumes," so value is conditional upon the object being a product of Labour. But he still sees the measure of value as determined solely by utility. Hegel recognised the system of Needs and Labour as a process of real abstraction and real measure, but he did not deploy what he developed in this part of his Logic to reveal the dynamics of bourgeois society. This Marx did.

Hegel is fully cognisant of the expanding and revolutionary effect of the market economy (essentially the bourgeois labour process) on the State and social life as a whole, but he accepted the creed of the Political Economists that in the market "self-seeking turns into a contribution to the satisfaction of the needs of others" (*PR* §199). Participation in Civil Society develops the habit of work and fosters an infinite range of skills, and a growing understanding of 'how the world works'. But the division of labour makes the labour of each individual less and less complex and makes people more and more dependent on one another:

> the abstraction of one man's production from another's makes labour more and more mechanical, until finally man is able to step aside and install machines in his place.
>
> *PR*, §198

In Hegel's ideal bourgeois society, every family is able accumulate capital to support a family enterprise. Unfortunately, the dynamic of capitalist development shows no evidence to support such an ideal. Do the measures Hegel advocates for the self-regulation of Civil Society and by the State hold out the possibility of realising this line of development? Hegel himself does not seem to believe this is likely.

§5   Hegel Debunks Successive Solutions to the Capitalist Crisis

Following the sections on the Courts and Public Authorities, Hegel meditates on the possibilities open to moderate the destructive historical tendencies of the market.

Charity is too dependent on contingency and private inclinations, and society should struggle to make charity unnecessary by "discovering the general causes of penury and the general means of its relief, and by organising relief accordingly" (*PR* §242). Hegel advocated for a *guaranteed social minimum income*, but he points out that it is not poverty itself, but

> there is born in the rabble the evil of lacking self-respect enough to secure subsistence *by its own labour* and yet at the same time of claiming to receive subsistence as its right. Against nature man can claim no right, but once society is established, poverty immediately takes the form of a wrong done to one class by another. The important question of how poverty is to be abolished is one of the most disturbing problems which agitate modern society.
>
> *PR*, §244ad., emphasis added

So transfer payments cannot alleviate the evil of growing inequality arising from the lack of work, and especially fulfilling and meaningful work, given the concentration of capital, increased labour productivity, and the growth of the factory system. Whether relief is provided by the State or by wealthy philanthropists "this would violate the principle of civil society and the feeling of individual independence and self-respect in its individual members." Alternatively, the state could create jobs for the unemployed, but "evil consists precisely in an excess of production and in the lack of a proportionate number of consumers who are themselves also producers, and thus it is simply intensified" (*PR* §245). So job creation is no solution either.

The only remaining solution is the founding of colonies to which the impoverished rabble can go to "return to life on the family basis in a new land" (*PR* §248), whether by state-organised colonisation or by the private initiative of individual families. Thus:

> This inner dialectic of civil society thus drives it ... to *push beyond its own limits* and seek markets, and so its necessary means of subsistence, in other lands ...
>
> *PR*, §246, emphasis added

This solution is ultimately self-defeating and offers only temporary relief before finding itself in even deeper crises as possibilities for colonisation are exhausted.

§6   The Classes of Civil Society: the Rich 'Lead' the Poor

Hegel's notion of class can be confusing, coming to it from our times when wealth is usually taken as being the main determinant of class. Hegel sees that at the same time as market economy fragments people, it also sorts people into classes according to the type of work done and its location within the whole economy. The classes are therefore: (a) The AGRICULTURAL CLASS, (b) the BUSINESS CLASS and (c) the CIVIL SERVANTS. Hegel sees these as forming a syllogism as respectively the immediate, reflecting and universal classes. The nature of the work activity of a class binds individuals together in common endeavours in which they come to share important attitudes and develop virtues characteristic of their class, notwithstanding intra-class antagonisms and differences in wealth and power.

The remarkable thing about this view is that the rich and powerful in each sector of the economy are lumped together with their underlings in the same class. This is clearly a different concept of class, but we should not be too quick to dismiss it. In Hegel's times, even to a great extent in Britain where class differentiation was more advanced than in Germany at the time, class consciousness had not differentiated along rich vs poor lines in the way it would as the nineteenth century went on. Of course, there have always been resentment and antipathy between rich and poor, between masters and servants, but in the practicalities of life and the real patterns of interaction with the whole community, Hegel's idea of class reflected a reality. Apprentices and journeymen (belonging to the 'business class') aspired to become masters and many would. Peasants aspired to own more land, hire wage workers and become rich landowners. In other words, class is largely 'aspirational'. There was always an underclass of navvies and vagrants, but even these would aspire to gain employment and recognition in one or other of the classes. In Britain, in Hegel's day, Whigs and Tories fought over the Corn Laws, with workers and peasants respectively supporting 'their own side'. The process of modernisation of industry and the concentration of capital ensured that the classes Hegel theorised would fade in social and political significance over time. In Hegel's day, there was no workers' movement, and Hegel did not foresee its emergence. What he saw was that in each branch and sub-branch of the economy individuals found a voice through their most 'prominent' figures. The rich and successful represented and *led* the marginal and less well-off.

Even today, one cannot fail to notice that the rural population votes overwhelmingly for conservative parties generally led by men from the upper crust of rural society. Political maps invariably manifest strong geographical differentiation reflecting older notions of class. Whichever way class lines configure themselves, it is through class conflict that class consciousness is developed and people become conscious of universal questions, beyond their mundane experience. Consequently:

> The family is the first precondition of the state, but class divisions are the second.
> *PR*, §201ad.

§7   The Public Authorities are Part of Civil Society, not the State

The Administration of Justice in Civil Society
The task of actualising Abstract Right falls to the justice system which applies the law to the reality of Civil Society, publicises these laws and enforces them.

At the time Hegel was writing, the states of the German Confederation each had inherited legal codes, but the situation was a mess; it was frequently the case that neither the public nor the courts knew what was legal and what was not legal.

Hegel claimed that it was urgent that existing laws be drawn into a proper legal code in which the principles of jurisprudence were clearly expressed in determinant laws expressing universal principles and applying them to particular cases. This is a task for the courts not for legislators. "In the course of applying the laws, clashes occur, and in dealing with these the judge's intelligence has its proper scope" (*PR* §211ad.). There will inevitably be discrepancy between the principles of Right and the content of actual laws, which nonetheless have obligatory force. But it is the responsibility of the courts to continuously review the laws in the light of the endlessly growing complexity of civil society, giving determinant form to legal principles. The State also provides further material through legislation to be incorporated in the development of the body of law.

As part of the actualisation of Right, Hegel is insistent that the laws be written down, expressed in accessible language, published and explained to the public and that all legal proceedings be open to the public. He required consistency in sentencing and favoured the use of the jury system to secure the sense that justice is being done when people are brought before the courts.

Hegel claimed that it makes no difference how the judges (who are taken to be the key figures in the justice system) are appointed (*PR* §219n.), because the *concept* of justice is the same whether the judge is elected, nominated from above or whatever. Hegel seems confident that the *concept* of a role or institution is the determining factor in their performance as against the mundane motivations such as individuals' social origins, remuneration, methods of advancement and so on. Hegel never specifies how the Courts or Public Authorities are to be appointed or controlled. Indeed, he recognises that this will vary from country to country according to cultural traditions; inevitably it will be 'messy' and complex, like everything in Civil Society; he does not try to lay down a blueprint for these processes, but limits himself to formulating the concepts which determine their role in the State.

Nowadays, we are too materialist to believe in such an idealist procedure; we take an intense interest in how officials are selected and appointed, how their performance is monitored, rewarded and controlled – in public roles even more than in business. But the historical trajectory of institutions tends to support Hegel's idealist view – the Law evolves rationally notwithstanding the privileged social origins of judges, and Science advances notwithstanding social pressures towards conformity and the various problematic mechanisms for academic assessment and peer review.

Perhaps the best stance here is that if we accept the concept of justice which Hegel elaborated and address the question of how a concept of justice could be realised in Civil Society which would be appropriate for *our* times. Nowadays, the administration of justice is not a function of Civil Society at all, but rather an arm of the State. Still, in the US for example, judges and police chiefs are elected locally and in many countries, regional governments make laws. What marks Hegel's concept of the administration of justice is that it is *endogenous to Civil Society*. History has demonstrated however, I think, that oppressive forms of power are entrenched in Civil Society and it is usually the State which has to intervene to protect emergent rights, such as freedom from racial discrimination. But sometimes the reverse happens, and the State intervenes to suppress local initiatives which are progressive.

The principles for which the courts are responsible are those elaborated in the first part of the work: Abstract Right. The Public Authorities and Corporations, on the other hand, have responsibilities which go beyond the maintenance of law and order.

The Public Authorities: Self-regulation of Civil Society

The Public Authorities are responsible for the *positive welfare* of all individuals in Civil Society, whatever their circumstances. Such responsibilities encompass regulation of food and the relevant inspections, fixing of prices, management of innovation of all kinds, ensuring that appropriate medical, public health and education services are provided whether or not from the public purse, intervening in favour of children where families fail in their responsibilities, assisting disabled people in whatever way possible, ensuring public safety and transport infrastructure, etc., etc.

As with the Courts, Hegel does not specify how the Public Authorities are to be constituted which would be peculiar to each country according to their own historical development, but the concept is the same:

> the right actually present in the particular requires, first, that accidental hindrances to one aim or another be removed, and undisturbed safety of person and property be attained; and secondly, that the securing of every single person's livelihood and welfare be treated and actualised as a right, i.e. that particular welfare as such be so treated.
>
> *PR*, §230

and

> If man is to be a member of civil society ... he has rights and claims against it just as he had rights and claims in the family. Civil society must

protect its members and defend their rights, while its rights impose duties on every one of its members.

PR, §238ad.

In our own times, it is the town and municipal councils which most closely
resemble Hegel's "Public Authorities," though generally with a far more limited
scope of responsibilities than what Hegel imagined. The scope of Welfare State
is closer to that of Hegel's Public Authorities; it was the intervention of the
workers' movement in the development of bourgeois society which pushed
the responsibility for the provision of welfare services to the state rather than
Civil Society organisations. I think the reasons for this are the same as the issues raised in connection with the Administration of Justice, viz., that only the
State provides the commanding position from which oppressed groups (such
as the proletariat) can counter the entrenched power of the established groups
in Civil Society; but the converse is also true inasmuch as the State intervenes
in instances where the workers' movement has established strong social positions. The economy of scale in our times seems to mandate that welfare be
organised at a national or at least regional level, but this is at the expense of
the spiritual benefits of mutualism. But Hegel's conception of Civil Society as
a self-governing community, distinct from the State remains, irrespective of
issues of scale.

As noted above, Hegel concludes the section on the Public Authorities with
reflections on the crisis tendencies of capitalism which pose the Public Authorities with insurmountable contradictions. The last section before moving
on to the State is the Corporations, which are taken under Public Authorities,
but they are not Public Authorities and deserve separate consideration.

§8   The Corporations

The Corporations, as Hegel sees them, arise in the 'business class', archetypically the artisan and merchant guilds, pursuing the particular self-interest of
sections of this class "no wider in scope than the purpose involved in business."
Hegel sees the Corporations, like the guilds, uniting employees and employers, but excluding day labourers and those with a casual interest in the trade.
They act like a 'second family' for their members, concerned with the whole
range of members' welfare. Through membership of the Corporation, families
are secured a 'recognised' place in urban society, just as the extended Family
and the Civil Service provide for the members of the agricultural and universal
classes respectively.

However, as was the case in mediaeval times, the Corporations operate "under the surveillance of the Public Authority." (*PR* §251).

> As the family was the first, so the Corporation is the second ethical root of the state, the one planted in civil society. ... the two fixed points round which the unorganised atoms of civil society revolve.
>
> *PR*, §255

The contradiction between the universal character of the Public Authorities for which controller and controlled relate only externally to one another, and the restricted and particular aims of the Corporation can be resolved only by the State.

Historically, the Corporations grew during the mediaeval period. Oxford and Cambridge Universities, the East India Company, the city governments in the Hanseatic League of 15th century Germany, and the colonial governments in New England were all generically artisanal Guilds. But by the 19th century, the Guilds had become marginalised by the growth of trade, unceasing technical innovation and the intrusion of the State. But also, the growth of class divisions on one side and the irresistible tendency of the leadership of the Guilds to harden into self-perpetuating cliques meant that participation of the working class in the Guilds gave way to the formation of trade unions and other specifically working class mutualist organisations. Hegel's observation that the Guilds had been 'abolished' in Britain is thus not quite accurate: they were dying. The great strike of 1825 demonstrated that the spirit of the Guilds still lived in the working class, but had turned against bourgeois rule.

It seems that the idea of a State which rests upon particularist organisations on one side and the public administration of justice on the other has some merit, though in point of detail it seems to have been overtaken by social change.

The reader should read Hegel on Ethical Life now.

The State

§1   The State is the March of God on Earth

The State is the crowning concept of *The Philosophy of Right*, the realisation of Freedom and the basic unit of World History, with supreme Right as against the individual.

> The state is the actuality of the ethical Idea. It is ethical mind ... knowing and thinking itself, accomplishing what it knows .... The state exists immediately in custom, mediately in individual self-consciousness, knowledge, and activity, while self-consciousness ... finds in the state, as its essence and the end-product of its activity, its substantive freedom.
>
> *PR*, §257

and:

> The state is absolutely rational inasmuch as it is the actuality of the substantial [and] ... has supreme right against the individual, whose supreme duty is to be a member of the state.
>
> *PR*, §258

and:

> The march of God in the world, that is what the state is.
>
> *PR*, §258ad.

but:

> The state is no ideal work of art; it stands on earth and so in the sphere of caprice, chance, and error, and bad behaviour may disfigure it in many respects. But the ugliest of men, or a criminal, or an invalid, or a cripple, is still always a living man.
>
> *PR*, §258ad.

It is very likely that the modern reader will have difficulty in swallowing this. Recall though, that Hegel's Germany was not the Germany of Bismarck, Hitler or Merkel, but more like the Vietnam of Ho Chi Minh with Kant and Beethoven thrown in. The "State as the realisation of Freedom" has to be seen in this light.

But the real gap between a progressive modern attitude to the State and Hegel's is that Hegel in no way saw the State as "an organ of class rule, an organ for the oppression of one class by another" (Lenin, 1917), as Marx and Engels (1848, 1884) and many readers of this book would see it.

State as Moderator of Class Struggle

Insofar as the State was used as a weapon of a feudal nobility against the bourgeoisie (which was still the main axis of class struggle in Hegel's day), Hegel would have seen this as either a deformation of the state or a symptom of a state which was still not worthy of the name of 'State' at all. Suppression of riots, crime and other disorders was a function of Civil Society, not the State – issues which Hegel would have seen in the frame of 'social problems', not political challenges.

We have recalled how Hegel insists that the historical origins of the State are "no concern of the Idea of the State," that the State may have originated in violence, but its *raison d'être* and concept was Freedom. Along the same lines, he notes that "Town and country constitute the two moments, still ideal moments, whose true ground is the state, although it is from them that the state springs" (*PR* §256n.) and "The family is the first precondition of the state, but class divisions are the second" (*PR* §201ad.). This implies that the State arises as a solution for the class struggle between the agricultural class, i.e., the nobility, and the business class, i.e., the bourgeoisie. But the point is that this phase of the State is to be transcended, and the essential meaning of the State is *unity*, specifically, the unity of the single individual and the universal. This is the meaning of: "the family was the first, so the Corporation is the second ethical root of the state" (*PR* §255). It is self-evident that class conflict and atomisation ("the civil life of business ... turns in upon itself, and pursues its atomising task" *PR* §256n.) which is a result of the market must be overcome, before the unity of the universal and individual can be attained. But Hegel is insistent that it is not the role of the State to moderate the conflict between members of Civil Society – that is a task of Civil Society itself:

> If the state is confused with civil society, and if its specific end is laid down as the security and protection of property and personal freedom, then the interest of the individuals as such becomes the ultimate end of their association, and it follows that membership of the state is something optional. But the state's relation to the individual is quite different from this. Since the state is mind objectified, it is only as one of its members

that the individual himself has objectivity, genuine individuality, and an ethical life. Unification pure and simple is the true content and aim of the individual, and the individual's destiny is the living of a universal life.
    PR, §258n.

The State is meant to rest only lightly upon Civil Society, the embodiment of the universal self-consciousness of its citizens, the realisation of their Free Will, both in oversight of national affairs and in their action on the world stage.

Internal and External Relations

The State acts as an Individual in relation to other states. Hegel allows that there can be alliances and treaties, but he absolutely rejects the idea of a World Government or any supra-national entity that has authority over a State. Every State has the right to make War, and the idea of a "perpetual peace" which Kant had proposed, was anathema to Hegel. In relation to internal matters, Hegel was a collectivist; in relation to external relations, Hegel was a libertarian. "The one and only absolute judge, which makes itself authoritative against the particular and at all times, is the in- and for-itself existing Spirit (*an und für sich seiende Geist*) which manifests itself in the history of the world" (*PR* §259n.).

But the State is not an absolute power.

The State has no business meddling in religious matters. This separation of spheres also goes to Science, Art and Philosophy. Hegel counts all these pursuits as 'higher' than Right inasmuch as they are components of Absolute Spirit, which transcends Objective Spirit. The State has no business in restricting or directing the practice of Science or Art. The question of allocating funds for public pursuit of Science or Art had simply never arisen in Hegel's times, but while the practice of these "modes of existence" were undoubtedly essential to humanity, it was equally essential that they flourished independently of civil and political life. (See *PR* §270 and its remarks and footnotes).

Conversely, Hegel is at pains to point out that the clergy has no place in affairs of State, and he likens the idea of "the unity of church and state" to "oriental despotism." Churches are landowners and employers like any other actor in civil society and is subject to the same laws, and Hegel subsumes them under Corporations. He also describes exclusion of Jews from civil rights as "folly." The conclusion is clear: religious practice has no privileged place in political life.

The separation of powers is an essential principle in Hegel's concept of the State. The State is an autonomous *organism* and its various 'powers' are 'Moments' or organs in just the sense that the various organs of the body: each organ exclusively performs its specific function for maintenance of the whole organism. The unity of the whole is true irrespective of the fact that historically the components of the whole may have originated independently. In becoming organs of the State they are transformed:

> The state is an organism, i.e. the development of the Idea to the articulation of its differences. Thus these different sides of the state are its various powers with their functions and spheres of action, by means of which the universal continually engenders itself in a necessary way; in this process it maintains its identity since it is presupposed even in its own production. This organism is the constitution of the state; it is produced perpetually by the state, while it is through it that the state maintains itself. If the state and its constitution fall apart, if the various members of the organism free themselves, then the unity produced by the constitution is no longer an accomplished fact.
>
> *PR*, §269ad.

The internal and external powers of the State are united only in the Crown, and the first division of powers is that between the civil and military powers. Conflicts within Civil Society are the business of Civil Society and the military have no role there at all.

The other powers of the State are the components of the State's Constitution: the Crown, the Executive and the Legislature. Note that the judiciary is *not* included here as a 'power of the State' because the judiciary is not part of this sphere – it belongs to Civil Society. Hegel never foresaw the possibility of the intervention of the Courts in conflicts between the powers of the State, which he saw as being resolved by negotiation.

Marxists have rejected the notion of separation of powers ever since Marx (1871) noted that the Paris Commune was "a working, not a parliamentary body, executive and legislative at the same time." Personally, I don't think this has worked out all that well, and it is worth re-assessing the doctrine of separation of powers in the light of Hegel's argument.

§2   The Crown

Hegel's idea of the State was a constitutional monarchy. The Prussia of his time was an *absolute* monarchy and all progressive people in Germany aspired to a *constitutional* monarchy, not a Republic such as existed in the United States.

Among EU nations today, Belgium, Denmark, the Netherlands, Spain, Sweden and Britain are constitutional monarchies and are hardly less perfect realisations of Freedom than Portugal, Bulgaria, Croatia, the Czech Republic, Finland, France, Germany, Greece, Hungary, Ireland, Italy, Poland and Portugal which are republics. While the idea of socialism is patently incompatible with constitutional monarchy, it needs to be understood that (at least as Hegel saw it), a constitutional monarchy is the more perfect insofar as the monarch has *no political function* beyond placing his or her signature on legislation and participating in ceremonies of various kinds. Hegel's model, as outlined in *The Philosophy of Right*, has not quite reached that point, but it is clear enough that this is the *concept* of constitutional monarchy. Hegel's monarch remained Commander in Chief of the armed forces, but again, the concept of constitutional monarchy is that even this role is entirely *symbolic*. Symbolism is something real, and in the matter of achieving the unity of the individual and the universal, it is of the utmost importance. It is of course precisely the symbolism that makes constitutional monarchy so repulsive to the socialist or otherwise radical social movement activist. This needs to be kept in mind in reading what Hegel has to say about the Crown.

Constitutional Monarchy and the Personification of the State

In Hegel's conception, the State is divided into three powers: the LEGISLATURE, which determines the Universal by making laws, the EXECUTIVE, which determines Particular cases under the Universal, and the CROWN – "the will with the power of ultimate decision ... the different powers bound into an Individual unity" (*PR* §273). The State thus reproduces the structure of the concept derived in the Logic, as the unity of Universal, Particular and Individual.

In relation to the Crown, there are two important issues: (1) Why the Crown must be an individual, not a committee or indeed an empty space, and (2) Why the Crown must be chosen by primogeniture from a noble family.

(1) I am not aware of any state – monarchy or republic, or even any organisation, which does not have a Head who is an individual, differing mainly by whether that individual normally plays a symbolic role or is a real ruler and commander-in-chief or somewhere in between. The only exceptions to this rule that I know of are protests and social movements which through immaturity, incapacity or as an ideological signal, refuse this individual moment of their self-concept.

Hegel explains why a State must have an Individual Head.

> this freedom which makes the ultimate self-determining certitude – the culmination of the concept of the will – the function of a single consciousness. This ultimate self-determination, however, can fall within

the sphere of human freedom only in so far as it has the position of a
pinnacle, explicitly distinct from, and raised above, all that is particular
and conditional ...

PR, §279n.

[This] is not to say that the monarch may act capriciously. As a matter
of fact, he is bound by the concrete decisions of his counsellors, and
if the constitution is stable, he has often no more to do than sign his
name.

PR, §279ad.

To be free, the State of which you are a member must be free, free to make decisions which are unquestionable and subject to no committee or such which
would thereby usurp that decision. Even the Houses of the Legislature each
have a Speaker who conveys messages to and from the Legislature. The Quak-
ers make do with a Clerk and many voluntary organisation have a President or
Secretary who merely formally conveys decisions, etc., but is not the *pinnacle*.
But Hegel insists that this role of being the actual subject is seen as the pinnacle, since the monarch must unite not only a deliberative committee, but an
entire nation.

The personality of the State is actual and the unity of the State secured only
when it is a *natural person*. Absolute monarchies, from which constitutional
monarchies originate, had this power of personality, but these States were subject to the whims and caprice of the monarch. But in the *mature*, stable State,
the processes of decision-making have developed to such an extent that all
necessary and possible deliberation has already taken place when the document is ready for signing – at least in normal, stable times. In exceptional times
or times of crisis, the necessity of a natural person with the authority of the
State is crucial. In such times the only rational decision procedure is for a natural person with the highest possible standing and the best possible advice to
make their decision. Hegel rejects all ideas of an 'artificial person' to take the
place of the monarch (*PR* §279n.). The only guarantee is a Head of State whose
own development is tied up with the development of the nation itself and is
symbolically identified with the whole nation.

Have you ever asked yourself what form the "withering away of the state"
(Lenin 1917) could take? Does it not mean precisely the withering away of commanding or executive functions to merely symbolic or ceremonial ones? and
not necessarily their actual *abolition*.

This brings us to (2) – why Hegel thinks that a monarch self-selected by
primogeniture from the same noble family is the only rational determination
of Head of State.

Hegel believes that a person representing the traditional owners of the
land best fulfils the symbolic role of the Crown. That this person is wealthy
and privileged and lives in a mansion is incidental; in Australia, it would
be the senior Elder of the Ngunnawal people who would play that role. It
is the deep identification with the land where the government sits which is
important.

In principle, the monarch has no particular interest or talent:

> In a completely organised state, it is only a question of the culminat-
> ing point of formal decision (and a natural bulwark against passion. It
> is wrong therefore to demand objective qualities in a monarch); he has
> only to say 'yes' and dot the 'i', because the throne should be such that the
> significant thing in its holder is not his particular make-up. ... Monarchy
> must be inherently stable and whatever else the monarch may have in
> addition to this power of final decision is part and parcel of his private
> character and should be of no consequence.
>
> *PR*, §280ad.

It is very important that nothing particular is required of the monarch and
consequently that the monarch is selected by an 'automatic' process which is
immune to particular interests, etc. Primogeniture, which forbids the monarch
from choosing his or her own successor, is therefore the ideal means of determining the holder of the Crown:

> that the unity of the state is saved from the risk of being drawn down into
> the sphere of particularity and its caprices, ends, and opinions, and saved
> too from the war of factions round the throne and from the enfeeblement
> and overthrow of the power of the state.
>
> *PR*, §281ad.

And according to Hegel: "elective monarchy is the worst of institutions"
(*PR* §281n.) because it guarantees the primacy of particularity and 'drags down'
the monarchy into 'factions and opinions'.

The 1999 Australia Republic referendum debate manifested the popular
prejudice that the Head of State must not be a 'politician' (and Hegel would
agree) but at the same time there was a fervent desire that the Head of State
must be *elected* by the 'people' and not the Parliament. This is of course a confused notion. As to the notion of 'the people', Hegel says:

> ... on the wild idea of the 'people'. Taken without its monarch and the ar-
> ticulation of the whole which is the indispensable and direct concomitant

of monarchy, the people is a formless mass and no longer a state. It lacks every one of those determinate characteristics – sovereignty, government, judges, magistrates, class-divisions, &c., – which are to be found only in a whole which is inwardly organised.

PR, §279n.

Nonetheless, it is Hegel's idea that the Crown, as a natural person, can establish a direct relation to the people, a role which is inaccessible to the Executive and Legislature or *any* committee.

It is almost self-evident that a Constitutional Monarchy is unsuited to the kind of State to which readers of this book would aspire, but we should not be too quick to dismiss the arguments by means of which Hegel has rationalised this institution.

§3   The Executive, the Civil Service and the Public Authorities

Hegel mentions a "supreme council" which the Monarch appoints as his Counsellors. It is not entirely clear, but I think the concept intended is a Cabinet appointed on merit by the Crown, from the senior members of the Executive. This differs from the Westminster model in which the Cabinet is recommended to the Head of State by and from the Legislature, and is closer to the U.S. model, except that the Crown is not the Chief Executive like the US President, but plays a mainly ceremonial role.

The Executive is the Senior Civil Service, a self-appointed meritocracy open to individuals according to their talents and education – "every citizen the chance of joining the class of civil servants" (*PR* §291). The Executive is responsible for interpreting and administrating the law determined by the Legislature. But the Executive and its lower ranks in the Civil Service 'oversee' the real work which is done *within* Civil Society by the Public Authorities and the Courts.

This apparent *duplication* of functions between the State and Civil Society has deep roots in mediaeval society, in which agents of the King (*thegns* in old England) supervised Courts distributed around the land. Positions in the Corporations and Public Authorities would be "a mixture of popular election by those interested with appointment and ratification by higher authority" (*PR* §288). In mediaeval times, this entailed a continuous struggle over control of these Civil Society organisations, but the concept of Constitutional Monarchy suggests that the force of appointment from above wanes as the stability and cultural level of Civil Society and the State matures, though in reality, this has not transpired.

The people working in the Executive branch of the State and in the Courts and Public Authorities are members of the 'universal class' – the class of civil servants, and Hegel, perhaps naïvely, presumes that the character and motivation of these individuals will be shaped by their commitment to the universal interest.

§4   The Legislature, the Estates and the Classes of Civil Society

Exactly how the Houses of the Legislature and the Estates are to be structured and operate is left open by Hegel and is somewhat unclear. All we have to go on is the real models that were available in the Europe of his times and earlier.

The Estates were a political institution of mediaeval times which survived into the 19th century. The constitution of the Estates varied from country to country and century to century, but mostly there were three: the nobility (which was initially the only Estate, but was referred to in the plural in reference to the various fiefdoms of the nobility), the bourgeoisie (generally organised via the Corporations) and the clergy, with its own hierarchies. In Hegel's case, the clergy are excluded, so there are just two Estates. The civil servants were not included in the Estates and there was no precedent for the civil service being treated as an Estate.

The Estates differ from the classes of Civil Society because the Estates are *political* entities, generally convened periodically to deliberate on political issues and appoint representatives to the Legislature or to petition the King. The classes however are not formal organisations at all but are constituents and products of the System of Needs and Labour, reproduced by the Family. The Estates appear to be a duplication of the Classes of Civil Society (indeed, Hegel has the same word, *Stände*), but this is not really the case – the Estates are the projection of the civil classes on to political life.

Hegel never spells out the relation of the Estates to the Houses or the gives us any hint as to how the Legislature should operate or how the two Houses interact with each other. It seems though that each House elected representatives to one of the Houses (much as the House of Lords and House of Commons operated in Britain), each of the Houses determined laws by their own processes and then came to a three-way consensus with the Executive, to produce an Act for the Crown's signature. Hegel is at pains to avoid a situation where the Legislature could come into direct conflict with the Executive, and dividing the Legislature into two Houses seems to be a device to secure this.

§5   The Young Marx vs. Hegel on the State

In the Spring of 1843, the young Karl Marx made critical notes on the section of Hegel's *Philosophy of Right* on the State (although he references earlier sections in the course of his commentary), abandoning the work in disgust at §313, which is about where we have got to in this commentary just now.

At this point in his life, Marx read Hegel as a Feuerbachian – that is, criticising Hegel for inverting the subject-predicate relationship, and most of his commentary is rather tiresome ridicule of Hegel's idealistic forms of argument and expression. Marx regarded almost everything Hegel said as a rationalisation of the status quo. Most of the substantive criticisms he made have been at least mentioned here, but some were more significant than others. Criticisms worth making particular note of are as follows:

Marx observes how in Hegel's scheme, the State reinforces already existing hierarchy and privilege in civil society and further that there is a 'civil society' within the civil service:

> The *corporations* are the materialism of the bureaucracy, and the bureaucracy is the *spiritualism* of the corporations. The corporation is the bureaucracy of civil society, and the bureaucracy is the corporation of the state. In actuality, the bureaucracy as civil society of the state is opposed to the state of civil society, the corporations. Where the bureaucracy is to become a new principle, where the universal interest of the state begins to become explicitly a singular and thereby a real interest, it struggles against the corporations as every consequence struggles against the existence of its premises. On the other hand once the real life of the state awakens and civil society frees itself from the corporations out of its inherent rational impulse, the bureaucracy seeks to restore them; for as soon as the state of civil society falls so too does the civil society of the state.
>
> MARX, 1843, p. 45

This passage is followed by an extended criticism of bureaucratism and hierarchy, upon which Hegel relies for the rationality of the State – the civil servant "is like a hammer *vis-à-vis* those below, he is like an anvil in relation to those above" (p. 53). And the civil servant's "office is indeed his substantial situation and his bread and butter. Fine, except that Hegel sets direct education in thought and ethical conduct against the mechanism of bureaucratic knowledge and work! The man within the civil servant is supposed to secure the civil servant against himself" (p. 53).

Marx criticises the mediating role Hegel gives to the Estates:

> The Estates preserve the state from the unorganised aggregate only through the disorganisation of this very aggregate.
>
> At the same time, however, the mediation of the Estates is to prevent the isolation of the particular interests of persons, societies and corporations. This they achieve, first, by coming to an understanding with the interest of the state and, second, by being themselves the political isolation of these particular interests, this isolation as political act, in that through them these isolated interests achieve the rank of the universal.
>
> Finally, the Estates are to mediate against the isolation of the power of the crown as an extreme (which otherwise might seem a mere arbitrary tyranny). This is correct in so far as the principle of the power of the crown (arbitrary will) is limited by means of the Estates, at least can operate only in fetters, and in so far as the Estates themselves become a partaker and accessory of the power of the crown. (p. 68)

Marx claims that this arrangement is aimed at *preventing* the people from forming an organised will, rather than at giving the people a means of *expressing* that will.

Marx rejects with contempt Hegel's 'deduction' of primogeniture and monarchy:

> Hegel has accomplished the masterpiece: he has developed peerage by birthright, wealth by inheritance, etc. etc., this support of the throne and society, on top of the absolute Idea. (p. 74)

and further rejects Hegel's dismissal of a 'representative constitution', i.e., universal suffrage. In considering the complex mediations Hegel creates between the various civil powers, Marx comments in exasperation:

> The sovereign, then, had to be the middle term in the legislature between the executive and the Estates; but, of course, the executive is the middle term between him and the Estates, and the Estates between him and civil society. How is he to mediate between what he himself needs as a mean lest his own existence become a one-sided extreme? Now the complete absurdity of these extremes, which interchangeably play now the part of the extreme and now the part of the mean, becomes apparent. They are like Janus with two-faced heads, which now show themselves from the front and now from the back, with a diverse character at either side.

What was first intended to be the mean between two extremes now itself occurs as an extreme; and the other of the two extremes, which had just been mediated by it, now intervenes as an extreme (because of its *distinction* from the other extreme) between its extreme and its mean. This is a kind of mutual reconciliation society. It is as if a man stepped between two opponents, only to have one of them immediately step between the mediator and the other opponent. It is like the story of the man and wife who quarrelled and the doctor who wished to mediate between them, whereupon the wife soon had to step between the doctor and her husband, and then the husband between his wife and the doctor. (p. 87)

In the course of a long diatribe against Hegel's obsession with mediation, Marx says:

Actual extremes cannot be mediated with each other precisely because they are actual extremes. But neither are they in need of mediation, because they are opposed in essence. They have nothing in common with one another; they neither need nor complement one another. The one does not carry in its womb the yearning, the need, the anticipation of the other. (p. 88)

Hegel and Marx on Universal Suffrage
Hegel argues consistently for highly mediated forms of representation and against universal suffrage. Marx responds by pointing out:

The question whether all as individuals should share in deliberating and deciding on political matters of general concern is a question that arises from the separation of the political state and civil society. (p. 118)

and

It is not a question of whether civil society should exercise legislative power through deputies or through all as individuals. Rather, it is a question of the extension and greatest possible universalisation of voting, of active as well as passive suffrage. This is the real point of dispute in the matter of political reform, in France as well as in England.

Marx does not proffer solutions to this problem, but makes an extended criticism of Hegel which brings out the contradictions entailed in his construction of representative politics.

Without meeting the problems raised by Marx, Hegel makes a powerful argument against universal suffrage.

> As for popular suffrage, it may be further remarked that especially in large states it leads inevitably to electoral indifference, since the casting of a single vote is of no significance where there is a multitude of electors. Even if a voting qualification is highly valued and esteemed by those who are entitled to it, they still do not enter the polling booth. Thus the result

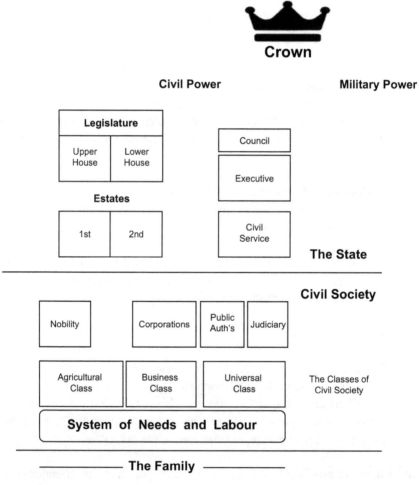

FIGURE 5   The structure of the state

of an institution of this kind is more likely to be the opposite of what was intended; election actually falls into the power of a few, of a caucus, and so of the particular and contingent interest which is precisely what was to have been neutralised.

PR, §311n.

According to Hegel, the deputies in the Legislature have to do with the various *branches* of society, and the electorate must not be seen an agglomeration of atoms (*PR* §311). Deputies should represent the various real *groups* in society and give them equal weight (Fig. 5). Universal suffrage on the contrary requires every individual to cast their vote privately, as an isolated atom.

Hegel believes that the public must be educated in national affairs, and he sees the assemblies of the Estates as the means of achieving this, while political discussion "at his fireside with his wife and his friends" can never go beyond "building castles in the sky." Participation in assemblies is essential for political education, and this can only be achieved in the bodies mediating between the associations of civil society and the Legislature.

'Public opinion' is the name given to "individuals ... in their having and expressing their own private judgments, opinions, and recommendations on affairs of state" (*PR* §316). Public opinion is therefore "a repository of genuine needs and correct tendencies of common life" but "infected by all the accidents of opinion, by its ignorance and perversity, by its mistakes and falsity of judgment," and Hegel quotes Goethe:

> the masses are respectable hands at fighting, but miserable hands at judging.

The remainder of *The Philosophy of Right* covers sovereignty, external relations, war, international law and World History. Consistent with my focus on those passages and works which I believe are of especial interest to social movement activists, I will leave it to the avid reader to explore the remainder of *The Philosophy of Right* on their own.

CHAPTER 20

Critique of Hegel's *Philosophy of Right*

§1   You, Marx and Hegel on the State

Hegel's *Philosophy of Right* has turned out to be a flawed work, but nonetheless a project which was exemplary in its intent and method. Hegel's critical-logical reconstruction of the State was intended as an element of a reform program, directed against the reactionary absolute monarchy which ruled Prussia at the time, and one which, as a philosophical treatise, would have enduring significance. It is just such a critical-logical reconstruction which any social change activist should be interested in making today.

Much has changed since the book was written in 1821. In particular, the main axis of the class struggle is no longer that between the landed aristocracy and the urban bourgeoisie (though the contradiction between rural and urban communities persists), but between a working class, now largely atomised by the modern labour process and anti-union strategies of government, and a bourgeoisie benefiting from a formerly unimaginable concentration of wealth.

Whereas Hegel could see the state as an arena of struggle for dominance in civil society, many of us today take it that the dominant class in civil society (now the bourgeoisie) wields the state as an instrument for the suppression of both organised and spontaneous revolt against capitalist exploitation. The ground was already shifting when Hegel died in 1831, and it is now more than 135 years since the death of Marx, and the nature of the labour process and therefore of the working class has also changed dramatically.

So, we have a lot of work to do, and I don't think there is a single claim in *The Philosophy of Right* which can be simply taken as read. It has all to be worked over again. Nonetheless, the fundamental idea of the book, as set out in the Preface, remains, to my mind, utterly convincing – we have to understand what in the existing state of political affairs is rational, i.e., historically necessary and therefore in that sense progressive, and understand what in the existing state is irrational and deserves to perish. Specifically, we can use the categories of *The Philosophy of Right* as stimuli to focus our attention on various aspects of the political world, using Hegel as both a frame of reference for reflecting upon today's issues, and using today's issues as a reference point for disclosing what is valid or not in Hegel's work. So reading *The Philosophy of Right* is something you can come back to again and again as you wrestle with political and social problems.

Let us review some of Hegel's major errors.

The highly misogynistic 'deduction' of the place of women in society is a pointer to the danger of taking any social phenomenon to be *natural* and of ignoring the *protests* of those who are suffering injustice. All social and historical phenomena are constructed by human activity and can be made otherwise than how they are. Everything is as it is for a reason, and generally that reason is social, cultural or political.

The superficiality of Hegel's treatment of economic value was exposed by Marx. The contradictions of bourgeois society which generated ever increasing inequality of wealth were staring Hegel in the face, but all Hegel could do was describe and bemoan them. It took Marx to show how these pathologies were rooted in the concept of value. It took the Women's Liberation Movement at least a decade and the life-work of thousands of feminist writers to expose the social roots of women's oppression. Likewise, the critique of political economy was Marx's life work and he wrote in the context of a powerful movement of industrial workers across Europe. The critical resolution of problems like the oppression of women or the exploitation of wage labour are not tasks which can be done in an off-hand manner. Hegel's real accomplishment was his Logic, and it is this work which is truly enduring in a way his relatively superficial treatment of many of the problems which came up in *The Philosophy of Right* will never be. In any case, the flashing lights over women's relegation to domestic labour and the exploitation of wage labour should have alerted Hegel to contradictions which were festering below the surface of social life.

Beyond these observations, and remarks I have made above, I will draw attention to a couple of important issues which I think Hegel has not satisfactorily resolved.

§2   Civil Disobedience is No Crime

Hegel is a fundamentalist in that he holds that the ethical is that which is ultimately determined by custom and law. He recognises that all laws and customs absolutely *must* fall into contradiction with themselves when some limit is exceeded, not to mention that there are manifestly unjust laws and bad governments. However, he gives the entire responsibility for recognising the contradiction and determining a resolution to the State, insofar as a universal principle is entailed. But he also tells us that if the citizens simply go on adhering to old customs and laws in the face of injustice, then the spirit of a people dies.

My claim is that Hegel contradicts himself here. In fact, civil disobedience is the *sine qua non* of social progress. However, what Hegel also tells us – and

I think he is correct here – that when a law is broken as a matter of principle, then the actor must accept all the consequences of their action. This means that the actor must think long and deeply before taking any such action, do so openly, not hoping to 'get away with' it, but on the contrary hoping to bring things to a head by their action.

Further, Hegel tells us that laws are drafted around the conflicting interests of social *groups*, not individuals. Consequently, civil disobedience must always be a *social act* and not an individual initiative.

I hope that it is unnecessary to point out that Hegel's concept of the social-historical hero who flouts the conventions of their times and founds new states, is no licence for a self-appointed Lenin or Che Guevara to rob banks. There is no such licence. According to Hegel, once a state is founded, there is no place for such heroes.

§3   Human Rights, Abstract Right and Ethical Life

The overall architecture of *The Philosophy of Right* is worth meditating upon. The book begins with Abstract Right, i.e., private property – the be-all and end-all of bourgeois liberal political philosophy. The second phase of the book is Morality, the be-all and end-all of liberal moralism. This *does not* mean that Hegel makes private property and morality the 'foundations' of his political theory though. On the contrary, Hegel always begins his books with what is given to ordinary consciousness, and transforms it into a scientific concept and *negates* it. Truth always begins from falsehood. The result is Ethical Life which nonetheless preserves private property and personal responsibility. This is a sound starting point for social and political theory.

However, a lot has happened since 1821. The 'rights discourse' is a little confusing in this context. What is usually meant by a 'right' is something belonging not to Abstract Right, but to Civil Society. The kind of rights encompassed by Abstract Right go far beyond the right to own private property, and include such rights as the right to control one's own body, the right against torture or unjust imprisonment, the right to be heard in a court and be judged by one's peers, etc. They also include the right to one's tools of the trade and a subsistence. But there are lots of 'rights', such as freedom of speech, the right of assembly, the right to education and health which are rights secured (or not) by civil society and consequently are not necessarily *universal* rights. It is here in struggles within Civil Society that these rights can be established.

However, it is questionable whether the 'rights discourse' is the proper way to frame these rights which belong to civil society. Isn't it possible that a principle like Solidarity, which cannot be subsumed either under a rights discourse or morality, should take a more central place in our social theory? Solidarity does not easily fit into the framework of *The Philosophy of Right* because Hegel's work is based on individual rights, even though it is a distinctly communitarian theory.

I think that in the same way that Hegel preserved Abstract Right and Morality in his conception of Ethical Life, there is a need to develop an ethic of collective action, that would sit somewhere between the second and third parts of *The Philosophy of Right*.

The reader could also reflect on how Hegel conceives of the distinction between the State and Civil Society. Is this viable in our times? What would it mean in the context of efforts to extend access to democratic participation? What do we make of all Hegel's elaborate mechanisms of mediation which are his substitute for universal suffrage?

There is one right that self-evidently belongs to the sphere of the State, which is derided by Hegel, but cannot be dismissed in the way Hegel did.

§4   Universal Suffrage and Participatory Democracy

The demand for universal suffrage was one of those rights which had been sprouting in the soil of early modern society at least since the English Revolution of the 1640s, but which, like the demand for women's emancipation and the demand for freedom from the exploitation of wage labour, Hegel ignored and set aside as "building castles in the sky." But surely we now know that such demands are the harbingers of great social struggles to come.

The 'right to vote' is understood as a right which extends to every *person*, like Abstract Right, but clearly it is part of the State, not Abstract Right or Civil Society. Unlike the kind of 'rights' for which Civil Society is responsible it is not an 'individual right' – dependent on person circumstances and economic exigencies, but a 'human right'. Notwithstanding all the criticisms which Hegel made of universal suffrage, criticisms which have been largely shared by Marxists, and if the opinion polls are to be believed, are nowadays shared by the majority of voters themselves, it is impossible to conceive of a 'democratic socialist republic' (or whatever you want to call the kind of state you aspire to) which does not include, as a marker of citizenship – a universal right to vote.

It matters not that universal suffrage is used, alongside private ownership of the means of communication and the means of production, as a means of manipulating the mass of the population and perpetuating systems of exploitation. As Marx (1848) put it in the *Communist Manifesto*: "the first step in the revolution by the working class is to raise the proletariat to the position of ruling class to win the battle of democracy." If you can't win a general election you certainly can't organise the expropriation of capital.

Hegel showed us how the political role of the Crown *withers away* from Chief Executive and Commander-in-chief, to a clerical officer who signs documents and officiates at ceremonies, as the state becomes more mature and stable and the cultural level of the masses increases. The same notion applies to all the institutions of State. Universal suffrage cannot be abolished (other than to usher in a despot), but must be *transcended*.

PART 4

Conclusions

∵

CHAPTER 21

Marx's *Capital* and Hegel's *Logic*

§1   Turning Hegel on His Head

Marx's aphorism is valid:

> My dialectic method is not only different from the Hegelian, but is its
> direct opposite. .... With him it is standing on its head. It must be turned
> right side up again.
>
>   MARX, 1873

But without explanation, it is rather unhelpful for *understanding*, let alone *using* Marx's dialectic. (See also 2§16 above).

Firstly, consider this criticism Marx aimed at Hegel:

> The totality as it appears in the head, as a totality of thoughts, is a product
> of a thinking head, which appropriates the world in the only way it can, a
> way different from the artistic, religious, practical and mental appropria-
> tion of this world. The real subject retains its autonomous existence out-
> side the head just as before; namely as long as the head's conduct is merely
> speculative, merely theoretical. Hence, in the theoretical method, too,
> the subject, society, must always be kept in mind as the presupposition.
>
>   MARX, 1858

The "real subject" is social practice. A form of social practice cannot be observed and made intelligible by a theoretician until it *has come into being*. The
progress of knowledge has the appearance of an accomplishment of thinking,
but in fact it is the *real* progress of *social practice*, subsequently 'reflected' in the
theories of successive philosophers. (Practical intervention into social practice
rather than 'reflection' offers a wider scope for understanding a natural or social phenomenon.)

Now this is implicit in Hegel's advice in the Preface to *The Philosophy of
Right* about the Owl of Minerva taking flight only at dusk, but Marx takes this
advice *seriously*, whereas Hegel was all too inclined to believe that the *intellectual elite* of society (including himself) could theorise in advance of the real
development. Hegel's idealism is also reflected in the fact that Hegel always

looked to the intellectual and social elite to *solve* social problems and regarded the masses as a more or less destructive force of Nature, whereas Marx on the other hand looked to the workers as the vehicle of social progress. This orientation to the 'earth' rather than the 'stars' is how I interpret "turning Hegel right side up again."

I mentioned at the outset that concepts are forms of activity and that Hegel's "Spirit" can be interpreted as human activity. The paragraph from Marx just quoted shows that Marx took the same position. There is much in Hegel's writing that makes it hard to believe that Hegel did not *also* see it this way, but whatever may have been in his head he always wrote as if it were the spiritual entities which were the primary component and human action merely derivative. Indeed, his whole style of writing can be described as 'idealistic'. However, ideas and activity are inseparable and any theory which bases itself on one and not the other is untenable.

The way I'd like to explain the relation between Marx and Hegel is to mediate the relation between them with Goethe's 'Romantic Science'.

§2   Goethe, Hegel and Marx

During his Italian Journey (1787/1962) and in correspondence with his friend Johann Gottfried Herder, the great naturalist and poet, Johann Wolfgang von Goethe, arrived at the concept of *Urphänomen* by observing the variation of plants at different altitudes and latitudes. Each plant, he believed, was a realization according to conditions, of an underlying form which he called the *Urpflanze*. This idea was inspired by Herder's *Schwerpunkt* – the 'strong point' of a people, their defining experience or industry, which (in Marx's words) "is a general illumination which bathes all other colours and modifies their particularity" (Marx 1973/1858, p. 107; c.f. Herder 2004/1774).

The *Urphänomen* was the simplest particular instance of a complex process or organism which exhibited the essential features of the whole. Thus in one simple, sensuously perceived instance, one could grasp the whole as a *Gestalt* and this *Urphänomen* would provide the starting point for a whole science. Goethe died shortly before microscopes developed sufficient power to reveal the microstructure of plants and animals and the *cell* was discovered. Goethe could never have imagined what the microscope would reveal, but the *Urphänomen* anticipated the cell, which, alongside evolution by natural selection, laid the foundation of modern biology.

Hegel explicitly credited Goethe with this discovery as the inspiration for his own method which begins from the Abstract Concept, the simplest concept, the "germ cell" which provides a science with its starting point, given to it from outside the science itself. For Hegel, this 'Ur-concept' cannot be the product of intellectual intuition as it was for Goethe's "delicate empiricism," but on the contrary was a product of critical thought. Hegel built his entire system out of this idea of the logical unfolding of a concrete science from a simple abstract 'Urconcept' (this is my term, not Hegel's).

For Marx, the starting point was not an abstract concept, but an elementary form of social practice, an *Urpraxis* (again, that's my term, not Marx's). Let us look at how this worked out with Marx's life work: *Capital*.

§3   Capital

In his first draft of a critique of political economy, *The Grundrisse* (1973/1858), in the passage "Method of Political Economy," Marx committed himself to a research program modeled on Hegel's *Logic*, and by 1859 he had settled on exchange of commodities as the "Urpraxis" of bourgeois political economy, and realized this idea in the completion of Volume I of *Capital* (1996/1867). Before tracing this development in *Capital*, let us trace Marx's philosophical journey to his critical appropriation of Hegel's Logic exhibited in *Capital*.

Activity and Concepts

In the very first words which belong to his mature views, Marx (1976/1845) criticises philosophical materialism for accepting the standpoint of natural science: that of an observer contemplating an independently existing object. Objects exist, distinct from thought; however, it is only thanks to 'practical-critical' activity that the object is perceived and reconstructed in thought. Marx insisted that neither abstract thought nor sensuous perception form the subject matter of science, but *activity*. By 'activity' (or 'praxis' or 'social practice') is meant not an outer manifestation of inner thoughts, but rather a *whole* from which thinking and behaviour may be abstracted. But a form of social practice may exist for centuries before anyone formulates an adequate concept of it, and likewise, utopian concepts may exist without any real basis in social life.

So Marx explicitly substituted systems of *social practice*, social formations, for Hegel's *Gestalten des Bewußtseins* (Formations of consciousness), real activities rather than their shadows.

In the first Preface to *Capital* (1867), Marx asks why, more than 2,000 years since Aristotle first puzzled over the concept of exchange-value, it was only in the 19th century that the secret of the formation of exchange-value and its ramifications were disclosed. According to Hegel, the growing understanding of economic categories such as exchange-value, was a result of the theoretical work of political economists who scientifically developed the content of the concepts of political economy. Most people would understand the progress of natural science in much the same way: as a long train of problem-solving, each building on the solutions of those before them. But this doesn't stand up does it? Human activity develops in its own way. Gradually, over millennia, all the aspects of the concept of exchange-value were actualised as real relations, ultimately in the form of money and capital. In modern bourgeois society, the concept of exchange-value has reached its ultimate development, and the theorist has only to reflect on what is *before her or his eyes*, through the development of activity itself – science appropriates concepts which have already 'worked themselves out' in practical life.

To make sense of Hegel's idea, concepts have to be understood as in the first place forms of activity, not as the product of theoreticians. Theoreticians can only study what is to be found in practical activity, at least implicitly if not explicitly. So even though Hegel may have lost sight of this, and mistakenly taken social progress to be the work of theoreticians, his *Logic* retains its validity, provided only that concepts are interpreted as forms of practical activity, and only derivatively as subjective thought-forms or figures of categorical logic.

The Method of Political Economy

In the *Grundrisse* (1973/1858), Marx explained the history of any science as being made up of two phases as follows:

> It seems to be correct to begin with the real and the concrete, with the real precondition, thus to begin, in economics, with e.g. the population, ... However, on closer examination this proves false. The population is an abstraction if I leave out, for example, the classes of which it is composed... Thus, if I were to begin with the population, this would be a chaotic conception of the whole, and I would then, by means of further determination, move analytically towards ever more simple concepts, from the imagined concrete towards ever thinner abstractions until I had arrived at the simplest determinations.

and then:

> From there the journey would have to be retraced until I had finally arrived at the population again, but this time not as the chaotic conception of a whole, but as a rich totality of many determinations and relations....

The concrete is concrete because it is the concentration of many determinations, hence unity of the diverse. It appears in the process of thinking, therefore, as a process of concentration, as a result, not as a point of departure, even though it is the point of departure in reality and hence also the point of departure for observation and conception. Along the first path the full conception was evaporated to yield an abstract determination; along the second, the abstract determinations lead towards a reproduction of the concrete by way of thought. (p. 100)

This passage describes the structure of Hegel's *Logic*. The starting point of a science is the mass of measurements abstracted from the flow of economic reporting. This phase is represented in Hegel's Doctrine of Being, a phase of observation and measurement which precedes scientific reflection as such. The journey begins when these measurements are worked over, reflected on and worked up into patterns and laws and a theoretical description of the data. This first phase of the development of a science ("the path historically followed by economics at the time of its origins," p. 100) is complete when it arrives at the 'simplest determination', the singular entity which exhibits the essential relations of the whole process. This first phase is accomplished in the history of the science by means of *immanent critique* of the concepts abstracted from Being, and is represented by Hegel in the Doctrine of Essence.

The second phase is reconstructing the whole, now not as a chaotic conception, but as a systematic whole, a whole which exhibits in developed form the essential features with which we are familiar in the unit from which we began the reconstruction. This second phase – *systematic dialectic* ("obviously the scientifically correct method." p. 101) is represented by Hegel in the Doctrine of the Concept. For Marx, this *Urphänomen* would be not a phenomenon or a concept, but an inter-action observable in social practice, a familiar social act which we can viscerally understand, an *Urpraxis*. In the case of political economy, this would be act of exchanging commodities. In each stage of the reconstruction, the concepts logically derived from the *Urpraxis*, are validated by their objective existence in social practice. The resulting concrete reconstruction (which in the Logic Hegel represented as 'Spirit') differs from the data with which the analysis began ('Being') because it is a *systematic whole* rather than a mere succession of abstract qualities.

Marx realised this plan of work, his own part in the history of political economy, through many years of immanent critique of the rival theories of political economy, followed by a systematic reconstruction of bourgeois society in *Capital*.

The Commodity

In the first Preface to *Capital*, where Marx is talking about the problem of value in political economy, he says:

> The human mind has for more than 2,000 years sought in vain to get to the bottom of it, whilst on the other hand, to the successful analysis of much more composite and complex forms, there has been at least an approximation. Why? Because the body, as an organic whole, is more easy of study than are the cells of that body. In the analysis of economic forms, moreover, neither microscopes nor chemical reagents are of use. The force of abstraction must replace both. But in bourgeois society, the commodity form of the product of labour – or value-form of the commodity – is the economic cell-form.
>
> 1996/1867, p. 8

Marx's use of the metaphor of "cell" cannot but remind us of Goethe's *Urphänomen*, which the science of biology realised in the cell. The first chapter is devoted to an exposition of the commodity relation. Marx derives the concepts of value in the first three chapters of *Capital*, unfolding from the exchange of commodities, the concepts of Quality, Quantity and Measure, paralleling the first book of Hegel's *Logic*. By beginning with the abstract concept of commodity and then unfolding from this concept a concrete conception of value in bourgeois society, Marx followed the structure which Hegel used in of *all* of the books of the *Encyclopaedia*.

In particular, Marx set out from the discovery that the commodity relation is the unity of two independent actions represented by two forms of value: the use-value of the commodity entailed in the consumption of the object (its social quality), and the exchange-value of the commodity entailed in the production of the object and realised in the market (its social quantity). The homology between the categories of Hegel's Ontology and the early chapters of *Capital* reflects the fact that money has been doing the work of reducing all the products of human labour to a single measure, carrying out the work of logic, but as *a real process*, rather than as an intellectual exercise. Given the social nature of Hegel's categorical logic, it is to be expected that the categories of the logic should have a real existence in corresponding social processes. However, I do not accept the suggestion by Chris Arthur (2015), that this homology is a result of Hegel's study of the British political economists. It was the Soviet philosopher Ilyenkov who highlighted this process of *objective abstraction* in his works on *Capital* (1982/1960) and the ideal (1977), which is the basis for this homology. Hegel's own critique of political economy turned out to be rather fatuous.

Unit and Germ Cell

It might strike us as odd to begin from commodity exchange. Although, as Marx says in the opening words of *Capital*: "The wealth of those societies in which the capitalist mode of production prevails, presents itself as 'an immense accumulation of commodities,'" exchange of commodities is a rare occurrence in modern bourgeois society; generally, we *buy* and *sell* commodities. The third section of Chapter 1, shows the historical genesis of exchange from its earliest appearance in exchanges between tribal peoples, leading up to the use of gold as a universal equivalent and later the issuing of paper money by states. In this way, he showed that money is *essentially* a commodity and that wage-labour is a commodity bought and sold on the labour market and used by capitalists purchasers.

This exhibits one of the aspects of the *Urpraxis* which I drew attention to above. The *Urpraxis* arises from problems at a lower level of development. But with the formation of the self-reproducing *Gestalt* it generates, the *Urpraxis* itself goes through a series of transformations.

The *Urpraxis* *is the "Simplest Social Form"*

In his *Notes on Adolph Wagner* (1989/1881, p. 544) Marx says: "I do not proceed from the 'concept of value' ... What I proceed from is the simplest social form in the which the labour product presents itself in contemporary society, and this is the '*commodity*'." This is the same as when Hegel takes *private property* as the *simplest social form* of Freedom and makes it the starting point of *The Philosophy of Right*.

The commodity is a *form* of value, but 'value' is an intangible, neither 'a geometrical, a chemical, or any other natural property' (1996/1867, p. 47) – it is a suprasensible quality of a commodity. Value is in fact an artefact-mediated *social relation* which can therefore only be grasped conceptually. Nonetheless, the commodity is a form of value which, thanks to everyday experience, *can be grasped viscerally*. This means that the critique of the concept of commodity works upon relations which can be grasped viscerally by reader and writer alike. By beginning with the (concept of) commodity Marx mobilizes the readers' visceral understanding of commodities, and as he leads us to each successive relation. So long as that relation exists in social practice, then not only is the writer's intuition validated by the *existence* of that relation, but it also allows the reader to securely grasp and verify the logical exposition.

Marx's decision to begin not with 'value' but with the 'commodity' illustrates Marx's debt to Goethe's 'delicate empiricism', and is crucial for his praxis implementation of Hegel's *Logic*.

I am not aware of any evidence that Marx even knew about Goethe's *Urphänomen*, far less set about appropriating it. Marx worked at a certain cultural and historical juncture and placed himself in a particular social position in the unfolding social crisis. If any philosopher is the proximate source of Marx's philosophical turn to praxis, then it would be the follower of Gottlob Fichte, Moses Hess (1964/1843). Also, much of what Marx had to say about Hegel is far from complimentary. The triadic relationship between these three holistic thinkers, Goethe, Hegel and Marx, is real notwithstanding that Marx never set out to make any kind of triad. In the 19th century, all Germans, Hegel and Marx included, were raised in the long shadow of Goethe, whose impact on German culture cannot be overstated. However, Goethe's natural scientific ideas were probably the least-known of his ideas, and were largely discredited by mid-century. But the impact of Goethe (who Marx listed alongside Dante and Shakespeare as his favourite poet) is undeniable.

Both Goethe and Hegel were one-sided in their method; the further development of science and culture, made it possible for Marx to transcend both Goethe's Empiricism and Hegel's Idealism.

Further, by making the *Urphänomen* of his science a real act of social practice, not an *imagined* social practice, but one whose norms had already been produced by the development of bourgeois society and could be the subject of observation and intervention, Marx turned Hegel's version of the *Urphänomen* inside out, recovering an important element of Goethe's *Urphänomen*.

'Everything' vs. a Gestalt

In Marx's view, bourgeois society was essentially a market place. But Marx did not believe he could explain *everything* about the modern world on the basis of the commodity relation. The state and family life were not (yet?) market places.

Marx was drawn into political activity by his outrage at press censorship, inequality, aristocratic privilege and the slow progress of liberal reform in Germany, but he came to see that it was not the nobility or the state which was at the root of these social problems, but the *market*. By taking an exchange of commodities as the *unit of analysis* (Vygotsky 1987/1934), he had chosen a unit which already contained what he saw as essential to bourgeois society. Thus the complex whole which Marx set out to understand was to be taken as just thousands and thousands of commodity exchanges. *Capital* provided a concrete analysis of how the production of commodities leads to the exploitation of wage labour on one side and the accumulation of surplus value on the other – but he did not pretend to provide an analysis of the state and world history. Hegel, by contrast, took private property – the germ cell of Freedom – rather than *exchange* of commodities as the 'Urconcept', and claimed to unfold from private property the *entirety* of the state and world history. Marx's aims were rightly more modest.

Commodity and Capital

But *Capital* is a book about capital, not simple commodity production. In Part I of the book, the first three chapters, Marx analyses the circulation of commodities and money, but from this analysis he demonstrates the emergence of a *new* relation, that of capital, a new type of commodity. C–M–C (commodity exchange mediated by money) is transformed into M–C–M', production of commodities mediating the accumulation of money. Thus Marx derives a *new* 'molar'[1] unit of analysis, a second *Urpraxis* – the capitalist company or unit of capital, and marks the emergence of the modern forms of capital. Beginning from Chapter 4, Marx unfolds from this second *Urpraxis* a dialectical exposition of the movement of capital.

This theme in holistic science, where there is both a micro unit or *Urphänomen* (cell, quality, commodity) and a molar unit (organism, concept, capital) was first identified by the Soviet activity theorist, A.N. Leontyev (2009/1981). It is actually the molar unit which is the subject matter of the study, the key to understanding of which lies in the micro unit. What homology is there between Part II and the succeeding chapters of *Capital*, and Hegel's Concept Logic? Very little. The very general homology which can be found arises from homology between the subject matters (accumulation, competition). It can be argued that the formation of a uniform rate of profit across an economy, despite an organic composition of capital which varies from firm to firm, has an homology with the formation of the Idea from abstract concepts in Hegel's Concept Logic. But in any case, the homology arises from parallels in the subject matter itself, based on money as a real abstraction of human labour, not from Marx emulating Hegel. The structure of *Capital* is not a mirror of any work of Hegel's. The concepts of political economy unfold according to their own logic, and it would be a mistake to try and match *Capital* concept-for-concept with any of Hegel's books.

---

1 'Molar unit' comes from chemistry where it means that quantity of a substance which contains as many molecules as 12 gm of carbon-12, i.e., $6{\times}10^{23}$ molecules.

§4   Summary

In summary, there are two phases in the formation of a science (the two volumes of Hegel's *Logic*, the two processes outlined in Marx's "Method of Political Economy"); firstly, a protracted period leading up to the point when a theorist has the abstract starting point (*Urphänomen*) for the science properly so called, and then the concretisation of that abstract concept in the development of the science. Equally there are two phases in the *formation* of a social formation like capitalism: first the protracted period of history leading up to the point when its germ cell emerges, followed by the concretisation and universalization of that concept, entailing the transformation of all other relations in the social formation.

Hegel did not discover the *Urphänomen* – he appropriated it from the poet-naturalist John Wolfgang von Goethe and turned it inside out. It provided the abstract beginning of his philosophy, and each of the sciences he worked out began with an abstract concept appropriated from the preceding science. This was the same idea which the communist Marx appropriated from the idealist philosopher, Hegel, and made the starting point for his critique of capital.

For Marx as for Hegel, a concept is a (normative) form of social practice, but whereas Hegel suffered from the illusion that a theorist could unfold from a conceptual ideal everything that was implicit within it, Marx consistently held to the view that the logical development had to follow the development of social practice at every stage, making intelligible what was given in social practice. Marx further took the simple concept to form the starting point for elaborate social formations to represent a finite *artefact-mediated action*, rather than an universal like 'value'.

Note that Marx took the same approach in his study of the workers' movement in their struggle for state power, amending the *Manifesto of the Communist Party* only in the light of the actions of the workers' movement in the Paris Commune (See Lenin 1917). He never built any socialist castles in the air.

The importance of the idea of the *Urpraxis* is that it provides you with a pointer as to how you can use Goethe, Hegel and Marx in your theoretical reflections on your experiences as an activist. I have never found that "turning Hegel back on his feet" to be helpful in that respect.

CHAPTER 22

Soviet Psychology

§1 Vygotsky, Concepts and Artefact-mediated Actions

In everything I have written above I have relied on an interpretation of Hegel's Logic in which the subject matter is *human activity*. As I pointed out, I am by no means alone in reading Hegel in this way: Walter Kaufman, Charles Taylor, Robert Williams and Robert Pippin are examples of widely respected Hegelians for whom the Logic is about human activity, and this is a widely accepted approach to Hegel's ideas.

This reading entails the claim that concepts are *forms of activity*. However, for all of these writers, 'human activity' is a general conception for which claims such as "concepts are forms of activity" are relatively opaque. What is distinctive about my reading of Hegel is that it is informed by the Cultural Psychology of Lev Vygotsky (1896–1934) and the Activity Theory of Alexei Leontyev (1904–1979) and the Marxism of Evald Ilyenkov (1924–1979). This current of thinking is referred to as Cultural Historical Activity Theory (CHAT). CHAT has given me an understanding of concepts as forms of activity, based on experimental psychological research, which is consistent with Hegel. CHAT also provides insights, especially to do with *collective learning*, which cannot be extracted from Hegel.

Despite the fact that CHAT was suppressed to a greater or lesser degree during the Stalin era, and only gradually became known in the West in the 1960s, it is now widely used across the world in Linguistics and Psychology, and in especially Educational Psychology and Child Development.

This is not the place for an exposition of CHAT, but I will indicate a number of concepts which I have appropriated from CHAT and have already utilised above.

Artefact-mediation

An 'artefact' is a material object or process which is used in human activities and/or is the product of such activities. There are two types of artefact, signs and tools. However, these do not form two distinct classes of object, since being an artefact depends on how the artefact is *used*. A 'sign' is an artefact which is used by a subject to act on the mind, either the subject's own, or that of another subject. A 'tool' is an artefact which is used by a subject to act on other material objects. 'Tools' are *not* concepts or methods or other intangibles, despite the way this term is used in common speech – both tools and signs are material objects or processes – what Hegel called 'external means'.

Examples of signs are words, whether spoken or written, as well as gestures, symbols like flags and logos, clothing styles, etc. Signs which are products of technical development, such as maps, computers, telephones, etc, are sometimes called 'psychological tools'. Examples of tools are domestic animals, crops, hammers, machinery, and so on. There is a grey area between signs and tools, but the essential difference is whether the artefact is being used to influence or control someone's mind (such as a spoken word), or to expand the scope and effectiveness of an activity (such as an automobile).

Vygotsky saw that *every action is mediated by the use of an artefact.* Hegel made the same point (See Hegel's theory of action, Part 1, above) and Marx makes reference to this important observation in *Capital* (vol. 1, ch. 6.1), but neither Hegel nor Marx highlighted the full significance of this fact.

When one person interacts with another, there are not just two people involved – the entire cultural history of the world is implicated in the signs mediating their interaction. This simple insight is of enormous significance and is indispensable to understanding cultural change, as well as how individuals appropriate cultural practices. The mediating artefacts have a history of their own, prior to and independent of the actors using them, and in the process of using artefacts, the actors participate in the cultural evolution of those artefacts, and *thereby* to the cultural and historical development of human activity.

Other Hegelians have attempted to render Hegel's works into an explicit 'pragmatic' interpretation – i.e., an interpretation based on human interactions, but none have included this moment of artefact mediation. In such readings, how history and culture manifest as coherent and developing processes is rendered mysterious. The approach usually taken to incorporate the mediating signs and tools into actions and interactions, is to subsume the artefact into the action, subsume the subject's body into the subject and render the material world generally into a 'background'. But if we view speech or gesturing without clearly distinguishing between the subject and the culturally inherited means being used, then we cannot satisfactorily analyse the interaction.

Further, as Hegel points out, when a person acts, the mediating element of their action, their tools, may be the private property of others, and this has profound social and psychological impact on the action, as for example in the case of the worker whose means of production is owned by their employer.

The concepts of 'artefact' and 'artefact mediation' allow us to clearly conceptualise the factors in play in any situation, both those which manifest the subject's will and those which reflect social and cultural development. Hegel included these concepts in his theory of action, but Hegel scholars have over-looked them by exclusively focussing on the section on Morality.

An important implication is that Spirit can be said to subsist in the total-ity of artefacts, for it is all the written and spoken words and all the technical means at the community's disposal, which together determine the norms of the community – with *material force*. As material objects and processes, they change in coherent ways and persist over long periods of time. This idea was reflected in Hegel's aphorism: "The tool is the norm of labour" (1802/1979).

The mediating artefacts are what is universal in an interaction, whereas the meaning attached to the artefact is particular.

Analysis by Units

On the basis of his reading of Marx's *Capital*, Vygotsky (1934) introduced the idea of a 'unit of analysis'. 'Unit of analysis' is a concept which had been widely used for more than a century, but Vygotsky gave it new depth of meaning. The unit of analysis is the smallest object which figures in a given theory – the reso-lution of the theoretical microscope, so to speak. So for sociology and psychol-ogy this is usually the individual, while political science may take social groups as their unit of analysis. Vygotsky's idea was that the chosen unit of analysis was the concept of the whole which was to be analysed. In other words, he adopted the approach outlined in the previous chapter in which I referred to the unit as the *Urpraxis*. By using this term, 'unit of analysis', Vygotsky made the dialectical method accessible to a wide scientific audience.

Vygotsky demonstrated the idea of unit of analysis in four distinct appli-cations, that is, he founded four distinct theories based on the selection of a unit of analysis for each problem area. For understanding the relation between speech and thinking, i.e., the intellect, he took '*word meaning*' as his unit of analysis – "a unity of thinking and speech but as a unity of generalisation and social interaction, a unity of thinking and communication" (Vygotsky, 1934) and showed how speech and intelligence each had distinct genetic roots, but at a certain point in the child's development, intersected and "thinking be-comes verbal and speech intellectual" (1934).

He also made a study of personality development, for which the unit was a *perezhivanie*, an untranslatable Russian word meaning an experience together with its assimilation by the subject. The personality develops through a series of such life-changing experiences, the sum of which is the personality.

He made a study of disability using *defect-compensation* as the unit. The defect and the compensation refer not to the subject him or herself, but to the *relation* between the subject and the community in which they live.

In his study of child development, he used "*social situation of development*" as his unit – the concept of the social role the child occupies, in which the child's needs and their means of satisfaction are co-determined. The child develops when they begin to overflow the limits of their situation, leading to a period of crisis, etc.

By taking the method of Marx's *Capital* and applying it to such a variety of different problems, Vygotsky pioneered an approach to holistic science which any serious person involved in social change activism should be able to emulate.

Germ Cell

Further developing Vygotsky's reading of Marx's *Capital*, later followers of Vygotsky in what is known as Activity Theory recovered Marx's idea of 'germ cell'. The germ cell is the unit of analysis, but the concept recognises that the way the unit first appears in development – the simplest social form of the unit – undergoes development, achieving its true form only after successive transformations. So for example, in *Capital*, the germ cell is the commodity relation, but as Marx showed, through a series of transformations, value eventually takes on the money form.

In his writings on the Egyptian Revolution and the part played by the workers' movement, Brecht de Smet (2015) showed that the *strike* is the germ cell which can, under the right conditions, grow into revolutionary political action. It is obviously important for a social movement activist to be able to recognise the germ cell of greater things when it makes its appearance. This idea is consistent with Hegel's theory as elaborated in the Doctrine of Essence.

Concepts as Systems of Activity

Using 'sign-mediated actions' as his unit of analysis, Vygotsky made a study of concept formation in young children. Subjects were asked to solve a problem, and were given cards or blocks each marked with a sign to help them solve the problem. This technique is called the '*method of double stimulation*', a concept which sheds light on how the intellect interacts with perception.

By observing how the children went about searching for a solution, Vygotsky was able to describe the series of concepts formed in terms of artefact-mediated actions. In this way, Vygotsky gave a definite and experimentally demonstrated form to the idea of concepts as forms of sign-mediated action. He also developed a typology for the formation of concepts in children, prior to the formation of a *true concept*. This typology has no equivalent in Hegel's Logic, but is of very great psychological and social interest in itself. As it happens, it also gives very precise scientific form to the difference between what Hegel counts as a concept, and what is currently taken to be a concept by non-Hegelian science – juvenile precursors to true concepts.

So far as I can see, Vygotsky never read Hegel, or least not more than a few pages, but his appropriation of Hegel is better than any other. I believe that the circumstances of the times in which he worked (c. 1924–1934), a revolutionary period, when everything was being rethought, and Marxism has undergone a kind of rebirth, made such a remarkable intellectual achievement possible.

§2   A.N. Leontyev on Activities

Vygotsky's younger associate, A.N. Leontyev, was lucky enough to survive the purges and continued working through to the 1970s. Scientific debate was virtually impossible in the Stalin era, and certainly not in the domain of social theory, but it seems to me that much of what Vygotsky achieved Leontyev failed to understand. Nonetheless, he made discoveries of his own which have been crucial for my understanding of Hegel.

Leontyev put forward a system of psychology in which there would be a hierarchy of three units: operations, actions and activities.

The actions are artefact-mediated actions, just as Vygotsky had formulated the idea. Leontyev pointed to the *difference between the goal and motivation* of the action as its defining feature, in Hegel's terms, the difference between the purpose and the intention.

The operations are actions, except that they are carried out without conscious awareness. Actions develop into operations by repetition and habit, while operations develop into actions by conscious mastery. An action is generally composed of many operations, each controlled by the conditions.

The activities are aggregates of actions (by the same, but generally by different people) in which all the actions share the same motivation (the reason for doing the action), but are oriented to different goals, which only collectively achieve the shared motive. For example, the goal of a factory worker may be their wage, but nonetheless, they understand that the motive for the work is the employer's profit.

This approach was clearly suitable as a foundation for, not just a psychology, but a social theory. Conditions in the USSR were however unpropitious for such a project.

I have many criticisms to make of A.N. Leontyev's theory, but this concept of activities is what provided me with the key idea for an activity reading of Hegel. Ironically, Leontyev did not see his concept of activities as relevant to a theory of concepts. Also, he conceived of activities in functionalist terms, rather than in terms of projects which may not only reproduce, but also change society.

CHAPTER 23

Once Again: Hegel for Social Movements

This book was written as a companion to the reading of Hegel, and as not a substitute for reading Hegel. If you continue with your study of Hegel, this will likely be a life-long project, but I hope that what you have read here will be both an encouragement and a help for your future study. Hegel does not offer any new strategies, guidelines or models for social movements. Studying Hegel is related to social change activism much like practicing your scales is related to playing the piano. It will make you a much better player, but the score is what confronts you in social life, not what is written in a book.

I will now conclude this work with a couple of conclusions I have come to from my experience mainly in the workers' movement, and aided by my study of Hegel, Marx and Vygotsky.

§1 Collaborative Projects

I have come to the conclusion that for the solution of the problem of socialism, it is necessary to choose a unit of analysis and that this unit must be an *Urpraxis*. The usual unit of analysis for social theory – social groups of one kind or another, is good only for describing social reproduction and cannot reveal the dynamics of *social change*; theories based on the individual as a unit of analysis are barely worthy of the name social theory at all. Furthermore, all contemporary human science is affected by the departmentalisation of the academy, which itself reflects the rupture of the modern world view into great societal forces and institutions on one side, and individuals and their families on the other, arranging the deck chairs on the social Titanic. Social revolution demands that this dichotomy be transcended.

The unit of analysis I use for understanding social life in general and revolutionary change in particular is the *Collaborative Project*, or 'project' for short. A project is not an aggregate of people but of actions, explicitly *artefact mediated actions*. So just as in writing *Capital*, Marx used two units of analysis: exchange of commodities, C-M-C, and buying in order to sell at profit, M-C-M', I use both a micro unit, artefact mediated actions, and a molar unit, collaborative projects.

'Project' is by no means an esoteric concept these days, in fact it is even fashionable. And my meaning differs from the everyday concept only in that I do not include individual actions as projects, which is part of the reason that I say 'collaborative' projects. Almost invariably people *join* projects, and only rarely have the privilege of launching one. It is only by participating in projects that a person effects anything in this world.

However, what is posed by the adoption of collaborative project as a unit of analysis are two interrelated studies: the study of the *internal dynamics of collaborative projects*, and the study of the *collaboration between projects*, both conflictual and cooperative. And my remarks for the remainder of this chapter go to *this* question, the question of collaboration *between* projects, for it is upon this problem that I believe the future of socialism rests.

Life Cycle of a Project

Projects are not eternal, but have a life cycle: they begin with a group of people unconsciously sharing a social position of some kind for which a problem or opportunity arises; a solution is floated which brings people together to participate and it becomes a social movement; strategies, tactics and aims change and subsequently, the project either withers away or becomes institutionalised, and the concept around which it mobilised enters into the everyday culture of the given community. This is the process Hegel described in detail in his Logic.

The relevance of collaborative project as a unit for social change today, at this juncture, reflects the developments in the productive forces themselves. Just as parties have become ineffectual in bringing about fundamental social change, capitalist firms have changed their form in ways reflective of the changing demands of our times. The Left itself now already looks like so many independent projects. That's life! The communist parties which coordinated the activity of millions of members is gone long, long ago, along with the great capitalist firms which directly employed all the people who worked for it. Projects have *become* the real unit of social change, not in theory, but in social reality.

Collaboration

A project is a collaboration. I call projects 'collaborative' because in a project numbers of autonomous individuals collaborate towards a universal, though ever-changing, end. But the more important aspect of collaboration is that *between* projects. Collaboration *as such* means projects fusing together in a common endeavour and sharing a common identity, but it is only collaboration between projects which succeed in changing people's minds. In such collaborations, the separate identity of each project is maintained. Projects can collaborate in one of three ways: colonisation (or philanthropy), exchange (or bargaining) and *solidarity*.

§2   Solidarity

My point is this: people will participate in projects and give it their best shot. The problem is that we have to *learn how* to collaborate with *other* projects. Above all we have to learn the meaning of solidarity. It is on this alone that the future of socialism depends.

As the Rules of the International Workingmen's Association declared in 1864:

> That all efforts aiming at the great end hitherto failed from the want of solidarity between the manifold divisions of labor in each country, and from the absence of a fraternal bond of union between the working classes of different countries.
>
> MARX, 1864

The French workers had invented the word *solidarité* on the barricades of Paris in the first working class uprisings against the bourgeoisie. 'Solidarity' had entered the English language from the French at the Chartist Convention in London in April 1848 and been popularised by *The People's Paper* of Ernest Jones and Julian Harney – leaders of the left-wing of the Chartists and founders of the Communist League, for whom Marx and Engels wrote the *Manifesto of the Communist Party*.

The French had learnt the hard way that without solidarity the army could defeat them one barricade at a time, as they had in 1832. By 1848, the Chartist movement, which had united 5/6 of the population of Britain against the ruling capitalist class had also learnt their lesson the hard way.

Self-emancipation

The Rules of the International Workingmen's Association began with the maxim: "the emancipation of the working classes must be conquered by the working classes themselves" (Marx, 1864). These two principles: self-emancipation and solidarity, together make the irreducible and inseparable foundations of the workers' movement.

That self-emancipation is necessary is almost self-evident; if the working class is to take public political power it can learn and equip itself for that task only through the work of freeing itself and abolishing the conditions of its own exploitation. No-one can do that on their behalf. Self-emancipation is the way in which working class self-consciousness, in effect, the working class itself, is constructed. Without self-emancipation there can be no working class, only billions of individual wage-workers, socially and politically controlled by capital.

The opposite of self-emancipation is attaining freedom as the gift of another party. Such a thing is actually impossible; a class which is freed by the action of another class or group is only thereby subordinated to their liberators, even if these be well-meaning. How then is a socialist group to foster the liberation of the working class if the liberation of the working class is to be *their own* achievement? The answer to this lies in the principle of *solidarity*.

The need for solidarity arises from the fact that the working class does not come into the world readymade as a single, homogeneous, organised stratum of society. It comes into the world divided into strata, trades, national, religious and ethnic groups, and spread across the globe in numerous cultural and linguistic communities, and the working class has become more not less diversified since. Energies are dissipated in numerous projects, very many of which contribute in some way to the socialist project, but independently and often in conflict with each other.

The modern working class can realise its own emancipation only by the collaboration of these disparate projects. The aims and methods of projects will differ, but the autonomy of every project within a broad movement remains until at some future time, maybe, they voluntarily create and submit themselves to a shared discipline.

When one group finds themself under attack, *provided they fight back*, then others have a duty to come to their aid. This duty and its practice is called 'solidarity'. The results of solidarity are three-fold. In the first place, as a result of the aid received from others, the struggling group may survive. Secondly, they learn who their friends are, and coming at their hour of need, they will not ever forget this.

But more importantly, through their joint struggle, whether successful or not, their collective self-consciousness, agency and self-confidence is enhanced.

However, this is not automatically the case; sometimes 'helping' someone is a violation of solidarity. If another group comes along and 'saves' them, then the 'rescued' group may be grateful, but their working class self-consciousness is not enhanced but at best subsumed under that of the rescuing party, who in any case, as often as not, do more damage than help.

The principle of solidarity, which guides how different sections of the workers' movement come to each others' aid, avoids such dangers and ensures that the self-consciousness of both the struggling party and the party offering solidarity is enhanced in the very process of bringing them closer together.

It is a simple rule:

when coming to the aid of another party, do so under *their* direction.

You do it their way, not your way. If your own beliefs are such that you cannot place yourself under their direction, if you believe that they are so misguided, then solidarity is impossible. But if they can contribute in some way to socialism then ensuring that they are not defeated is important, and you will surely be able to find *some* way of supporting them according to their own practices. This may be by donating to their fighting fund or sending a message of solidarity or whatever. But if you are going to participate in the struggle of another section of the workers' movement, then the principle of solidarity demands that you do so *under their direction*. The working class is unified by voluntary association, not by conquest or persuasion.

To be clear, I am not just making a call for unity on the Left. This is neither possible, nor actually desirable. Preparing and building a movement which can overthrow capitalism and make something *better*, is the most complex task imaginable, and it will not be planned or directed. It will be diverse, with many centres. But nor am I making a libertarian, anarchist call for self-expression and multiplicity.

People have to learn how to collaborate; people have to learn how to practice solidarity. People will do what they will. If people are not struggling for social justice, then there is nothing we can do to bring that into being. We cannot accelerate the *Zeitgeist*. The job of activists is to show people how the practice of solidarity builds a movement for self-emancipation.

A world in which solidarity is universal is already socialism.

To be clear, again, I am not arguing for a loose movement of diverse projects. That is what already exists. I am not arguing against building a party to win seats in Parliament; I am not arguing against building a monthly journal of Marxist theory, or a direct action group opposing evictions or an antifascist group to defend communities against attack, or building a cadre of professional revolutionaries. All these are part of the struggle for socialism. It is not a question of one or the other, but of how they can bind themselves together in bonds of solidarity.

It is *solidarity* which is the *Urpraxis* of the socialist project.

References

Abidor, M. (2018). May Made me. An Oral History of the 1968 Uprising in France. Oakland, CA: AK Press.

Arthur, C. (2015). 'Marx, Hegel and the value-form', In *Marx's* Capital *and Hegel's* Logic. *A Reexamination*. ed. Fred Moseley and Tony Smith, Chicago, IL: Haymarket Books.

Bakhtin, M. (1975/1986). Toward a Methodology for the Human Sciences. *Speech Genres and Other Late Essays*. Austin, TX: University of Texas Press.

Beaton, L. (2013). A reflection on the feminist movement, in *Collaborative Projects. An interdisciplinary Study*, ed. Andy Blunden. Leiden, Netherlands: Brill.

De Smet, B. (2015). A Dialectical Pedagogy of Revolt. Gramsci, Vygotsky, and the Egyptian Revolution. Leiden, Holland: Brill.

Derrida, J. (1967). *De la grammatologie*. Paris, France: Éditions de Minuit.

Descartes, R. (1637/1911). Discourse on the Method of Rightly Conducting the Reason and Seeking for Truth in the Sciences. Cambridge, UK: Cambridge University Press.

Engels, F. (1880). *Socialism: Utopian & Scientific*. MECW vol. 24.

Engels, F. (1884). The Origin of the Family, Private Property and the State. Chapter IX. *MECW volume 26*, pp. 256ff.

Friedan, B. (1963). *The Feminine Mystique*. New York, NY: W.W. Norton & Co.

Goethe, J.W. v. (1787/1962). Goethe To Herder, 17 May 1787 in *Italian Journey, The Collected Works*, Volume 6, pp. 298–299, London: Collins.

Hegel, G.W.F., (1802/1979) *System of ethical life* [1802/3]) *and First Philosophy of Spirit* [1803–4]), translated by T.M. Knox. NY: State University of New York Press.

Hegel: *The Letters*, (1984) Trans. C. Butler and C. Seiler, Bloomington, IN: Indiana University Press.

Hegel, G.W.F, (1807/1996) *The Phenomenology of Mind. The Sociality of Reason*. Trans, with an Intro & notes Terry Pinkard, Cambridge UK: Cambridge University Press.

Hegel, G.W.F., (1816/1969) *The Science of Logic*, trans. A.V. Miller, London UK: George Allen & Unwin. § represent paragraph numbers in the internet version of this book at http://www.marxists.org/reference/archive/hegel/works/hl/hlooo.htm.

Hegel, G.W.F., (1817/1955) *Hegel's Lectures on The History of Philosophy*. trans. John Sibree, New York, NY: Dover.

Hegel, G.W.F. (1821/1996) *Philosophy of Right* (Preface). Amherst, NY: Prometheus Books.

Hegel, G.W.F., (1821/1952) *Hegel's Philosophy of Right*, translated with Notes by T.M. Knox, Oxford, UK: Oxford University Press.

Hegel, G.W.F., (1830/2009) *Hegel's Logic*, tr. Wm. Wallace. Pacifica, CA: Marxists Internet Archive Publications. a.k.a. "The Shorter Logic."

Hegel, G.W.F., (1830/1970) *Hegel's Philosophy of Nature*, in 3 Volumes, tr. M.J. Petry. London, UK: George Allen & Unwin.

Hegel, G.W.F., (1830/1971) *Hegel's Philosophy of Mind*, Part Three of the Encyclopædia of the philosophical sciences, tr. Wm. Wallace. New York, NY: Oxford University Press.

Hegel, G.W.F., (1831/1969) "Preface to the Second Edition," *The Science of Logic*, trans. A.V. Miller, London, UK: George Allen & Unwin.

Herder, J.G. (1774/2004). *Another Philosophy of History* and Selected Political Writings. trans. I.D. Evrigenis and D. Pellerin, Hackett Publishing Company.

Hess, M. (1843/1964). The Philosophy of the Act. In *Socialist thought. A documentary history.* ed. Albert Fried and Ronald Sanders, Chicago, IL: Aldine Publishing Co.

Ilyenkov, E.V. (1960/1982). *The Dialectics of the Abstract and the Concrete in Marx's* Capital. Moscow: Progress Publishers.

Ilyenkov, E.V. (1977). The Concept of the Ideal, in *The Ideal in Human Activity*. Kettering OH: Marxists Internet Archive Press.

Kant, I. (1787/2007). *Critique of Pure Reason*. Trans. Norman Kemp Smith. Palgrave Macmillan.

Kuhn, T. (1962). *The Structure of Scientific Revolutions*. Chicago, IL: University of Chicago.

Lenin, V.I. (1917). *The State and Revolution*. Chapter 3. *LCW* volume 25.

Leontyev, A.N. (2009/1981). *The Development of Mind*. Kettering OH: Marxists Internet Archive Press.

Marx (1843/1970). *Marx's Critique of Hegel's Philosophy of Right*. Ed. Joseph O'Malley. Cambridge, UK: Cambridge University Press. Page nos. from *MECW* volume 3.

Marx (1845). Theses on Feuerbach. pp. 6–8. *MECW, vol. 5.*

Marx (1848). The Manifesto of the Communist Party. *MECW vol. 6*, p. 477.

Marx (1852). The Eighteenth Brumaire of Louis Bonaparte, *MECW vol. 11.*

Marx (1857/1973). The Method of Political Economy, *The Grundrisse*. London, UK: Penguin Books.

Marx (1864). Provisional Rules of the Association, *MECW vol. 20*, p. 14.

Marx (1867/1887). *Capital*, vol. I. *MECW, vol. 35.*

Marx (1867). Preface to first German edition of *Capital. MECW*, vol. 35.

Marx (1871). The Civil War in France. Second Draft, 6) The Commune. MECW vol. 22, p. 537.

Marx (1881). *Notes on Adolph Wagner's Lehrbuch der politischer Oekonomie. MECW, vol. 24.*

Russell, B. & Whitehead, A.N. (1910–1913) *Principia Mathematica*. Cambridge, UK: Cambridge University Press.

Vygotsky, L.S., (1934/1987) 'Thinking and Speech', *Collected Works, Volume 1*, New York: Plenum Press, pp. 39–285.

Index

CPSIA information can be obtained
at www.ICGtesting.com
Printed in the USA
JSHW011421010620
5985JS00006B/14